THE NEXT WELFARE STATE?
UK Welfare after COVID-19

Christopher Pierson

D1612498

First published in Great Britain in 2021 by

Policy Press, an imprint of
Bristol University Press
University of Bristol
1–9 Old Park Hill
Bristol
BS2 8BB
UK
t: +44 (0)117 954 5940
e: bup-info@bristol.ac.uk

Details of international sales and distribution partners are available at
policy.bristoluniversitypress.co.uk

British Library Cataloguing in Publication Data
A catalogue record for this book is available from the British Library

ISBN 978-1-4473-6118-3 hardcover
ISBN 978-1-4473-6119-0 paperback
ISBN 978-1-4473-6120-6 ePub
ISBN 978-1-4473-6121-3 ePdf

Cover design: blu inc, Bristol
Front cover image: Alamy/Quality stock
Bristol University Press uses environmentally responsible print partners.
Printed and bound in Great Britain by CMP, Poole

This book is dedicated to all those who swim against the tide – but never lose their nerve or their sense of fun. Especially those who do that off Battery Rocks – and in particular Abby, Bec, Bek, Belinda, Clare, Diane, Ella, Jane, John, Jude, Julia, Julie, Lucy, Mike, Peter, Rachel, Sally, Tori and Sammy the generic seal.

I mean to inquire if, in the civil order, there can be any sure and legitimate rule of administration, men being taken as they are and laws as they might be ...

I shall be asked if I am a prince or a legislator, to write on politics. I answer that I am neither, and that is why I do so. If I were a prince or a legislator, I should not waste time in saying what wants doing; I should do it, or hold my peace.

Jean-Jacques Rousseau, *The Social Contract*

Contents

List of figures and tables

Figures

Tables

List of abbreviations

AI	artificial intelligence
CGT	Capital Gains Tax
CJRS	Coronavirus Job Retention Scheme
CPI	consumer price index
FSM	free school meals
FTE	full-time equivalent
GDP	gross domestic product
HBAI	household below average income
HMRC	Her Majesty's Revenue and Customs
IFS	Institute for Fiscal Studies
LFS	Labour Force Survey
OADR	old-age dependency ratio
OBR	Office for Budget Responsibility
ONS	Office for National Statistics
OTS	Office of Tax Simplification
RPI	retail price index
SEU	Social Exclusion Unit
UBI	Universal Basic Income
UC	Universal Credit
VAT	Value Added Tax
WID	World Inequality Database

Acknowledgements

I have received plenty of advice, some of it quite helpful, at every stage of this project. I am especially grateful to all of the following: Daniel Béland, Francis Castles, Jennifer Curtin, Nick Ellison, Carl Emmerson, Hannah Lambie-Mumford, Nick Manning, Kimberly Morgan, Herbert Obinger, Eric Shaw and Paul Williamson.

Laura Vickers-Rendall, Caroline Astley, Emma Cook and the rest of the editorial team at Policy Press were consistently brilliant.

Very special thanks to Lucy who provided a room with a view and read everything at no notice.

Introduction

I finished writing this book just as we passed the anniversary of the first nationwide UK COVID-19 lockdown (on 23 March 2021). It was a year unlike any other. Most importantly and distressingly, it saw more than 10,000,000 cases of the disease and in excess of 140,000 COVID-related deaths across the UK.[1] In response to the rapid spread of the disease in March 2020, the government took infection control measures that involved suspending basic civil liberties – including freedoms of movement and association – and shut down significant sectors of the economy (essentially those that involved person-to-person contact). Education, for both school- and university-level students, was severely disrupted. Twelve months on, many of these regulations were still in place and the government was still effectively ruling by decree.[2] It had committed enormous sums of money – close to £350 billion – to counter the effects of the pandemic, fairly evenly divided between support for households and businesses on the one hand and public services, especially the NHS, on the other. Public debt for 2020/21 was on a similarly unprecedented (peacetime) scale – at around 17 per cent of Gross Domestic Product (GDP).[3]

In whatever way we choose to define the welfare state, it was transformed by the pandemic – though many of the changes were supposed to be 'temporary'. Millions of people of working age became dependent upon the state for an income in a way they could never have anticipated. The number of people on Universal Credit (UC) – the government's principal welfare benefit – doubled from 3,000,000 to 6,000,000 in the nine months from March 2020 to January 2021.[4] Through 'furloughing' for employees and support grants for the self-employed, the government avoided the mass unemployment – and the associated collapse of spending power – that the rapid contraction of the economy would otherwise have precipitated. The recession was still severe – GDP declined by around 10 per cent in the year to April 2021, according to the Office for Budget Responsibility (OBR) – but the hope was that recovery could be fairly rapid once more 'normal' trading conditions were restored. The government repeatedly found that its temporary measures – for example, furloughing and the £20 per week uplift in UC – had to be extended. Given this experience, the projected rapid fall-off in COVID-related government spending after 2021 looked extremely optimistic. This applies not least to the public health budget where the very large increases through 2020 and 2021 were projected to fall away (rapidly) thereafter – even though there would be a great deal of additional healthcare need created both by the pandemic itself and by the interruption to normal healthcare services that it had caused. The damage to the public finances which dealing with the pandemic occasioned will take at least a generation to fix. The UK economy will be permanently and significantly smaller.[5]

One of the very few good things about COVID-19 was that it pushed Brexit off the top of the news agenda – where it had sat more or less unchallenged ever since David Cameron's calamitous and career-defining Bloomberg speech in January 2013 had committed a future Conservative Government to an in–out referendum on EU membership. Following Britain's exit from the EU at the end of January 2020, haggling over the 'future trading relationship' rumbled on throughout the year, at a COVID-safe distance, before a rather bedraggled rabbit was pulled out of the negotiatorial hat at the last possible moment (24 December 2020). Brexit always had an important welfare state component, especially if we are willing to see the latter in the rather broader terms of a political economy of welfare (which includes the world of work). At its very simplest, the professional (economists') consensus is that Brexit will reduce the size of the economy, probably by as much as COVID-19 – that is by around about 3 per cent in both instances.[6]

But the politics of welfare also has another and more complicated relationship to the politics of Brexit (see Sobolewska and Ford, 2020). While the referendum was ostensibly about the single issue of Britain's membership of the EU, it came to stand for very much else besides. Not least, it was seen to crystallise the social and economic divisions between typical 'Leavers' and 'Remainers', with the former being older, less well educated and non-metropolitan. Upon some accounts, the referendum was an opportunity for 'Leavers' to express their general dissatisfaction with a perceived-to-be socially liberal majority led by an increasingly remote governing elite and a surrogate way of articulating a hostility to immigration (whether from the EU or elsewhere) that it had become increasingly socially unacceptable to express. For some observers, it was the peculiarly British form of a wider right-wing populism, seen also in continental Europe and the US (see Norris and Inglehart, 2019). This populism always had a welfare state component – but exactly what this was is not clear. In part, hostility to EU migration simply reflected a very long-standing belief (on the right) that the UK's 'generous' welfare state system was being exploited by variously defined non-natives. And the 'Leave' campaign certainly made much of the idea that precious resources which could have been spent on public services in the UK – most famously the £350 million a week lost to the NHS – were being siphoned off to pay for the Brussels gravy train (see Iacobucci, 2018). Sometimes this elided with a distinctive 'welfare chauvinism' – a view that favoured welfare spending but wanted to see this focused upon a variously defined 'native' population (a tendency reported in other European welfare states too; see Keskinen et al, 2016; Fenger, 2018; Greve, 2019). Those with low wages and comparatively few of the skills valued in the new economy, for example, were persuaded that cheap foreign labour was forcing down their wages. Denials of such claims by professional economists proved to be worse than useless, since these economists were themselves widely seen as a part of that liberal elite which had, in the name of globalisation and cosmopolitanism, disadvantaged 'Leaver' communities for a generation.[7] Some analysts even detected a complicated feedback mechanism at work in the Brexit politics of welfare. Thiemo Fetzer (2019), for example, argued that the increment of support needed to get a 'Leave' vote over the line in 2016 was actually created by the Conservative–Liberal Democrat Coalition Government's policies of welfare austerity after 2010.

The coincidence of COVID and the completion of the Brexit process makes it unusually difficult to determine cause and effect. It seems that both COVID and Brexit will have a (roughly similar) impact upon the size of the UK economy ('scarring'). But other processes, 'in the depths', may be more difficult to observe and explain. A good example is change in the size and nature of the UK population. Of course, COVID-19 led to excess deaths in the UK – perhaps as many as 100,000. Shockingly, these deaths, concentrated in the over 75s, were enough to have a discernible impact upon future projections of state pension costs.[8] But it seems that much greater demographic shifts may also have been under way. The work of O'Connor and Portes (2021) suggests that there were enormous shifts in population after March 2020 – with the overall population of the UK decreasing, maybe by as much as 1,000,000, with more than half of this loss being from London. Much of this decline they attribute to foreign-born workers going home. Shifts on this scale in such a time frame – if they really exist – are almost unprecedented. But was this COVID or Brexit? And how could we tell?

This is a book about welfare after COVID. But it is very much not a book that is solely concerned with what COVID has done to the political economy of welfare in Britain. As I will set out to show in Chapter 5, the impact of COVID upon the welfare state has been substantial and it will last. But it is built upon an underlying infrastructure of welfare which has itself been constantly changing, ever since it first emerged in something like its modern form more than 70 years ago – and which neither COVID nor Brexit will make go away. In fact, if anything, COVID and Brexit have *reinforced* pre-existing patterns of welfare inequality, rather than changed them. It is *this* long-standing welfare state order with which I am principally concerned. And I am especially interested in what has happened to the welfare state as an imagined mechanism for achieving political change – above all, as 'a strategy for equality'. To be absolutely clear, there is nothing *necessarily* progressive about the welfare state and it has never belonged *exclusively* to the centre-left. But there used to be smart progressive people in Britain who thought that a rightly-constructed social security regime could be an avenue of real social change. I plan to find out what happened to make that vision go wrong – and what alternatives, if any, we now have.

Looking backward

The welfare state in which I grew up looked very different from what we have today. I was born in an NHS hospital (that had once been a workhouse), received free medical and dental care throughout my adult life and could look forward (at 66) to a lifelong and (for now) 'triple-locked' retirement pension. This world had changed decisively from that in which my parents had grown up. I was four inches taller than my father. My mother, one of the smartest and hardest-working people I ever knew, left school when she was 15. I arrived at university in my 20th year, with no fees to pay, a grant to meet my living expenses and a completely unselfconscious sense of entitlement.

That was in 1976 – the year when James Callaghan famously declared that it was no longer possible to spend your way out of a recession (!). It was the year after Tony Crosland had told a local government conference in Manchester that 'the party is over' and, in so doing, declared that the golden age of the welfare state (if such it was) had ended. None of this made much of an impression on me at the time. Though I had firmly arrived on the left by this time, Labour Governments, trades unions and the welfare state were all a bit dull for me – dull, but not, I rather innocently believed, likely to go away any time soon. I read voraciously but, unlike many of my peers, I wasn't drawn to what they thought of as the *really* radical politics. I was staggered then, as I still am now, by the extraordinary depth of Marx's understanding of (his) capitalism. But I could only have been reckoned a 'proper' Marxist (even of a quirkily revisionist kind) for a few months, maybe from October 1976 to April 1977. I still think that Marx provided the most profound reading of capitalism that we possess but I didn't think that what he had said was 'true' in a way that it seemed to me you had to do in order to be a Marxist.

Since I didn't think that the revolution was coming, I was drawn to what might be possible if the mainstream parties of the left – Labour in the UK, Social Democrats in Europe and beyond – wanted to do something more than defend what they had already achieved (which I thought was considerable). At that time, 'the welfare state' had become the generic shorthand name for the agenda of gradual change that these parties had pursued. It was, at its simplest, the politics of gradually advancing the well-being of those who were disadvantaged in societies like ours, particularly because they were sellers of their labour-power, through the mechanisms of actually existing representative democracy. My hope was that these mainstream parties of the left could get past their rather dreary incrementalism and find something that would *really* change the character of the societies in which we lived. And this was why the first book I wrote after my PhD thesis, and published in 1991, was called, aspirationally if enquiringly, *Beyond the Welfare State?*

Meanwhile, the rest of Britain was experiencing the 1980s and a full-scale assault on the world in which I had grown up. From the mid-1970s onwards, the welfare state had come under sustained attack: at first, from the neo-Marxist left and then, to considerably greater political effect, from a fashionable New Right. As Thatcherism marched triumphantly across the land, two things went largely unremarked. The first was just how hopeless social democrats in Britain were in defending their own post-war achievements. Perhaps because the governing record of Labour after 1950 had contained so much fudge and compromise, it seemed unable to say much more than that the welfare state was 'a good thing' and all civilised countries should either have one or be one. Crosland's *Future of Socialism*, which was one of very few post-war books of any standing in the British Labour tradition, seemed completely out of step with the new times. In the face of the rigour and fireworks of both the New Right and the neo-Marxist left, this response seemed to be (as it was) completely inadequate. The other remarkable thing – only really to be observed at the other end of the 1980s – was that the welfare state was still there! Indeed, social expenditure had grown more rapidly under the first Thatcher Government than at any other time since the Second World War (Pierson, 2006: 162). It was clear that the welfare state must be something other than the last refuge of the feckless or the sole protector of the destitute. Ironically, it turned out that both the New Right and the neo-Marxists were wrong. They had both argued that capitalism and the welfare state were incompatible (and that one of them would have to give way). But the truth was much closer to an earlier conventional wisdom – often associated with the name and work of Karl Polanyi (1944) – that capitalism *cannot* survive *without* a welfare state.

As the 1990s dawned, it seemed that everyone – including those who wanted to see a revival of the mainstream left – would have to make more space for markets (including labour markets). Under these new circumstances I, like others, turned to an exploration of the slightly improbable logic of market socialism. There were plenty of good ideas here – including the belief that a sole reliance upon a *labour* income would leave its recipients often poor and always vulnerable. But in so far as its greatest claim to support was its *feasibility* – as in Alec Nove's (1983) landmark text on *The Economics of Feasible Socialism* – it was a grave disappointment. As a political strategy, it looked deeply implausible. It was while working on this topic – and preparing the accompanying study of *Socialism After Communism* (1995) – that

I first began to think much harder about the place in all of this of ideas and practices of *property*. This had, of course, been a quite crucial category for all the early socialists – Marxist and non-Marxist – and for the still earlier architects of a certain kind of liberalism. Reading again, but carefully this time, John Locke's crucial chapter 'On Property' (from the *Second Treatise on Government)*, I was astonished that so much could have come to rest upon an argument that seemed to be so full of holes *and* which ended up with conclusions that none of the preceding argument could possibly have justified (Locke, 1988 [1688]). It was at this point that I decided that it was necessary to go much further back and down, and that any adequate account of an alternative left strategy would have to rely upon a comprehensive re-reading of how we understood property relationships in contemporary capitalist societies (like ours).

I spent most of the next 20 years working on a history of the idea of private property which went back not just to Locke but to Pythagoras – and that attempted to cover everything that was relevant in the world of ideas in the West in the period in between and beyond (Pierson, 2013–20). Here are the headline conclusions. First, property is deeply implicated in almost everything we do. Second, almost all the existing arguments we have in defence of its present allocation are either wrong or point in directions other than (often, opposite to) those that their architects imagined. Third, property is a social relationship and, as societies or communities, we need to decide which property rules we want to live with and by. Fourth, while it is generally good to have rules about property, there are no natural rights (to property) which place a limit upon these institutional arrangements. And fifth, if we want to understand how societies like ours work and how we can change them, we have first to understand how their property regimes work (and for whom they work).

All of which brings us to this book, in which I consider what is happening to our (broadly conceived) welfare state now, by placing it firmly in the context of our (still broader) property regime. To change either, or both, of these, we need first to understand the (intimate) relationship that ties them together. Among other things, I shall argue that social democrats were once keenly aware of this connection but that, somewhere along the line, and to their irreducible loss, they forgot it. Before we can go anywhere, we need to remake that connection.

The welfare state as a 'strategy of equality'

The welfare state is not a uniquely social democratic accomplishment. It origins are as much liberal and a little bit conservative and there was a time when nearly *everyone* wanted to claim that the welfare state was theirs. And it is definitely not going away. It remains what governments – local and central – do, most of the time. It constitutes a key part of the infrastructure of our shared lives – in health and education, for example. And it provides healthcare and secure incomes for older people – in what is a steadily ageing society. But, very clearly, its standing has changed. It is certainly no longer, as once it seemed to be, a shorthand for what social democrats want to do. There is a real question about whether it still can be, as R.H. Tawney had famously anticipated in the 1930s that it should be, 'a strategy of equality'.

It is worth taking a moment to look (again) at what it was that Tawney actually said. 'The Strategy of Equality' is the fourth chapter of Tawney's rather broader treatise on *Equality* (Tawney, 1964 [1931]). In it, he argues for 'the extension of social services and progressive taxation, which mitigate disparities of opportunity and circumstance, by securing that wealth which would otherwise have been spent by a minority is applied to purposes of common advantage' (1964 [1931]: 126). While inequalities of wealth should and would be reduced by this intervention, Tawney was more concerned with the ways in which collective provision can be used to secure more equal outcomes in terms of health, education and protection against such contingencies as sickness, disability and unemployment. Income and wealth would not be equalised – but they would count for much less. Above all, Tawney believed that the state's power and resources could be deployed to guarantee its citizens social *security*.

By the time Julian Le Grand published *The Strategy of Equality* some 50 years later, the idea had subtly changed. Le Grand's 1982 book is principally an empirical survey of the failure of the welfare state to do the work of redistribution. But it also reflects what that strategy had become by that time for the Labour Party: that is, a commitment to effect gradual social change and increase social equality *by maximising spending on the welfare state* (Le Grand, 1982: 8–12). This is, perhaps, why for a time the growth of the welfare state seemed to have become a barometer of social progress. But this was never Tawney's view. For Tawney, spending on social provision was only ever a part of a programme that included the empowerment of trades unions and the creation of not-for-profit businesses (either publicly owned and/or worker-controlled). And it was not a stand-alone strategy, but one 'which, *till a radical change has been effected in the balance of economic power*, will at every point be thwarted and checked' (Tawney, 1964 [1931]: 127; emphasis added). Addressing *this* challenge was the work of the much less-noticed fifth chapter of *Equality*: 'The Conditions of Economic Freedom'.

That we ended up with an account of 'the strategy of equality' different from that which Tawney was recommending matters. In the classic social democratic model of welfare – broadly, that which is critiqued in Le Grand's book – organised labour, in parties and unions, mobilises behind an incremental growth in entitlements based on social citizenship so as to countermand the inequalities generated by a mixed-market economy. The intention is that this redistribution is funded out of the progressive taxation of the open-ended growth which (only) such a mixed-market economy could deliver. In this way, the fundamental character of our society – and its entrenched social and economic inequality – could be gradually transformed, without making a change in its underpinning economic organisation. *This* social democratic model – which I shall argue had its last and rather deviant manifestation in the epoch of New Labour – is finished. In a sense, what to do about the welfare state is *the* political problem of social democratic politics, whereas, for a long time, social democrats had thought it was the solution. If we still want to pursue some sort of 'strategy of equality' we shall have to find it elsewhere – or perhaps more accurately, we shall need to change both the welfare state *and* the wider regime of inequality within which it is embedded.

In this short book, I consider how and why the welfare state in which I grew up disappeared, where we are now, and what we might do in the future. For all sorts of reasons, as I will show, we need something very different from what we have. And, as I also set out to demonstrate, things are certainly going to (continue to) change. If we don't want them to change for the worse, and the classic social democratic welfare state is no longer an option, we need to think very hard (and quite fast) about how welfare and progress (and existential survival) can be made to go together. Helping us to do that is what this book is for.

An outline of the book

I begin by considering the shape of our welfare regime at the end of ten years of Conservative-led government, and on the eve of the COVID-19 crisis. The story is messy but the overall outcomes are relatively clear. The decade was defined by the pursuit of austerity: the aspiration to reduce public debt and the budget deficit, above all, by curbing spending on welfare. This strategy was partially successful – taking the budget deficit back to the levels seen before 2008, and stabilising the overall debt. Pensioner incomes were largely protected, as were budgets in health and (to a lesser extent) education. Income and wealth inequality did not (quite) take off in the way that some had feared. But there were still very real costs to this retrenchment, and these were largely imposed on those who were least able to afford them. There were real-term cuts for those towards the bottom of the income profile and there was a substantial growth in the number of working-poor families. Perhaps the starkest indication of the costs of a decade of austerity was the major increase in child poverty. *All* parties had pledged to eliminate child poverty under the Child Poverty Act 2010 – but in the decade that followed the number of children living in poverty rose by around 600,000.[9]

If this is not what we want, what are the alternatives? Perhaps the most obvious place to start the search is with the extended period of ('new') social democratic government that preceded the Conservative ascendancy after 2010: that is, with the record of New Labour. This is the task in Chapter 2. Although we may feel that there is *nothing* which has not already been said about the Blair–Brown years, it is still important to undertake this work. This is a period that, largely as a result of its place in subsequent fighting within the Labour Party, has already entered the realms of mythology (see Goes, 2016). And it is an experience which, I suspect, is misunderstood or misrepresented by both its supporters and its opponents. In the welfare area, New Labour did some really important and progressive things – especially in relation to child and pensioner poverty, and in spending on healthcare and education. But it did so with rapidly depleting political resources. What it did achieve it achieved through fairly traditional means – raising taxes and funding public services, in a context of sustained economic growth. But social mobility stalled and high levels of wealth and income inequality went largely unchallenged. Despite all the things that were different about New Labour, it still pursued what was, at its core, a social democratic strategy – but one attempted under circumstances that made it ever more difficult to deliver *sustainable* change. It is a bit melodramatic to call it (with Yanis Varoufakis) a 'Faustian pact', but, for reasons I outline in this chapter, I think of New Labour as presiding over what was probably the *last* social democratic welfare state (Varoufakis, 2016: 211).

The third chapter takes us some way further back in Labour's ideational history – and to a rather different account of what the welfare state was for, and of its intrinsic *limits* as a 'strategy of equality'. Although, as we find it in the work of key figures such as Tom Marshall and Tony Crosland, the welfare state is an important part of this story, there is much else besides. Other prominent Labour thinkers – including Dalton, Cole, Durbin and Meade – saw that *just* doing the politics of tax and spend wouldn't work. As Cole had it, you couldn't just keep on 'squeezing the capitalist orange'. At some point, you had to think about who owned what and how you could change that. A sort of 'political Keynesianism' made it possible to defer that – very difficult – question, perhaps for a generation or even two, but it could not make it go away for ever. By the time that confronting the problem could no longer be delayed, the party seemed to have forgotten that it ever existed in the first place. Hence, the incomprehension in the face of the reversals of the 1980s – and beyond. We are unlikely to find the solutions that we need now in these sources from the 1930s, 1940s and 1950s. But we will certainly find that there were Labour thinkers then who asked the right questions – and there is something we can learn from reading them now, as we face a very different set of challenges in very different circumstances but, in relation to which, as they insisted, *who owns what is still the crucial issue.*

Chapter 4 looks at three of the most pressing and difficult of those coming challenges: ageing, the changing nature of work and climate change. Ageing is a deep-seated, unshiftable and growing challenge for whoever has custody of the welfare state. The world of work is changing rather unpredictably, but certainly in ways that render the traditional institutional management of the working life-course increasingly irrelevant and impractical. *All* previous social democratic solutions relied upon the dynamics of sustained economic growth to finesse/fudge difficult questions of distribution but, given the imperative of addressing climate change, this is a solution we can no longer afford. There are plenty of good and innovative ideas out there with which to address these new circumstances and I review what seem to me to be the most important and promising of these. But they are not (quite) enough. It is difficult, but we need to address the distributional challenges of the present head on. Now more than ever, we have to find a way of *reallocating wealth* which we have to learn to share in a different way – if we want to leave anything civilised behind us in a hundred years' time (that is within the lifespan of some citizens who are already born).

In Chapter 5 I ask (with even more circumspection) how will all of this be impacted by COVID-19? Some have thought that it might bring us a new era of mutualism and cooperation; others, that it will trigger a second and still more damaging epoch of austerity. Although no one can know, I suspect that the outcomes will actually be rather more prosaic. COVID will make everything more difficult and it will present us with some new and unanticipated challenges. Governments will have to do some very fancy fiscal footwork to deal with the mountain of debt that they have created. But when the crisis and its aftermath have passed (which will take some time), none of the underlying problems I have reported will have gone away. In the Conclusion, I review the argument and make some suggestions about what we would need to do if we wanted a politics of welfare and well-being that was adequate to these several challenges. Sadly, I fear that the prospects of our actually doing any of this are not very good.

It will be clear that this is a very personal take on the issues we face. It is also, in every way, a *British* story. (European social democracy looks very different, and it intellectual sources are very different. But it is still in deep trouble.) While I have tried wherever I can to provide a solid evidential basis for my claims, not everyone will accept what I say in substance, still less the judgement calls that I make. But I have tried very hard to be honest about the problems that we face – and the ways we might confront them. Very obviously, this is not the only way forwards, or out. But I am very confident that we can only get where we need to be once we square up to the question 'who owns?'. If we really are concerned about our collective well-being, we have no alternative.

1

Welfare in an age of austerity

My purpose in this first chapter is to establish just what the welfare regime in Britain looked like on the eve of the COVID-19 crisis. The decade of welfare austerity, signalled in George Osborne's Mais Lecture on 24 February 2010, had already come to a rather faltering close with Chancellor Sajid Javid's Spending Review at the end of the summer of 2019.[1] And this shift was consummated with the new Chancellor Rishi Sunak's first budget in March 2020, which promised growth in public expenditure of 2.8 per cent for the years between 2020/21 and 2023/24. This initiative committed the government to building and funding a public sector larger than it had been at any time between the 1980s and the financial crisis of 2008 (including *all* of the years of New Labour government prior to the crisis). This future scenario was almost immediately overtaken by (unanticipated) events. Thus, Rishi Sunak's first budget also included a series of emergency spending measures designed to deal with the developing crisis surrounding the outbreak of COVID-19. These turned out to be just the first, now rather modest-looking steps in what was to become an unprecedented peacetime programme of public spending, designed to save the economic life of the nation, while protecting its collective health. As we shall see in Chapter 5, COVID-19 took us into a new world of public expenditure and public indebtedness. The hard-won savings that had been eked out over a decade of austerity were blown away in a couple of months as the Treasury committed itself (initially) to an additional £218 billion of borrowing for 2020/21.[2]

While the pandemic, and the wealth of measures taken by the government to counteract it, has had a profound impact upon our welfare order (and our well-being), it has not simply 'undone' what was there before. As we shall see, while some changes will endure, and while the impact of some of the more temporary measures will have a lasting effect, much of what the government did was self-consciously designed to be short term – to 'do whatever it takes' to get us through the crisis. The longer-term consequences of these shorter-term changes – plus the impact of simultaneously moving to a post-Brexit world of work and trade – may take a generation to emerge. For now, they remain profoundly uncertain. But some things we do know. One is that the intensifying demographic challenge of an ageing population will not go away any time soon. We know also that, whatever may be the consequences for inequality of living in a post-COVID economy, these changes will have done little to address long-standing problems of substantive poverty, both generally and, more particularly, in the form of child poverty (even if, for a time, they might make the wealthy a little less wealthy). We shall still be struggling to find a workable solution to the problem of the future management and funding of social care – a challenge that successive governments have been avoiding for a generation.[3] And all of this is before we ask the question of how we can remake our way of life – economically, socially and culturally – so that it fits with the parameters of an urgent climate change crisis.

I return to these necessarily uncertain but profoundly consequential questions a little later in the book. I begin with something just a little bit more certain, though already shrouded in its own veil of myth and mystery: how we got to be where we are – and where that is. I begin by outlining the policy changes that made up the strategy of austerity in the decade after 2010. I then consider how these changes impacted on inequalities of income and wealth, on poverty, particularly child poverty, and on social mobility. I close the chapter with a consideration of the changing dynamics of inherited wealth.

The austerity welfare state 2010–20

It is probably right to think of welfare state policy making in the decade between George Osborne's Mais Lecture (24 February 2010) and Sajid Javid's Spending Review (4 September 2019) as operating under the spectre of austerity. In his Mais Lecture, Osborne insisted that the 'big problem' that loomed over the British economy was debt. Private debt had caused the last crisis and, were it allowed to continue as it was, public debt would trigger the next one. The imperative was to reduce public indebtedness, and to do so quickly – aiming 'to eliminate the bulk of the structural current budget deficit over a Parliament'. This was to be achieved principally by reducing public expenditure, which Osborne stipulated should bear 80 per cent of the burden of rebalancing the budget.[4]

That this meant reducing the size of the welfare state became clear in Osborne's Emergency Budget of June 2010. Arguing that the situation was even worse than it had previously supposed, Osborne committed the new Coalition Government to £61 billion-worth of cuts down to 2014/15. Since the government was signed up to real-terms increases in expenditure on the National Health Service, and as it chose to 'triple lock' pension upratings to the higher of increases in earnings, prices or 2.5 per cent and to sustain the level of expenditure on education, the burden of these cuts would fall the more heavily on other areas of public expenditure, reducing other departmental budgets by around a quarter. The bulk of these savings would have to come from what Osborne labelled 'the welfare bill'. But the squeeze also represented, he insisted, an opportunity to refashion this budget as 'a tool to support work and encourage aspiration'. The following savings were identified at the time of the Emergency Budget in 2010: a two-year freeze on public sector pay; a three-year freeze on Child Benefit; an acceleration in the increase in the State Pension Age to 66; a reduction in entitlement to Housing Benefit; various reductions in tax credits; and uprating of benefits in line with the (lower) consumer price index (CPI) rather than the retail price index (RPI). At the same time, the rate of Value Added Tax (VAT) was raised from 17.5 per cent to 20 per cent (generating a further £13 billion). Corporation tax was cut from 28 per cent to 27 per cent (in the first of a series of reductions that would see it fall to 19 per cent in 2017).[5] In the first of a series of such moves, the income tax personal allowance was raised to £10,000 (rising to £12,500 in 2020).[6] In the 2014 Budget, the government introduced a 'welfare cap' on the total of cash transfer spending on around half of the social security budget (excluding state pensions).[7]

Many of these changes were complicated and subject to revision throughout the period of the Coalition Government between 2010 and 2015 (and beyond). For many, the effects were, and are, cumulative. The public sector pay freeze was lifted in 2013 but increases were restricted to 1 per cent (until 2017), with the net effect that public sector pay was 2.5 per cent lower in real terms in 2017 than it had been in 2010.[8] When the freeze on Child Benefit ended in 2013, entitlement to support was partially withdrawn for households with one income above £50,000 and totally withdrawn where that salary was £60,000 or above. This impacted upon some 13 per cent of families with children. As these thresholds were not subsequently uprated in line with inflation, by 2019/20 this figure had risen to cover around 18 per cent of all families with children.[9] The Pensions Act 2011 accelerated the process by which women's retirement ages would be made the same as those of men, with both then rising to 66.[10]

In 2010, George Osborne described the system of Housing Benefit as 'in dire need of reform'. The principal reforms in the period 2010–15 consisted of a reduction in the rate at which rental costs would be met (as a proportion of typical local rental costs, within absolute limits) and the imposition of a 'bedroom tax' on those tenants whose properties were deemed to be 'too large' on the basis of their family size. A small proportion of tenants had their support reduced because they would otherwise breach the upper limit of a newly introduced benefits cap (from 2013/14).[11] Deductions for non-dependants were also increased in the period 2012–14.[12] In 2010, the Chancellor described the levels of payments of tax credits as 'unsustainable'. Here again, changes were complicated and introduced across time. The most important of these changes included abolition of the 'baby element' in the Child Tax Credit and a quicker tapering of payments as incomes rise. Similar reductions were made in relation to Working Tax Credits, with an increase in the minimum hours worked for entitlement and a reduction in payments for childcare costs (from 80 to 70 per cent).[13]

In the years that followed, there were a series of reforms in the treatment of those with a disability – aimed at reducing the numbers claiming benefits and bringing more people with a disability into the world of work. The Disability Living Allowance was replaced by the Personal Independence Payment. Incapacity Benefit was replaced with the Employment and Support Allowance. These changes involved more stringent medical tests (especially in relation to the capacity to work), greater conditionality and time-limiting of the non-means-tested entitlement for those in what was designated the Work-Related Activity Group. The 2010 Budget had identified these reforms as a way of 'significantly improving incentives to work' and there was also an expectation that this would represent a significant saving to the Treasury. In the end, savings were closer to £650 million than the £4.5 billion originally projected (on all of which, see Beatty and Fothergill, 2017: 951).

Some benefits were simply abolished. Council Tax Benefit ceased (in 2013) with grants of 90 per cent of the previous value of the benefit paid to local authorities to fund their own schemes. Under these circumstances, most councils chose to reduce the level of support previously made to those who had difficulty in paying (the government required that no additional costs were levied upon pensioners). The Health in Pregnancy Grant was abolished in 2011, while eligibility for the Sure Start maternity grant was tightened. The Coalition Government also decided to abandon the Saving Gateway and to cease further payments into the Child Trust Fund.[14]

The single most important *structural* reform in the period of Coalition Government was the introduction (from 2012) of UC: a single payment which was to incorporate and replace six of the main pre-existing working-aged benefits and credits: Jobseekers' Allowance, Employment and Support Allowance, Income Support, Housing Benefit, Council Tax Benefit, and Child Tax and Working Tax Credits. Much attention came to focus on the repeatedly delayed roll-out of the new system.[15] Critics also argued that the new pattern of payments – monthly and with a long wait for first payments – was unsuited to the many vulnerable and resource-strapped people who would need to apply for UC. Among the explicit aims of the new structure was an end to 'welfare dependency', a greater focus on work and 'work-readiness', increased conditionality and more responsibility for budget management among claimants themselves (including the greater use of benefit sanctions for non-compliance).[16] The government's own impact assessment estimated that once fully implemented there would be a net cost to the Exchequer of around £2 billion. An OBR evaluation in 2017 estimated net savings of around £1 billion in a budget of around £60 billion.[17] The overall cost implications of implementing UC are unclear. According to the Resolution Foundation, the tightening of some entitlements under UC may have been offset by a greater uptake of (previously unclaimed) benefits.[18] There were and are winners and losers – though it appears that it is the poorest who are most likely to lose income in the long run.[19] In any case, UC was not primarily a cost-cutting device. It was designed, above all, to change claimants' *behaviour*.

The return of a stand-alone Conservative Government in 2015 brought further austerity measures. The Summer Budget in 2015 saw: most working-age benefits frozen for a four-year period; income thresholds in tax credits and work allowances in UC reduced (by 40 per cent in the case of tax credits); the rate of tax credit tapers increased (from 41 to 48 per cent); a limit of two to the number of dependent children who counted in new tax credit and UC claims; a further reduction in the benefit cap; and social rent increases capped at 1 per cent with an anticipated saving to Housing Benefit (of around £2 billion). The intention overall was to secure further savings on the welfare budget of around £12 billion a year (by 2019/20).[20]

On the revenue side (and in keeping with the 80:20 rule), there was a modest growth in taxes across the decade. The increase in VAT from 17.5 to 20 per cent saw a steep hike (of about 1 per cent of GDP) between 2010 and 2012, after which it levelled out at around 6 per cent. Income tax as a percentage of GDP fell modestly between 2010 and 2020 (to below 9 per cent), reflecting repeated increases in the personal allowance and sustained sluggish growth in real wage levels. Despite a widely publicised lowering of the highest rate (from 50 to 45 per cent in 2013/14), the top 1 per cent of earners ended the decade paying around a third of all income tax (up from around a quarter in 2010). While there were repeated adjustments to National Insurance contributions across the decade, its contribution to overall revenue remained steady as a proportion of GDP (at just over 6 per cent). Overall, taxation rose by around 2 percentage points between 2010 and 2020 (from 32 to 34 per cent of GDP). As a consequence, *before* the emergency COVID-19 measures, the government's tax take from the economy was higher than it had been at any time under New Labour. And while most of the work of income redistribution was (and is) done by the benefit system, the tax regime remained broadly progressive, accounting for about 20 per cent of redistribution (of market incomes).[21]

This extended programme of welfare reform had multiple purposes. The reforms were designed to change incentives: principally, the incentive to take low-paid waged work though also, for example, to live in smaller and less expensive (rented) accommodation. They were also intended to focus resources on 'those in need' and to reduce 'welfare dependency'. But, they were supposed to reduce a welfare bill which George Osborne had described in 2010 as 'unaffordable'.

Austerity? Which austerity?

Austerity was real enough. A House of Commons briefing paper (from 2016) suggested that the welfare reforms were intended to save around £26 billion by 2016/17– roughly 10 per cent of the welfare budget. Looking forward to 2020/21, these savings were projected to increase to around 15 per cent. Of these (net) savings, around 40 per cent was accounted for by reductions in the uprating of existing benefits (freezes, or linking benefit increases to a lower index), 14 per cent by reductions in tax credits, 12 per cent by the tightening of eligibility for Child Benefit and 10 per cent by changes in the rules surrounding Housing Benefit. Despite the introduction of the Living Wage, and the work done by Child Tax Credits and Working Tax Credits, the cuts had a disproportionate impact on poorer families, and the children within those families. Figure 1.1 shows the distributional impact of changes made down to 2017 (projected to 2021/22), making it clear that the tax/benefit changes primarily disadvantaged those in the bottom half of the income profile.

Employment certainly increased across the decade (Figure 1.2). At the start of 2020 there were a record-breaking 33,000,000 people in work (representing 76.5 per cent of the population aged 16–64).

But persistent low levels of overall economic growth, slow increases in wages and widespread underemployment meant that growing numbers of these workers were also poor.[22] By 2017, wages had failed to return to their levels of a decade previously (Figure 1.3).

Those *without* work (and their children) were still much more likely to be poor. But, in terms of numbers, they were increasingly outweighed by those who were in work, but poor (and their children). In 2019, the Joseph Rowntree Foundation reported that 'more than half (56 per cent) of people in poverty are now in a working family, a significant change from 20 years ago when 39% were … [S]even in ten children in poverty are now in a working family'.[23] I return to the incidence of poverty later.

Despite these very real hardships, both Coalition and Conservative Governments failed to make the savings they had anticipated. In its retrospective survey in 2016, the OBR found that, in the event, only £5 billion-worth of the projected savings had actually been realised under the Coalition Government. The Summer Budget of 2015 had anticipated a further reduction in annual welfare spending of around £12 billion by 2019/20.[24] At the time, the OBR's estimate of likely actual savings from these reforms was £9.7 billion. Reviewing the position in 2019, the OBR found that savings were about £4 billion less than the Treasury had anticipated, with most of the difference being explained by the government's reversal of its own decision to reduce the generosity of tax credits and by the wholesale absence of savings from anticipated

Figure 1.1: Cash impacts of reforms made during 2010–15 and 2015–17 Parliaments, by household income decile

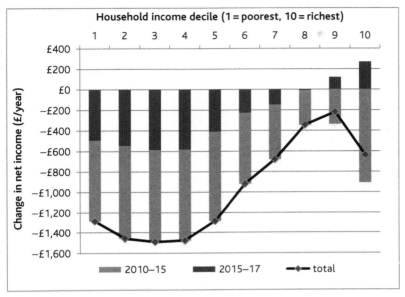

Note: Annual cash impact of 2010–17 reforms in 2021/22
Source: https://www.equalityhumanrights.com/sites/default/files/impact-of-tax-and-welfare-reforms-2010-2017-interim-report_0.pdf. The copyright in the document this publication has been adapted from and all other intellectual property rights in that material are owned by the Commission for Equality and Human Rights, known as the Equality and Human Rights Commission ('the EHRC').

reductions in the cost of disability benefits. Almost the only projected saving to have been larger than anticipated was that associated with the freezing of benefit rates for the four years after 2015/16 (and this because of higher than anticipated inflation).[25]

Still more important in government's failure to realise the savings they wanted was the decision to ring-fence budgets in the most expensive areas. Across the decade, governments decided not just to protect but, in practice, to enhance incomes for the growing number of old-age pensioners (under the terms of the triple-lock guarantee). By 2016/17, the state pension made up something like 42 per cent of the entire welfare budget and the increased generosity after 2010 had increased the state pension by 3 per cent relative to RPI inflation and a full 10 percentage points against the level of earnings (which barely grew at all between 2010 and 2016).[26] Expenditure on the old-age pension rose from £94 billion in 2009/10 to £103 billion in 2014/15.[27] Governments throughout the decade were also committed to real-terms increases in spending on public healthcare. The NHS budget rose from £111.7 billion in 2010 to £137.1 billion in 2020.[28] The government also

Figure 1.2: Employment rate (ages 16–64) in HBAI and LFS, UK

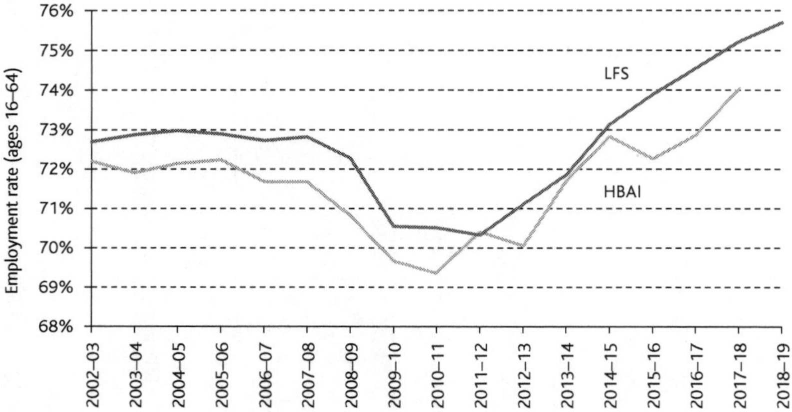

Note: HBAI = households below average income; LFS = Labour Force Survey
Source: P. Bourquin, J. Cribb, T. Waters and X. Xu, 'Living Standards, Poverty and Inequality in the UK: 2019'. London: Institute for Fiscal Studies. Available from: https://www.ifs.org.uk/uploads/R157-Living-Standards-Poverty-and-Inequality-2019.pdf

Figure 1.3: Real median weekly earnings of employees in HBAI and LFS, UK

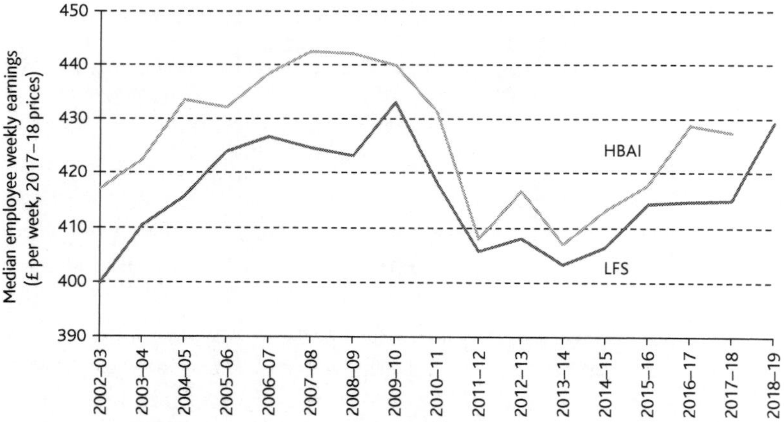

Note: HBAI = households below average income; LFS = Labour Force Survey
Source: P. Bourquin, J. Cribb, T. Waters and X. Xu, 'Living Standards, Poverty and Inequality in the UK: 2019'. London: Institute for Fiscal Studies. Available from: https://www.ifs.org.uk/uploads/R157-Living-Standards-Poverty-and-Inequality-2019.pdf

broadly maintained the value of spending on education, the third largest item on the public expenditure ticket.[29] Meanwhile, reform of the disability benefit regime failed to yield the anticipated substantial savings. Rates of economic growth remained sluggish (and below forecast) for the entire decade, meaning that tax revenues did less work than might have been expected.[30]

By the time Boris Johnson's Conservative Government came to abandon austerity, the picture was complicated but clear. The cuts were real enough – but the burden was very unevenly distributed, with the largest areas of expenditure being protected or, indeed, enhanced. In particular, the significant advances made in addressing child poverty (through to 2012) had been reversed and the numbers of the working poor had risen substantially. Anticipated savings were never achieved, while persistently low interest rates and growth repeatedly below official expectations meant that the fixation with 'reducing the size of the deficit' looked increasingly misplaced.[31] Eventually, the goal of eliminating the budget deficit had been, more or less reluctantly, abandoned. For those who needed it most, the welfare state had certainly become leaner and meaner. Increasing costs had been restrained, but not reversed. But as welfare states are principally systems of provision for older people and as this section of the population continued to grow and as its income and services looked set to remain protected, the prospects of an overall 'scaling back' of the welfare state seemed increasingly improbable – even *before* COVID-19.

Income inequality

This gives us a pretty good idea of what happened to welfare policy and budgets over the decade 2010–20 (down to the outbreak of COVID-19). But what is perhaps of greater interest are the social and economic *consequences* of these developments. One important aspect of this can be seen in changing levels (and forms) of inequality. We have seen a wealth of new work on inequality in the last decade (including Stiglitz, 2012; Therborn, 2013; Atkinson, 2015; Milanovic, 2016; Scheidel, 2017) of which the most widely noticed has been Thomas Piketty's *Capital in the Twenty-First Century* (2014) and *Capital and Ideology* (2020). The picture that emerges from this work is complicated, even if the headline message – that we have witnessed a resurgence of economic inequality in Western countries over the past four decades – seems clear enough. Piketty's story (in both books) shows the pattern of social and economic inequalities (and their justification) over the very long term. In particular, he reports a U-shaped curve in the 20th century, as the extremely high levels of income inequality prior to the Second World War were transformed through to the 1970s, from which time we have seen a re-emergence of inequality (Figure 1.4).[32]

In the context of austerity – which, as we have just seen, while not being quite what its architects had intended and supposed, was real enough – this long-term pattern fed into a story about rising inequality in Britain after 2010. This is an account that we can find in both popular and academic discourse (see, for example, the essays in Dorling, 2018). It is often evoked in explanations of the rise of populist politics and of why Brexit happened

Figure 1.4: Top 1 per cent national income share, UK, 1918–2019

Source: Graph provided by www.wid.world

(Fetzer, 2019; Norris and Ingelhart, 2019). But as an account of what actually took place in the decade 2010–20, it is slightly misleading. The really big changes in income inequality over the past 40 years came in the 1980s. For much of the period between 2010 and 2020, income inequality more or less flatlined. But it increased significantly towards the end of the decade (from around 2017). Thus, the Gini coefficient for disposable income rose from 33.4 in 2016/17 to 36.3 in 2019/20. This was still significantly *lower* than it had been in the last year of (Labour) government before the financial crisis of 2008 (when it reached 38.6). Some have argued that the Gini coefficient is not a good metric for measuring inequality (since its one number may reflect quite different inequality profiles). But other indicators (such as P90/ P10 and S80/S20) also show a significant rise across the decade.[33] When the Institute for Fiscal Studies (IFS) sought in 2017 to project the likely direction of income inequality for the next five years (through to 2021/22), it did anticipate that the situation would deteriorate significantly and that, for those at the 20th percentile, real incomes would fall – and this largely as a consequence of the changes to benefit provisions made after 2015.[34] In the event, these predictions have been rendered obsolete by COVID-19 and its aftermath.

Wealth inequality

It would be a mistake to focus too exclusively upon changes in *income* inequality. One of the key conclusions/outcomes of Piketty's work is a recognition that wealth – which has always been much more unequally

Table 1.1: Gini coefficient: wealth inequality in the UK

	2006–08	2016–18
Total wealth	61	63
Pension wealth (net)	77	72
Property wealth (net)	62	66
Financial wealth	89	91
Physical wealth	46	47

Source: https://www.ons.gov.uk/peoplepopulationandcommunity/
personalandhouseholdfinances/incomeandwealth/bulletins/totalwealthingreatbritain/
april2016tomarch2018#trends-in-total-wealth-inequality-in-great-britain

distributed than income – has recently experienced something of a renaissance as an indicator of people's (differential) well-being (though it never really went away). One simple indicator of this is the fact that total wealth in the UK had grown from being around three times the size of GDP in 1980 to be something like seven times as large as a much-increased GDP by 2015. This unequal distribution of wealth is at least as important as the unequal distribution of incomes. Probably, more so. And wealth is much more unevenly divided than income. Whereas the Gini coefficient for income is around 34, for wealth it stands at around 63 (perhaps higher; see Table 1.1). In 2016, UK households held more than £11 trillion – including £4 trillion in property and £4.5 trillion in private pension assets.[35] Britain is a wealthy country.

Again, the story in the really long term is that wealth was very unequally owned in the period prior to 1914. In 1900, 1 per cent of the population in the UK owned around 70 per cent of total personal wealth. Absolute levels and the concentration of ownership declined between 1910 and 1970. From the early 1980s, they began to rise once again. This is the period in which wealth for those at the very top of the distribution globally – the top 1 per cent, or top 0.1 per cent or the top 0.01 per cent – began to move away from everyone else (Figure 1.5). In the UK, the wealth share of the top 1 per cent increased from around 15.2 in 1988 to 20.6 per cent in 2009.[36] Milanovic (2016) estimates that between 1987 and 2013 the share of the world's bi-billionaires (those with assets of $2 billion or greater) in global GDP doubled (from 3 per cent to 6 per cent). Compounding these trends over a period of time would lead to the ever more pronounced concentration of wealth among a tiny minority of the hyper-rich (Piketty, 2014: 432–9).

If we focus on recent data for the UK from the Office for National Statistics (ONS), inequality in the ownership of wealth appears relatively stable since figures were first collated on their present basis in 2006, though there has been some further concentration, at both the bottom and the top. But the inequalities are of a different order from those we see in relation to income.

Figure 1.5: Top 1 per cent net personal wealth share, UK, 1895–2012

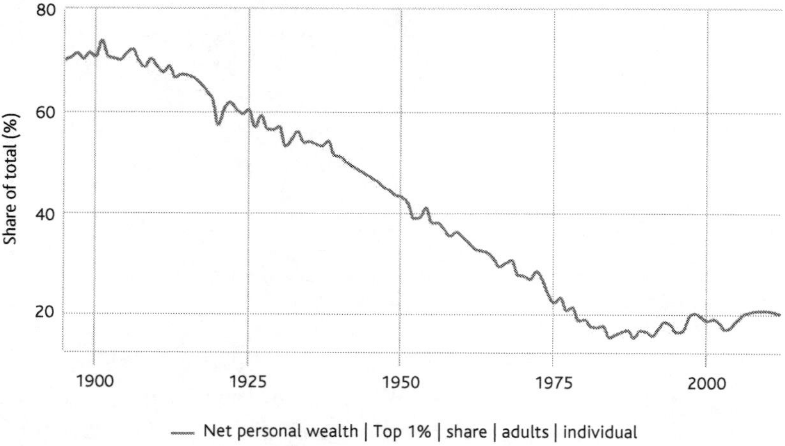

— Net personal wealth | Top 1% | share | adults | individual

Source: Graph provided by www.wid.world

Upon the ONS evidence, half of Britain's wealth is owned by 12 per cent of the population. The bottom 10 per cent own less than one tenth of 1 per cent – and on average their financial and property wealth is negative (that is, they are in debt). The mean-to-median ratio for all wealth in the UK (a simple index of unequal distribution) has increased incrementally to be close to 2.0 in 2018. But this conceals very substantial differences in the unequal ownership of differing forms of property. While pension wealth has become more equal since 2006 (as the numbers retiring with relatively generous private pension annuities increased), property wealth and financial wealth have become more unequal, with the Gini coefficient for the latter shading above 90.[37]

Housing property makes up around one third of all wealth in the UK – and it is more evenly distributed than wealth in financial assets. In *Capital in the Twenty-First Century*, Piketty had already pointed to the emergence over the 20th century of a patrimonial middle class: that is, a middle class made up of individuals and families who increasingly owned their own home. This was, he suggested, 'a social, economic, and political transformation of fundamental importance' (Piketty, 2014: 129–30). Homeownership was perhaps the most important means of diffusing the ownership of wealth after 1945 and, in Britain, it was extended down the affluence ladder by the selling-off of (discounted) social housing from the 1980s onwards. But Peak Private Ownership in Britain came in 2003, at 71 per cent. The present distribution of homeownership is skewed, with much lower levels of homeownership among younger people (compared to their parents at a similar age) and a lower proportion of younger people being able to step

Figure 1.6: Top 1 per cent's share of taxable income

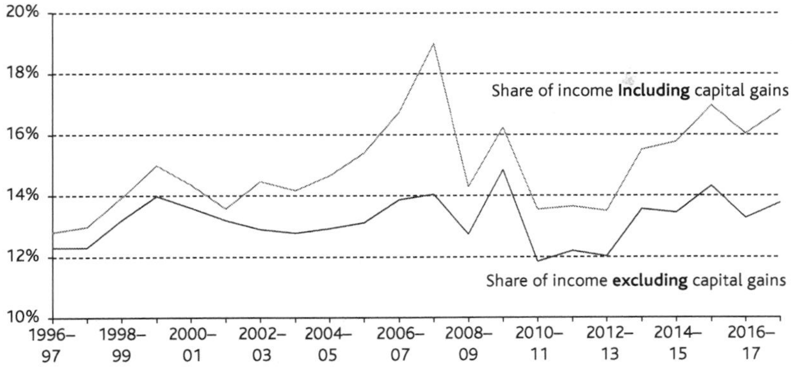

Source: https://www.resolutionfoundation.org/app/uploads/2020/05/Who-gains.pdf

onto the property ladder. But this is not just a cohort effect. Since 2006, homeownership has fallen by 12 per cent for those in the bottom half of the wealth profile. For those in the top 10 per cent, it shows very little change. The consequences of these changes will take several decades to emerge fully – but it is clear that the distributional issues here are both intra- and intergenerational (on which, see Christophers, 2018). It also shows that the salience of inheritance may be creeping down the income profile – as the emergent importance of the 'Bank of Mum and Dad' as a source of home loans makes clear.[38] I return to the issue of inheritance later in this chapter, and of property in housing and pensions in Chapter 2.

Finally, it is worth reporting the way in which the level and distribution of capital gains has changed, both before and after 2008. Although they fell in the immediate aftermath of the financial crisis, capital gains have increased rapidly over the past eight years, from around £24 billion in 2012/13 to £55 billion in 2017/18 (Figure 1.6).

Apart from the remarkable spike in income share just prior to the crisis, the most instructive element in contrasting income share of the top 1 per cent with and without capital gains is that while the proportion *excluding* capital gains returns (around 2013) to its pre-crisis level, the proportion *including* capital gains has risen steeply ever since 2012. This would point towards a further (and under-reported) concentration in the ownership of wealth between 2010 and 2020.

Poverty

Of course, inequality – whether of income or wealth – is always likely to be an area of concern. This would be true even if we lived in societies that ensured that everyone had the means of living a reasonably secure and comfortable life. In practice, societies that are very unequal do *not* generally secure the health and well-being of those at the bottom (see, for example, Wilkinson and Pickett, 2009). But, even if they did, they might not be good societies to live in. In any case, we have good reason to be concerned about the welfare of those at the bottom of the pile – irrespective of the overall profile of distribution (of whatever good it is with which we are concerned). This means we should independently take an interest in the question of poverty.

In doing this, we do well to circumnavigate the well-worn arguments about what *really* counts as poverty. Ever since we have had any conception of relative poverty, critics on the right have insisted that this is just a surrogate for arguing against inequality. If poverty is defined as a proportion of mean income, when incomes rise so do the numbers defined as being in poverty (even though they have not become any worse off).[39] I seek to avoid this claim by focusing principally upon *absolute* poverty, which is not vulnerable to the claim that increases in overall incomes will generally increase the numbers in poverty. (This is also the preferred metric of the Department for Work and Pensions.) In addition, I devote particular attention to *child* poverty, since here at least there is a (notional) party political consensus that it exists and that it ought to be eliminated – and virtually all of the arguments that 'blame' the poor for their own poverty cannot really be seen to apply (unless we think that poor children should not have chosen the *wrong* parents).[40] In general, I employ the following definitions given by the IFS:

- *Absolute poverty*: 60 per cent of median income in 2010/11, updated for inflation.
- *Severe poverty*: very low household income (below 50 per cent or 40 per cent of the median), low household expenditure, and/or experiencing 'material deprivation'.
- *Material deprivation*: being unable to afford a range of items (for example, warm winter coats for any children in the household) and activities (such as taking children to a regular leisure activity). A family is classified as materially deprived if it is unable to afford a certain number of these items, with more weight given to items that most families already have.

Absolute poverty rates (see Figure 1.7) fell steeply between 1997 and 2004. They were relatively flat for much of the next decade, before falling again, more slowly, after 2012. The steepest fall was in poverty among pensioners – driven, in part, by their more generous benefit treatment (maintained after 2010) but also a result of greater private pension wealth among new retirees. Absolute poverty among children was and remains above the average for the population overall.

Figure 1.7: Absolute poverty rates (After Housing Costs) since 1997/8, overall and by demographic group

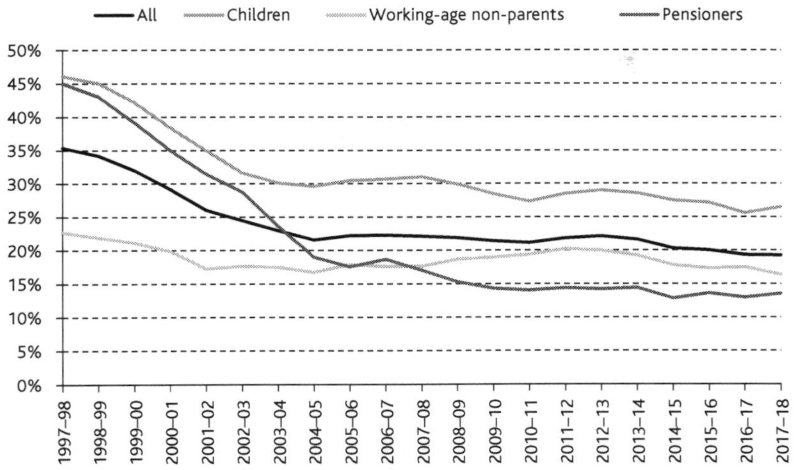

Source: P. Bourquin, J. Cribb, T. Waters and X. Xu, 'Living Standards, Poverty and Inequality in the UK: 2019'. London: Institute for Fiscal Studies. Available from: https://www.ifs.org.uk/uploads/R157-Living-Standards-Poverty-and-Inequality-2019.pdf

Severe poverty can be measured in a variety of ways and can be reported at various thresholds (see Figure 1.8). The IFS warns that these numbers may not reflect accurately what is going on – especially among those reporting the very lowest incomes. Nonetheless, certain trends are clear enough. Having peaked around 2000, measures of severe poverty fell through to 2008. They have fluctuated beyond that time, but with no clear trend. At whatever level we choose to set 'severe' poverty, these rates seem not to have fallen as much as the higher threshold measures of 'absolute' or 'relative' poverty. Generally, severe poverty is more concentrated among social renters and in workless families but there is a measurable increase in recent years in severe poverty among working/private-renting households.

Material deprivation is an alternative indicator of families' inability to afford certain 'basics' (buying a winter coat or celebrating a birthday, for example). This metric rose for both pensioners and children in the immediate aftermath of the financial crisis of 2008 (see Figure 1.9), before falling after 2013/14. Thereafter, it continues to fall slowly for pensioners. For children, the indicator is broadly flat after 2015 and it affects a much larger section of the relevant population (though indicators for the two groups are not directly comparable).

The *material deprivation* indicator for households in severe poverty shows a broadly similar trend to that for the pensioner population: increases through 2014 and a fall thereafter (though both sides of this 'peak' are rather steeper; see Figure 1.10). This differs from the other indicators we have for severe poverty (which saw no real trend between 2008 and 2018).

Figure 1.8: Share in both expenditure poverty (various thresholds) and headline income poverty, After Housing Costs

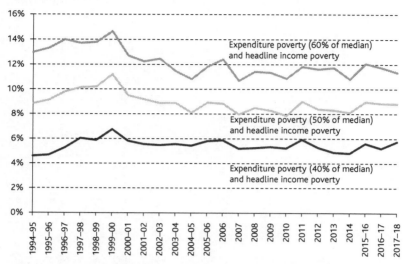

Source: P. Bourquin, J. Cribb, T. Waters and X. Xu, 'Living Standards, Poverty and Inequality in the UK: 2019'. London: Institute for Fiscal Studies. Available from: https://www.ifs.org.uk/uploads/R157-Living-Standards-Poverty-and-Inequality-2019.pdf

Figure 1.9: Child and pensioner material deprivation rates

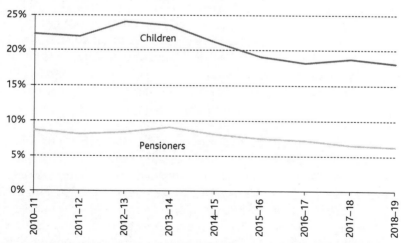

Source: P. Bourquin, R. Joyce, A.N. Keiller, 'Living Standards, Poverty and Inequality in the UK: 2020'. London: Institute for Fiscal Studies. Available from: https://www.ifs.org.uk/uploads/R170-Living-standards-poverty-and-inequality-in-the-UK-2019-2020%20.pdf

Figure 1.10: Income poverty rates (After Housing Costs) and material deprivation among working-age families (households below average income)

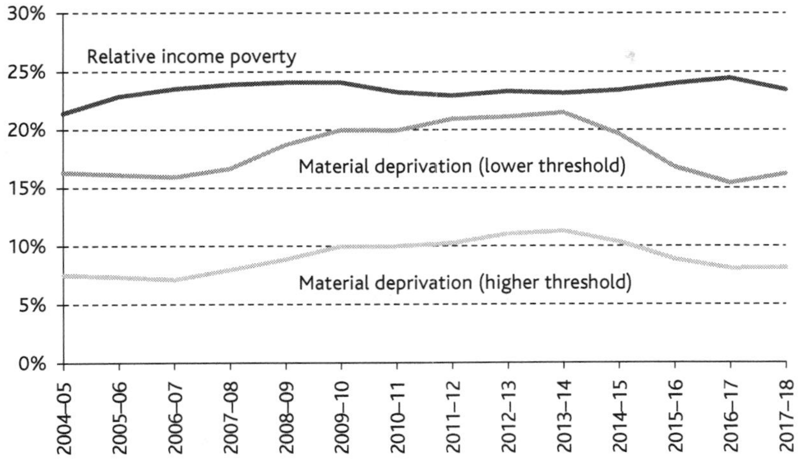

Source: P. Bourquin, J. Cribb, T. Waters and X. Xu, 'Living Standards, Poverty and Inequality in the UK: 2019'. London: Institute for Fiscal Studies. Available from: https://www.ifs.org.uk/uploads/R157-Living-Standards-Poverty-and-Inequality-2019.pdf

Child poverty

Child poverty was a particular focus of attention across the 2010–20 decade, as it had been in the ten years previously following Tony Blair's commitment (in 1999) to eliminate child poverty by 2020.[41] The Child Poverty Act of 2010, with all-party support, committed future governments to work towards this same target. The incoming Coalition Government, however, showed little interest in meeting this goal, with Osborne's Mais Lecture simply committing the government to reduce the numbers of children growing up in workless households – a target which it could reach (and did reach) without actually reducing levels of child poverty. The government renamed the Child Poverty Commission, which was legally responsible for reporting on progress in reducing child poverty, first as the Child and Social Mobility Commission and then as the Social Mobility Commission. As we shall see, social mobility is itself a crucial indicator of inequality – but it is not the same as child poverty. The explicit target for reducing the latter was finally dropped in 2015.

There is some disagreement about what precisely happened to child poverty after 2010, and of what is likely to happen to it in the immediate future. But there is little disagreement about the general direction of travel: child poverty worsened (though somewhat unevenly) between 2010 and 2020 (see Figure 1.11). In 2017, the IFS estimated that around 3,700,000 children were living in absolute poverty in the UK in 2015. They projected

Figure 1.11: Absolute poverty rates, After Housing Costs incomes

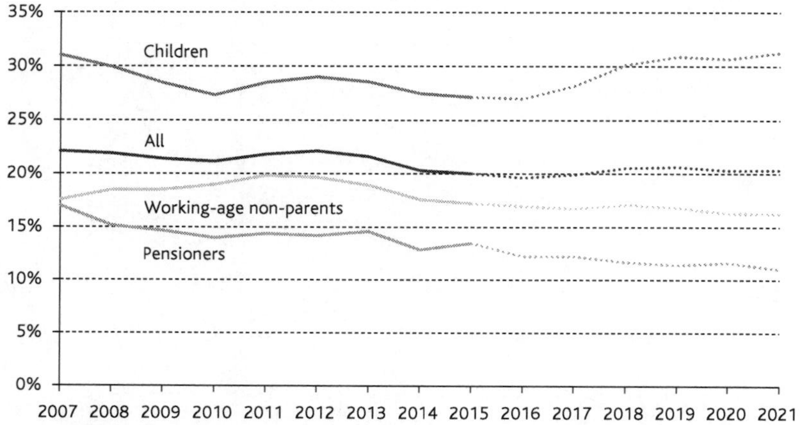

Source: A. Hood and T. Waters, 'Living Standards, Poverty and Inequality: 2017/18 to 2021/22'. London: Institute for Fiscal Studies. Available from: https://www.ifs.org.uk/uploads/publications/comms/R136.pdf

a rise in this number to 4,300,000 in 2021. This suggested an increase of 600,000 children living in poverty across a six-year period.[42] Data generated by the Department for Work and Pensions suggested that the three-year rolling average for the number of children in absolute poverty rose from 3,600,000 in 2010–13 to 4,100,000 in 2015–18. Of course, this incidence of exposure to poverty was very unevenly distributed across the population. In single-parent households, it stood at 47 per cent in 2017. In workless households, it was 73 per cent.[43]

Much of this increase in child poverty can be directly attributed to changes in the government's benefit regime. The IFS estimated that the numbers of poor children in workless homes – whose incomes are very heavily reliant upon benefits – would rise by 12 per cent through to 2021. Even in working-poor homes, the rise was estimated at 3.3 per cent. Much of the increase is to be found in families with three or more children, itself the result of planned tax and benefit reforms. Even as overall absolute poverty rates flatlined, the IFS anticipated significant increases for children (offsetting reductions for pensioners and working-age non-parents; see Figure 1.12). In sum, in 2020, there were around 4,000,000 children living in absolute poverty in the UK and their number was rising.[44]

Other poverties

There are, of course, other axes of poverty and we can also think about the distribution of disadvantage in terms of, for example, gender, ethnicity and age. I will return to some of these questions in this and later chapters. For

Figure 1.12: Absolute poverty rates, working-age only, After Housing Costs incomes

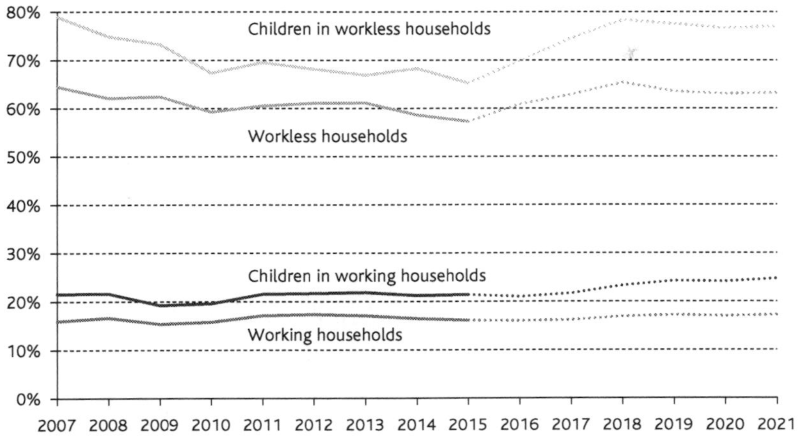

Source: A. Hood and T. Waters, 'Living Standards, Poverty and Inequality: 2017/18 to 2021/22'. London: Institute for Fiscal Studies. Available from: https://www.ifs.org.uk/uploads/publications/comms/R136.pdf

now, I offer just one example of these alternative axes of disadvantage: that is geographical region (Figure 1.13).

Although the regional bias can be found in other indicators of the increase in poverty – with some regions showing little overall increase and others (correspondingly) coming out above average – it is perhaps clearest in relation to child poverty. While absolute child poverty is projected to rise across all areas, it is much worse for some (the North-East, the East Midlands, Wales) than for others. Generally, it is the areas with the most disadvantaged families (and greatest reliance upon benefit income) that fare worst. In this, as with other indicators of poverty, London is a special and interesting case. While London and the South-East are generally the most affluent areas of the UK, the capital is also the site of some of its most concentrated poverty (including child poverty).[45]

Social mobility

The problem with a highly skewed distribution of income/wealth is not just that it makes some people very rich and others very poor. It is also that poverty excludes people – especially children – from the opportunity to participate fully in their societies. At the same time, it may mean that those who possess may (perhaps increasingly) be able to pass on their wealth and the advantages that go with this wealth (in terms of education and employment, for example) to their own children. We have good reason to

Figure 1.13: Absolute child poverty rates, selected years, After Housing Costs incomes

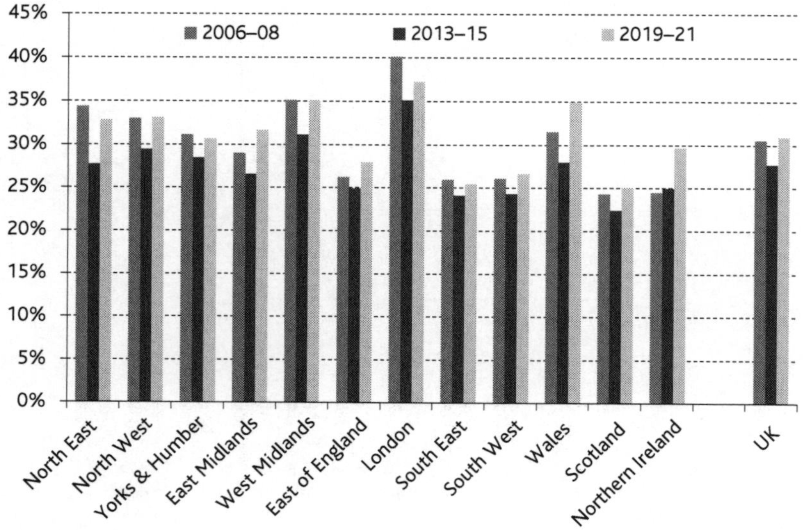

Source: A. Hood and T. Waters, 'Living Standards, Poverty and Inequality: 2017/18 to 2021/22'. London: Institute for Fiscal Studies. Available from: https://www.ifs.org.uk/uploads/publications/comms/R136.pdf

think that a very unequal society in which positions of prestige and well-being were awarded in relation to some sort of 'merit' would not be just. But we may think that a society that allocates such positions in a way that is unrelated to merit, or in which desert is somehow mixed up with prior wealth, is manifesting an additional layer of injustice. Similarly, a society in which people seem to succeed or fail in a way that is systematically related to something about who they are but which is unrelated to the good or opportunity in question – say their gender or ethnicity or sexuality – is burdened by an additional and significant form of injustice. This issue had a new salience after 1997 when *all* parties showed a renewed interest in the idea that a (very) unequal society might be (adequately) just if it allocated both opportunities and resources in ways which were 'deserved'– and which heightened social mobility (especially in relation to education) might support (see Bukodi and Goldthorpe, 2019: 3).

This question often becomes tangled up in a dispute about what *really* counts as 'equality of opportunity' – when is it real and when is it purely formal. I will largely avoid this more or less worn-out debate by focusing on social mobility primarily in terms of *outcomes*. As with the case of child poverty, there is something of a political consensus that social mobility is 'a good thing', just as child poverty is 'a bad thing'. Indeed, so persuaded of this was the Coalition Government that it abandoned the

Child Poverty Commission in favour of a Social Mobility Commission – arguing that what really mattered was not how many children lived below an (arbitrary) poverty line but whether these same children were likely to be able to move out of poverty in the longer term. Social mobility therefore deserves attention in its own right. Here I focus on evidence collated by the government's (cross-party) Social Mobility Commission.[46] In the next section, I turn to the question of the inheritance of wealth and its consequences.

In the academic literature, 'social mobility' is a multifaceted idea and measuring it presents a range of technical challenges.[47] And politicians, political parties and academics are not always talking about quite the same thing when they talk about social mobility. The underlying idea is clear enough. In a good society, your social destination (in terms of education, employment, income, health) should not be determined by your point of origin (in terms of gender, family background, wealth or geographical location, for example). Social mobility captures the idea that you can or should be able to 'move' (up *or* down) in terms of social outcomes irrespective of your point of departure. This social mobility may be observed *inter*generationally (that is, between parents and their children) or *intra*-generationally (that is, in terms of an individual's life course). And the measure may be *absolute* ('what proportion of the adult population is in a different social class from the one they grew up in?') or *relative* ('how big is the difference in mobility chances of someone from, say, a working-class background relative to someone from a professional/managerial background?').[48] Politicians often (and the Social Mobility Commission sometimes) confuse absolute and relative social mobility. Perhaps understandably, they tend to focus upon the *upward* element in mobility. Indeed, much of the time politicians seem (perhaps conveniently) to confuse overall improvement in living standards or well-being with increasing social mobility – even though relative mobility requires that people move 'down' as well as 'up'. More particularly, they sometimes argue that improved access to a resource (say, a university education) demonstrates that there has been an increase in social mobility, per se. But this is not quite the case. Everyone can have a home with an inside toilet (and a jolly good thing, too). But only one tenth of any fixed population can be in the top 10 per cent (for any given variable – say, wealth). In the latter case, for anyone to move in (or 'up') someone has to move out (or 'down'). This is important because, as we shall see, in Britain increased (absolute) social mobility has largely been the product of changes in the structure of opportunities (more 'room at the top') rather than the reallocation of privileges (greater movement between occupational positions). In these circumstances, what is now sometimes described as a decline in social mobility – for example, the claim that the current generation of 30-somethings is and will remain poorer than their parents – is rather an aspect of a changing class structure (or structure of opportunities) with rather less 'room at the top'.

Much of the data that we have concerns mobility in relation to occupational class (variously defined). It focuses upon educational and employment outcomes. In the 20-year survey compiled by the Social Mobility Commission in 2017, the overall judgement was that some progress had been made since 1997, but that the gap in outcomes between rich and poor was still (much too) wide – and that progress had slowed after 2010.[49] Thus, for example, the attainment gap at age five between children receiving free school meals (FSM, a surrogate for low income) and others was still around 17 per cent in 2016 (see Figure 1.14).

At the other end of their school life, there was a very substantial gap in examination outcomes which had hardly narrowed across time (even as absolute performance levels had improved; see Figure 1.15).

In terms of higher education, access to universities had expanded rapidly from the 1990s onwards and, after 2006, the percentage of students from disadvantaged areas accessing higher education almost doubled (from 11 to 20 per cent). But these students still found it extremely difficult to access the most selective institutions (see Figure 1.16). As the numbers at university expanded rapidly, the labour market value of being a graduate was reduced and the selectivity of the institution attended become increasingly important.[50]

A second key area for social mobility data is employment (and earnings). The Social Mobility Commission's *State of the Nation Report* for 2019 focused

Figure 1.14: Attainment gap at five: percentage point gap in reaching a good level of development at age five by free school meal eligibility, 2007–16 academic years, England

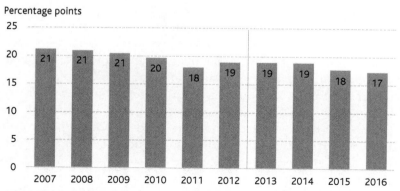

Percentage points

Note: A new framework from 2013 onwards means that direct comparison between pre- and post-2013 should be treated with some caution.
Source: Department for Education Early Years Foundation Stage Profile Result, various years

Figure 1.15: Percentage of pupils achieving five GCSEs A*–C or equivalent (including English and maths) and percentage point attainment gap by free school meal eligibility academic years 2002–11, England

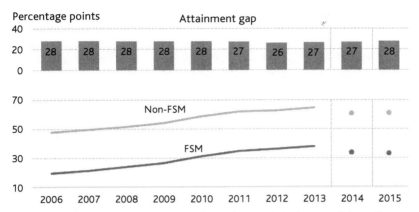

Source: Department for Education GCSE and equivalent result (various years), https://assets.publishing.service.gov.uk/government/uploads/system/uploads/attachment_data/file/622214/Time_for_Change_report_-_An_assessement_of_government_policies_on_social_mobility_1997-2017.pdf

Figure 1.16: Percentage of disadvantaged (POLAR3, Q1) 18-year-olds entering higher education by selectivity of institution, 2006–16, UK

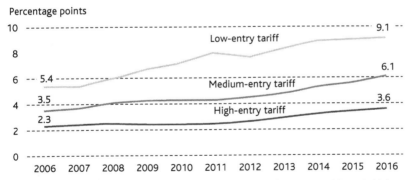

Note: The POLAR classification looks at how likely young people are to participate in higher education across the UK and shows how this varies by area. POLAR Q1 refers to students from areas with the lowest participation.
Source: UCAS Equality and Entry Rates Explorer, Trends through Time (2016), https://assets.publishing.service.gov.uk/government/uploads/system/uploads/attachment_data/file/622214/Time_for_Change_report_-_An_assessement_of_government_policies_on_social_mobility_1997-2017.pdf

on (relative) occupational mobility.[51] They found that, despite the changing jobs profile over the past 50 years – and the attendant increase in professional work and decline in manual occupations – those with a better-off family background were 80 per cent more likely to land a professional job than their working-class peers. Meanwhile, those with a poorer background were twice as likely to end up in a working-class job as were those from a professional household. They refer to these two phenomena as 'sticky ceiling' and 'sticky floor'. It was hard to rise and it was hard to fall. In a parallel observation, Abigail McKnight (2015) reports on a process of 'opportunity hoarding' as those at the top play the system in such a way as to ensure that their own children are protected against (the pressures of) downward social mobility (in part, by buying them a private school education).[52]

The same phenomenon is explored in depth in Friedman and Laurison (2019) *The Class Ceiling: Why it Pays to be Privileged*. They plot the movement from origins to destinations in working Britain (in 2014) as in Figure 1.17. Overall, most people stay close to where they started. If they move, they tend to move over comparatively short distances. 'Put another way, people from upper-middle-class origins have about 6.5 times the chance of landing an elite job compared to people from working-class backgrounds' (Friedman and Laurison, 2019: 13). And, as they further point out, 'getting in' is not quite the same as 'getting on'. Those (comparatively few) who make it up

Figure 1.17: Working destinations

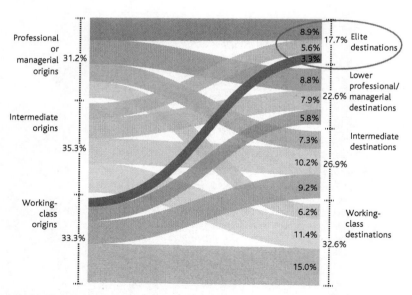

Source: Originally published in Friedman and Laurison (2019: 13). Republished with permission of Policy Press (an imprint of Bristol University Press, UK).

the ladder towards the most desirable (and well-paid) occupational positions still find themselves less well rewarded than those with more privileged origins. Friedman and Laurison (2019: 47) go on to argue that 'those in elite occupations from working-class origins earn on average £6,400 less a year than their colleagues from privileged backgrounds, [so that] those from upper-middle-class origins earn 16 per cent more than those from working-class backgrounds, even in the same set of jobs'.

Overall, it looks as though most of the advances in social mobility over the past 50 years have been *absolute* – that is reflecting a changing range of opportunities – rather than *relative* – that is reflecting greater mobility ('up' and 'down') between origins and destinations. If changes in future employment opportunities do not create (more) room at the top, we might anticipate that overall social mobility will stall, or perhaps decline.

We tend to plot patterns of social mobility in the very long term – as they concern the trajectory of individuals across the entire life course. As we shall see, social mobility was an important component of the New Labour vision of welfare reform, as it was, in a rather more subdued way, for subsequent Coalition and Conservative Governments. All of these governments looked to expand *educational* opportunities, in particular, as their preferred route to promoting social mobility – a focus which Erzsébet Bukodi and John Goldthorpe, the godfather of British social mobility studies, argue has failed (Bukodi and Goldthorpe, 2019). Given the long-term nature of social mobility, it is difficult to assess the performance of particular governments (especially in the short term). Overall, though, we can say, echoing the judgement of the Social Mobility Commission, that the policies of governments in this area after 2010 look to be 'not fit for purpose'.[53] I consider the New Labour record in this area in Chapter 2.

Inherited wealth

We have seen that there is good reason for us to be quite as much concerned with the distribution of wealth as of income. Inheritance is the key mechanism through which wealth is (unequally) transmitted between generations.[54] The 'return of inheritance' was a key theme of Piketty's *Capital in the Twenty-First Century* (Piketty, 2014: 377–429). Focusing upon the French case, Piketty found that inheritance as a source for individuals' wealth had declined through much of the 20th century – but it had begun to rise again from the 1980s. Piketty projected that this trend would continue for the foreseeable future. The decline and recovery in rates of inheritance is less pronounced in the UK (and the long-term records are less complete). When Tony Atkinson (2013) sought to replicate Piketty's analysis in the UK, he found that transmitted wealth (as a percentage of national income) had fallen from around 20 per cent before 1914 to below 5 per cent in the 1970s,

Figure 1.18: Lifetime inheritances as a share of lifetime income, by lifetime income quintile

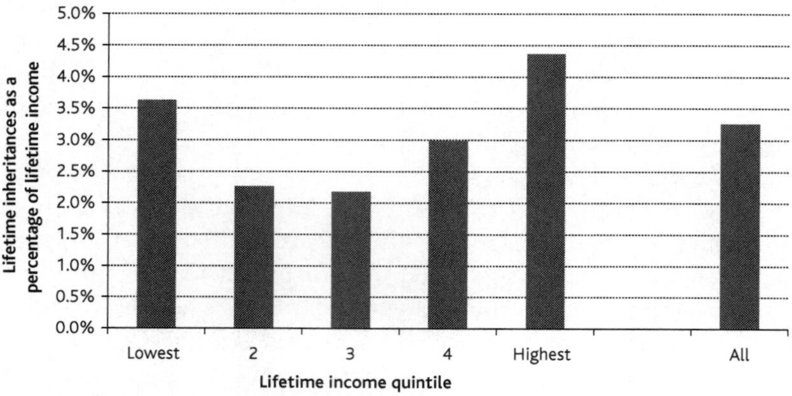

Source: Andrew Hood and Robert Joyce, 'Inheritances and Inequality across and within Generations'. London: Institute for Fiscal Studies. https://www.ifs.org.uk/uploads/publications/bns/bn192.pdf

and then recovered to around 8 per cent in 2008. He found it to be on a continuing upward trend. In 2017, the Resolution Foundation reported that the real value of estates transferred more than doubled between 1995/6 and 2014/15. They anticipated that this upward trajectory would continue, with the value of inheritances set to double again by 2035.[55] In short, inheritance is an increasingly important source of the wealth of younger generations. How it is distributed matters very much.

In some ways, this is a good news story. If income growth is likely to continue to be sluggish and with lower levels of homeownership among younger cohorts, a wealth boost from an older and more affluent generation – in short, the Baby Boomers – is welcome. But it may (still) be quite a long time coming. (The ONS estimates that the median age for current 20–35-year-olds inheriting is 61![56]) Much more significantly – and as we have already seen – the wealth that is to be passed on is very unequally held. Given this, the likelihood is that inheritance has and will exacerbate future inequalities. In the period 2012–14, for example, the highest income fifth of 40–59-year-olds inherited three times as much as the bottom fifth of the same age group (see Figure 1.18). Some 83 per cent of millennials who own their own home have at least one parental homeowner; 46 per cent of millennials who don't own have no homeowning parent.[57]

The picture is not completely straightforward. Among the population over 65, the wealthiest individuals are more likely to have received an inheritance in the past and this inheritance is likely to have been larger than for those further down the profile. But inheritance is also a significant source of wealth for (some of those in) the bottom fifth of the population and, as a *proportion* of lifetime earnings, these sums may be greater than for those in the middle of the wealth profile. Smaller inheritances are also proportionately more significant for younger cohorts (especially those aged 16–24).[58] And it is important to remember that wealth is differentially distributed *within* age cohorts. Baby Boomers may be wealthier than later generations (at the same age). But there were and are poor Baby Boomers – and affluent millennials. Pension incomes for those already retired vary hugely and, while it often said that it is those born in the 1980s and beyond who are less advantaged than those who came before them, the evidence suggests that the first cohort to be 'less privileged' than their forerunners may been those born in 1955 – about halfway through the 'baby boom'. There is also evidence that *within-cohort* inequality has increased for every generation born since the 1960s.[59]

We are used to thinking about inheritance as a long-term development and it does indeed share some characteristics with more recognisably 'demographic' phenomena – like societal ageing. We already know a lot about what is going to happen, and we may think of it less as the product of particular governments' choices and rather more as the (unintended) consequence of a lot of unrelated decisions taken over (a long period of) time. But in the UK over the past 10–20 years we can actually trace comparatively rapid change over a (societally) short period of time. Net wealth has grown rapidly. In many ways and for significant numbers of people, it has been more important than income from employment. It is *much* more unequally distributed than this employment income (albeit that this income from employment is itself *increasingly* unequally distributed). And we have seen that its intergenerational transmission will have a growing impact on future distributions of wealth. Of course, we *can* make (potentially different) decisions about *how* we choose to transmit this wealth between generations. But, in practice, both Coalition and Conservative Governments did remarkably little about inheritance during their decade in office – though in 2017 they did substantially increase the amount of wealth that can be left before the tax (at 40 per cent) is imposed. Inheritance Tax is remarkably unpopular (even when compared to other taxes). Governments have repeatedly resisted calls either to abolish it or to replace it with a more comprehensive tax on wealth and/or gifts and bequests. As it currently exists, it is peculiarly ineffective in reaching transmitted wealth or in raising revenue. I return to this question in Chapters 3 and 4.

The aftermath of austerity

The history of the welfare state since 2010 is messy – but the general lines of advance and retreat are clear. There were real cuts in provision between 2010 and 2020 – but these were focused on the poor, especially upon poor families with children and within this group upon poorer families with three or more children. Employment increased to record levels but being in work was increasingly no guarantee of avoiding poverty. At the same time, the three largest areas of social expenditure (old-age pensions, healthcare, education) were, to varying degrees, protected. This meant that, despite severe cuts in some targeted areas, overall savings were limited and the overarching ambition to eliminate the budget deficit was never achieved. The most drastic visions of rising inequality of income and wealth were not realised but, overall, distribution remained very unequal and things grew to be worse towards the end of the decade. Wealth and inheritance became more important but were ineffectively managed and/or taxed. Social mobility stalled. Social care remained a problem that was just too big and too difficult for governments to address. The welfare budget was continuing to rise – even in a context of lingering austerity – because of governments' commitment to protect the incomes of its largest groups of beneficiaries, those over the normal retirement age. Welfare states seemed certain to remain, by a very significant margin, the largest area of state spending and state activity. But even when the welfare state's work of redistribution had been done, the UK would remain a deeply divided and unequal society.

The problem for those who want something other – and, as they would see it, better – is this: what is that something else going to be? And, we might add, who is going to deliver it? I will get to these questions eventually. But first I want to take one step further back: to understand rather better what the social democratic welfare state project has been in Britain in the past and to understand its relationship to what has happened since 2010. The experience under New Labour (between 1997 and 2010) is a pivotal and, I think, much misunderstood part of this past. What went right and what went wrong under New Labour may tell us something useful about what is possible, and what is not possible, now. Exploring these questions is the subject of my second chapter.

The last social democratic welfare state

When the Labour Party was swept back into power on 1 May 1997, with an unprecedented majority and the realistic prospect of securing two full terms in government, the reform of the welfare state was high on its to-do list. What this actually meant was not always clear. Reportedly, when Tony Blair called Alan Milburn three days after the election to invite him to be the new minister of state for health, he told him 'We haven't got a health policy ... Your job is to get us one' (Timmins, 2017: 589). But the broad agenda for welfare, and its centrality to the New Labour project, seemed clear enough. Three of the five pre-election pledges made by the party concerned welfare: reducing class sizes, shortening NHS waiting lists and getting 250,000 young people off benefits and into work. There were two key components to this agenda: the first was to encourage the move 'from welfare to work', captured in the mantra 'work for those who can, security for those who cannot'; the second was to direct greater resources into public services, and to achieve a step-change in the quality of provision.[1] As we already have a number of excellent accounts of this reform programme, I confine myself here to a brief reminder of Labour's policy agenda (among others, Ludlam and Smith, 2004; Powell, 2008; Timmins, 2017). I devote rather more attention to the *outcomes* of these reforms, as this has been less comprehensively covered and is the source of considerable misunderstanding – and misrepresentation. In the final part of the chapter, I explore the claim that between 1997 and 2010 New Labour somehow manged to forge a 'new' sort of social democracy. In fact, I think that it is more appropriate to think of this as the *last* social democratic welfare state of its kind.

The New Labour programme

New Deals

The earliest and definitive expression of New Labour's first welfare commitment was the New Deal. Originally created for 250,000 under 25 year olds who had been unemployed for six months or more, the programme combined work or work experience, training or education, all with the support of a personal adviser. Benefit payments were made conditional upon participation in the programme. Further New Deals were introduced across time for the long-term unemployed, for lone parents, for the over 50s and for disabled people. The creation of Jobcentre Plus, with a single site for welfare claims and job search, was designed to move looking for work and the receipt of benefits closer together. At the same time, there was a series of steps to 'make work pay' (more): the reform of tax credits (focused on the low-paid in work); increases in state-funded childcare; and the introduction of a National Minimum Wage.[2]

Child-contingent benefits

The emphasis for the able-bodied of working age was to move 'from welfare to work'. The big commitments Labour made in terms of cash transfers were for those who were too young or too old to work. In a major speech on welfare reform made by Blair in March 1999, he declared it 'our historic aim ... to eliminate child poverty for ever' (Blair, 1999: 17). The more immediate ambition was to halve child poverty by 2010. Some of this pledge was to be met by increased funding of new or existing *services*, including the Sure Start programme. But much of it was to achieved through increased *cash transfers*, above all to the parents of poorer children. This constituted a step-change in social expenditure. Kitty Stewart estimates that spending on child-contingent benefits and tax credits more than doubled across the period of Labour government (from around £1,375 in 1997/8 to £3,003 per child in 2009/10). In terms of overall GDP (in a period of sustained growth), this represented an increase from 1.66 per cent in 1997/8 to 2.73 per cent in 2009/10 (Stewart, 2013: 12). These resources were targeted on poorer families. Van Mechelen and Bradshaw (2013: 98–101) estimate that the Child Benefit package in 2009 represented around 9 per cent of income for a single parent on average earnings but around 39 per cent for someone receiving the minimum wage. I will return to Labour's overall record on poverty a little later but these changes had a real impact on child poverty, which fell from 27 per cent in 1996/7 to 17.5 per cent in 2010/11 (Lupton et al, 2013: 49).

Pensions

The other area of major increases in cash transfers related to pensioners. The domain of pensions and pension reform, both state and private, was, and is, complicated. On the state pension, there were a number of significant institutional changes throughout the period of Labour government, including the introduction of the Minimum Income Guarantee and subsequently the Pension Credit. There were new universal perks: winter fuel payments, free TV licences, concessionary bus travel. The state's second pension system was reformed. And in 2008, the index-linking of pension payments was reconnected to earnings rather than prices. The changes were complex but the overall effect was significantly to increase pensioners' incomes – and substantially to reduce the incidence of pensioner poverty (see Timmins,

2017: 274–7). Between 1996/7 and 2010/11, the annual social security budget rose, in real terms, from £114 billion to £181 billion. Around a half of that increase was expenditure on pensioners (£37 billion), with much of the rest of it directed towards child-contingent benefits. As a percentage of GDP, spending on pensioners rose by 1.3 per cent. Largely as a consequence, levels of pensioner poverty (when measured After Housing Costs) halved (from 29.1 per cent in 1996/7 to 14.2 per cent in 2010/11).[3] New Labour tussled repeatedly – and with itself – over reform of the private pensions sector. By the early 2000s, it was clear that the existing system of company-based private pensions was in serious trouble, as a growing number of large companies either closed their schemes to new members or else radically changed the basis upon which they would make future payments. Following Reports of the Pensions Commission (which it had established in 2002), Labour legislated in Pensions Acts in 2007 and 2008 to require automatic enrolment in company-based pensions and to raise the retirement age (see Timmins, 2017: 577–85). I return to the distributional outcomes of these pension reforms a little later in this chapter.

Health

Two other areas of welfare state expenditure saw major growth throughout the Labour years, alongside almost permanent institutional reform. In healthcare, there was a series of reforms and reorganisations, many of which reflected the new logic of audit, targeting and 'performance management'. But this was accompanied by very substantial increases in capital expenditure and in staffing levels. Overall, healthcare expenditure more than doubled under Labour. Annual average growth in this budget was 5.8 per cent with a particular burst of effort under the second Blair Administration (in the years 2001/2 to 2004/5) when the rate reached 8.6 per cent per year. As a percentage of GDP, public health expenditure increased from 5.3 per cent in 1996/7 to 8.3 per cent in 2009/10. Although much attention was directed to the reduction in waiting times for various hospital procedures, there were also major improvements in survival rates for cancer and circulatory diseases across the period, much of which will have benefited older people in particular. Overall life expectancy at birth grew by 3.9 years for men and by 2.8 years for women. Reported levels of satisfaction with the NHS were transformed (Lupton et al, 2013: 40–1, 35; Vizard and Obolenskaya, 2013: 33, 83, 85).

Education

Famously, at the 1996 Labour Party Conference, Tony Blair had declared that his three priorities in government would be 'education, education, education'. As in healthcare, the overall Labour record on education was one of almost permanent reform and substantially increased expenditure. This covered the full spectrum from preschool to higher education – and, to a much more limited extent, beyond. By 2010, preschool education had been transformed, with some free provision for all three- and four-year-olds. In tertiary education, there was a significant growth in the number of young people going to university (rising to 46 per cent in 2010), including a modest increase in the numbers from disadvantaged households. This expansion was partially funded by the introduction of tuition fees. Schools saw an increase of 48,000 in the number of full-time equivalent (FTE) teachers and 133,000 more FTE classroom assistants. There was a major programme of new school building and refurbishment (some of it funded via the Private Finance Initiative). Real-terms expenditure on education rose by 78 per cent across the Labour period. As a proportion of GDP, it rose from 4.5 per cent in 1997/8 to 6.2 per cent in 2009/10 (Lupton and Obolenskaya, 2013: 16).

Social exclusion

The stated aim of the short-lived and revealingly named Department for Education and Employment (it was abolished in 2001) was 'to give everyone the chance ... to realise their full potential, and thus build an inclusive and fair society and a competitive economy'.[4] In the case of low-income pensioners and disadvantaged children (and disabled people), it was appropriate to recognise that the problem was poverty. For everyone else – and for disadvantaged children too – the problem was seen, as it was in education, to be *social exclusion*. In part, this was just a recognition of the long-established principle that deprivation is multiple. But it also reflected a belief that people's welfare in the longer term could only be fixed by increasing their 'real opportunities', not by giving them cash. As Alistair Darling had it, 'benefits cannot remove the causes of poverty' (cited in Timmins, 2017: 573). This refocus was recognised in the creation in October 1997 of the Social Exclusion Unit (SEU), based in Downing Street. The emphasis of the SEU was on increasing 'real' equality of opportunity – though far from exclusively – through expanded education and training (see SEU, 2004). For present and future workers, the emphasis was upon securing the circumstances that would allow for greater social mobility – and this meant increasing educational opportunity. As the SEU reported in 2004, 'a good education can allow individuals from a relatively deprived background to enjoy upward social mobility' (SEU, 2004: 17).

New Labour, new welfare state

This, very briefly, is the New Labour record on welfare policy between 1997/8 and 2009/10. It was a period of almost permanent institutional reform – designed, ostensibly, to bring greater accountability and efficiency to the delivery of public services – and of sustained growth in expenditure. At times, and especially during the second Blair Government (2001–05), social expenditure grew at an almost unprecedented pace. The steepest rises in expenditure as a proportion of GDP came at the very end of the Labour years – but this was largely a product of the financial crisis of 2008, and responses to it. For most of the New Labour years, more especially between 2001 and 2005, sustained economic growth funded a systematic expansion of welfare state services. Child poverty and pensioner poverty were significantly reduced. Many of these achievements were lost sight of as the Labour Party sought to distance itself from the New Labour years – first under Miliband and then under Corbyn (see Goes, 2016; Pogrund and Maguire, 2020). In any case, the pace of reform slackened after 2005, as the government became increasingly embroiled in the aftermath of the decision to invade Iraq and as rivalries between the Prime Minister and the Chancellor of the Exchequer descended into more or less open warfare. Before we consider whether all of this added up to some sort of 'new' welfare state, I want to look a little more closely at the social and economic *consequences* of New Labour's reform programme. In doing this, I parallel my evaluation of the Coalition and Conservative record between 2010 and 2020 in Chapter 1.

Income inequality

One of the banner headlines of New Labour's performance in addressing poverty and inequality – one most frequently cited by its critics – is that the Gini coefficient (measuring overall income inequality) reached a new peak in 2007/8. When, as I reported in Chapter 1, the Gini coefficient rose to 36.5 under a Conservative Administration in 2019/20, this was still significantly lower than the 37.2 it had reached under New Labour ahead of the Global Financial Crisis. When Labour left office in 2010, levels of overall income inequality were similar to what they had been in 1997/8 – but this owed much to a very steep fall in inequality after 2008, as the assets of the rich depreciated (for a time) while benefit levels were maintained.

This very summary account conceals as much as it discloses. It is true that the Gini measure shows increasing income inequality in the decade 1998–2008 – but the process varied through this time. In the period down to 2001/2 (the first Blair Government), income growth was strong fairly evenly across the population, except for the bottom 10 per cent. Between 2001/2 and 2007/8, growth was generally much lower: somewhat higher at the top end and significantly lower for the bottom quarter of the income profile. After 2007/8, it was the bottom fifth of the population

Figure 2.1: Income inequality as measured by the 50/10, 90/50 and 99/90 ratios

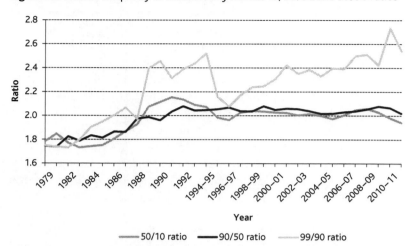

Source: J. Cribb, 'Income Inequality in the UK: 2013'. London: Institute for Fiscal Studies. Available from: https://www.ifs.org.uk/docs/ER_JC_2013.pdf

which did best: with incomes advancing quicker than for those further up the profile down to 2010, and falling more slowly thereafter. Increases in inequality also varied across the income profile. A key driver was the much higher growth of incomes at the top end of the profile: for the top 10 per cent, or 1 per cent, or 0.1 per cent. Across the pre-crisis years, the lowest incomes lagged, while income at the top end moved further away from those in the middle. Between these two 'tails' of the distribution, income inequality probably lessened (that is for those between the 10th and the 90th percentile). A Gini coefficient which excluded the top 10 per cent would more or less flatline between 1997 and 2010. This trend is captured in Figure 2.1.

A persistent problem with this data is the suspicion that, because of the tendency of middling incomes not to become more unequal, the Gini coefficient understates the levels of inequality between the top and bottom 10 per cent of the population. Figure 2.2 is an attempt to show how different ways of measuring inequality can give us a very different profile – though the direction(s) of change remains the same.

It is also worth recalling, as Obolenskaya and Hills (2019) do in their comparison of Labour before 2010 and the Coalition thereafter, that it makes a great deal of difference to the *experience* of inequality if the economy and wages are growing. In an expanding economy, the *absolute* condition of those worse off may improve, even if for others things are improving more quickly. In a flat economy (like that after 2010), the *absolute* position of the worse off may decline, even if inequality is being reduced.

Figure 2.2: Summary measures of income inequality, UK

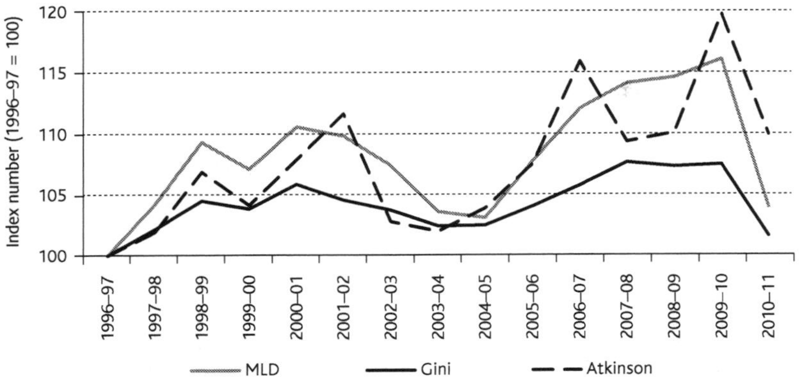

Note: MLD = Mean Logarithmic Deviation
Source: J. Cribb, R. Joyce and D. Phillip, 'Living Standards, Poverty and Inequality in the UK: 2012'. London: Institute for Fiscal Studies. Available from: https://www.ifs.org.uk/comms/comm124.pdf

Wealth inequality

In Chapter 1, I argued that we have probably focused too much of our attention upon *income* inequality and certainly not enough upon inequalities in the possession of *wealth*. For all of the reasons suggested there, I attempt here to give a rather clearer indication of what happened to personal wealth under New Labour. This is difficult. We lack for wealth the consistent time-series data that exist for income. A new (and much more comprehensive) basis for comparing wealth in the UK across time was put in place in 2006 (with the creation by the ONS of the Wealth and Assets survey).[5] But this break in the data series makes it difficult for us to construct a consistent account across the entire New Labour period. The long-run data we do have – from the Credit Suisse Research Institute and the World Inequality Database (WID) – points to a slow but steady increase in the share of wealth held by the top 10 per cent and the top 1 per cent through to 2009. The WID evidence suggests that the wealth share of the top 1 per cent rose from 19.3 per cent in 1997 to 20.6 per cent in 2009. The equivalent growth for the top 10 per cent was from 51.6 per cent to 54 per cent.[6] At the same time, the data we have on wealth is much more opaque than that which exists for incomes. The rich are much more skilled (and interested) in concealing the extent of their wealth, compared with the size of their incomes. And at the very top end of the profile, we have little sense of just *how* rich the very rich really are. This skews (and almost certainly underestimates) levels of wealth inequality. But it matters for at least two reasons: wealth is increasingly important as a source of differential well-being across the population; and it

Figure 2.3: Gini coefficient for wealth, various measures: 1995 to 2012–14, GB

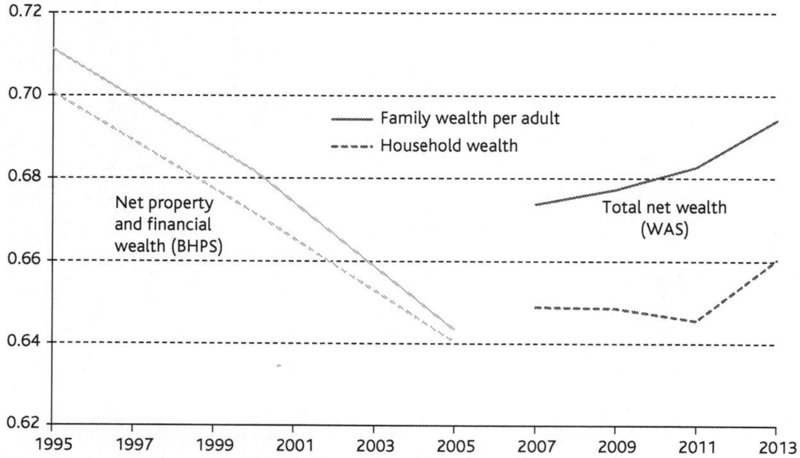

Note: BHPS = British Household Panel Study; WAS = Wealth and Assets Survey
Source: https://www.resolutionfoundation.org/app/uploads/2017/06/Wealth.pdf, p 22

is much more unequally distributed than income. The shape of the wealth inequality profile is almost certainly different from that which describes the distribution of income.

As we saw in Chapter 1, Britain is a wealthy country. By the end of New Labour's period in office, net personal wealth in the UK was around £10 trillion, reflecting mean net household wealth (including private pension rights) of around £232,000 (Hills et al, 2013: 13). But, as we also saw, this wealth was much more unequally distributed than income, with an overall Gini coefficient in 2011 of around 60 for wealth contrasting to around 33 for income. And different forms of wealth were differently distributed. Financial wealth was especially concentrated – with those at the top having billions of pounds' worth of assets, while those at the bottom had less than zero. But by some way the very largest forms of personal wealth were in housing and private pension rights. And with wealth, probably even more than with income, we see *generational* differences – unrelated in any discernible way to the efforts or intentions of those whose date of birth has put them into a particular cohort.

The more detailed material we have (from HMRC prior to 2006, from the ONS thereafter) shows a rather different pattern from the Credit Suisse / WID data (even though the absolute numbers before and after 2006 are not comparable). This is graphically captured in material published by the Resolution Foundation in 2017 (Figure 2.3). This shows a declining Gini coefficient in the earlier period (1995–2005) but a slow rise from 2006 onwards. The trends are broadly similar in the evidence collated by Alvaredo et al (2016: 25–32).[7]

Both of these sources suggest that this pattern is best explained by looking at changes in the distribution of the ownership of *property* – and that means, principally, in the housing stock. It seems clear that the decline in wealth inequality in the period 1997–2005 is largely to be explained by an increase in house values. Property in housing is a much more substantial part of the wealth of those further down the profile (compared to the rich). As housing put on value in the boom of the early 2000s, it added proportionally more value to the housing assets of middle-income households, even though the absolute increase in value was higher for those with more expensive properties. Since housing makes up such a large part of the nation's wealth (around £4 trillion in 2010), this had a tendency to reduce wealth inequality. And the overall Gini coefficient for wealth fell from around 70 to around 64 in the first half of the 2000s. After 2006, that number started to rise (albeit slowly).

Who owns housing really matters for the dynamics of wealth inequality. In periods of house price inflation, it will tend to have an equalising effect on the wealth-holdings *of all homeowners*. However, it will do nothing for those who *do not own*. Between 1995 and 2005, the value of property in housing rose by 100 per cent at the 90th percentile, but by 200 per cent for those at the 50th percentile. Those in the bottom 10 per cent owned nothing in 1995 and nothing in 2005. This change was enough to bring the Gini coefficient for housing wealth down from 65 to 56 (Bastagli and Hills, 2012: 10).

The reversal of trends in wealth inequality in the later 2000s had much to do with the change in patterns of housing tenure – a reduction in owner-occupation from a high of 71 per cent in 2003 to 64 per cent in 2011, a near-doubling in the size of the private rented sector in the same period to stand at 18 per cent, and a slow long-term decline in social housing from a high in excess of 30 per cent in 1980 to around 18 per cent in 2011. Of the 1,700,000 new households formed between 2001 and 2011, more than 90 per cent were in the social and private rental sector.[8] In 2001, 29 per cent of owner-occupiers owned outright; 41.5 per cent owned with a mortgage. By 2012, these numbers were at parity. Of the outright owners, 83 per cent were aged 54 or over. The smaller number of mortgagors reflects a decline in owner-occupation in the younger population and the growing number of outright owners the paying-off of mortgages by Baby Boomers. These changes are hugely consequential for the distribution of wealth. For those on middling incomes, the most important form of wealth ownership has long been the family home. When values appreciated rapidly, these owner-occupiers became wealthier. A smaller proportion of their children are able to enter into owner-occupation – either because they struggle to raise a deposit or because their incomes are just too low to service the necessary debt. Many of them are now in the much-enlarged private rental sector.

One result of these changes – as we saw in Chapter 1 – is the growing importance of the 'Bank of Mum and Dad', for those who have such access. Another is the increasing importance of inherited (household) wealth (to which I will return).

The other great reserve of wealth across a broad population consists in the implicit worth of pension resources. There are some well-established difficulties in measuring the value of pension rights for individuals.[9] But it is hugely consequential, with the net value of pension rights being estimated by the ONS at around £5.4 trillion in 2016, that is more than a third of all personal wealth in the UK. Addressing pensioner poverty has to be judged one of the key successes of the New Labour governments (see the later section in this chapter). And external evaluations of its reform to private pensions after 2007 have for the most part been positive.[10] The introduction of auto-enrolment workplace pensions also had a positive impact on inequality, lowering the Gini index by four points between 2006 and 2010.[11]

But this still meant that the Gini index for private pension wealth was (as it continues to be) in excess of 70. And while the introduction of auto-enrolment had a (perhaps one-off) impact upon inequalities in private pension wealth, other trends seem to be running in the opposite direction. There is very substantial inequality in private pension wealth *within* cohorts, including those who are at or beyond retirement.[12] But perhaps the most critical challenge is the difference *across* cohorts – and particularly the challenge for those who are 40 or younger. Making contrasts across cohorts is not easy, as pension saving and dis-saving is a lifelong activity. We should expect that someone who is 60 would have more (pension) wealth than someone who is 20 (just as we would think it is much more likely that they would be a homeowner). As with homeownership, both the scale and the consequences of inequalities will take several decades to emerge fully. But we know that earnings and homeownership among younger cohorts are lower than they were for older generations at the same age. And we know that defined-benefit pensions (several times more valuable than defined-contribution schemes) are in (terminal) decline. In many ways, pensions was a success story for Labour. The pensions Gini index fell, but only in a way that lessened the overall increase in wealth inequality driven by increases elsewhere.

Poverty

We established in Chapter 1 that a concern with poverty is not the same as a concern with (income or wealth) inequality. While most people would accept that poverty has a relative component – and to this extent inequalities matter – it is not primarily about comparisons across the entire population. And thresholds matter. Raising the living standards of those at the bottom of the profile is important, whatever the rest of the distribution looks like. Much of the graphic evidence of Labour's performance featured in Chapter 1 (see Figures 1.2–1.16). To maintain consistency in looking at the record of Labour and subsequent governments, I focus here on the trajectory of absolute poverty rates between 1997 and 2010. I also pay particular attention to Labour's record on child poverty. Since excellent and comprehensive treatments exist of what is by now quite a familiar story (notably Hills et al, 2013; Lupton et al, 2013; Obolenskaya and Hills, 2019), my own account here is brief.

Both absolute and relative poverty rates fell significantly in the New Labour years, across the general population, but more especially for pensioners and children. I focus here on the absolute poverty numbers (reported After Housing Costs; see Table 2.1). Using 1997/8 as a baseline, we can see an overall fall in poverty across the population between 1997 and 2011 of more than 10 per cent. Across the same time period, pensioner poverty fell from close to 3,000,000 (29.1 per cent) to below 1,000,000 (7.7 per cent). Although a part of this fall had to do with some better-resourced retirees (with larger private pensions) entering this section of the population, much of the sustained fall can be attributed to the government policies I outlined earlier. At the same time, there were a number of in-kind benefits (concessionary travel, the winter fuel allowance) and a large part of the much-increased budget for the NHS will have ended up being spent on pensioners. For children, absolute poverty fell from around 4,300,000 (34.1 per cent) in 1997 to 2,100,000 (16.1 per cent) in 2011. These children were also the beneficiaries of increased spending on school education and preschool provision. Almost all of the advance on child poverty was made *before* 2005. There was a small increase in the incidence of child poverty between 2005 and 2008.

Reflecting the government's priorities, the position of working-age non-parents was little changed through the Labour years. There was an increase in employment levels after 1997 – plus a minimum wage and various tax credits for the low-waged – but work did not really pay in the way that the advocates of 'welfare to work' had supposed. Reductions in poverty under Labour were largely the result of direct fiscal redistribution (Joyce and Sibieta, 2013: 197). We know that in the decade down to 2008 income inequality was increasing. Nonetheless, by the end of Labour's time in office, being old or being young were no longer key predictors of the likelihood that you would be poor. This was, in itself, a substantial achievement.

Social mobility

Social mobility had a special place in the New Labour story – and in the claims of some of its key architects to have forged a 'new' kind of social

Table 2.1: Relative poverty: percentage and number of individuals in households with incomes below 60 per cent of median After Housing Costs income

	Children		Pensioners		Working-age parents		Working-age non-parents		All	
	%	Million	%	Million	%	Million	%	Million	%	Million
1996/7 (GB)	34.1	4.3	29.1	2.9	26.6	3.3	17.2	3.5	25.3	14.0
1997/8 (GB)	32.4	4.1	27.7	2.8	25.1	3.1	15.4	3.2	23.6	13.2
1998/9 (GB)	31.7	4.0	26.0	2.6	24.4	3.0	14.8	3.1	22.7	12.7
1999/2000 (GB)	29.0	3.7	21.1	2.1	22.6	2.8	14.4	3.0	20.7	11.6
2000/1 (GB)	24.6	3.1	16.2	1.6	19.6	2.4	14.0	3.0	18.0	10.1
2001/2 (GB)	20.7	2.6	11.6	1.2	17.1	2.1	12.1	2.6	15.0	8.5
2002/3 (UK)	18.2	2.4	9.7	1.0	15.4	1.9	11.9	2.7	13.6	8.0
2003/4 (UK)	17.4	2.3	8.6	0.9	14.9	1.9	12.2	2.7	13.3	7.8
2004/5 (UK)	15.9	2.0	6.8	0.7	13.6	1.7	11.3	2.6	12.0	7.1
2005/6 (UK)	16.4	2.1	7.0	0.8	14.5	1.8	12.3	2.8	12.7	7.5
2006/7 (UK)	17.2	2.2	8.8	1.0	14.9	1.9	12.2	2.8	13.2	7.9
2007/8 (UK)	17.4	2.2	8.3	0.9	14.9	1.9	12.6	2.9	13.4	8.0
2008/9 (UK)	17.1	2.2	7.9	0.9	15.8	2.1	13.6	3.1	13.7	8.3

2009/0 (UK)	15.8	2.1	6.9	0.8	14.7	2.0	14.4	3.3	13.3	8.1
2010/1 (UK)	16.1	2.1	7.7	0.9	15.2	2.1	14.7	3.4	13.8	8.4
Changes										
1996/7 to 2004/5	−18.2		−22.3		−12.9		−5.9		−13.3	
2004/5 to 2007/8	1.5	0.2	1.4	0.2	1.3	0.3	1.3	0.4	1.4	0.9
2007/8 to 2010/11	−1.4	(−0.1)	(−0.6)	(0.0)	(0.2)	(0.1)	2.1	0.4	(0.4)	0.4
2009/10 to 2010/11	(0.2)	(0.0)	(0.0)	0.1	(0.5)	(0.1)	(0.4)	(0.1)	(0.4)	(03)

Source: Source: J. Cribb, R. Joyce and D. Phillip, 'Living Standards, Poverty and Inequality in the UK: 2012'. London: Institute for Fiscal Studies. Available from: https://www.ifs.org.uk/comms/comm124.pdf

democracy. If the key problem for the poor is seen to be not so much their poverty as their social exclusion, or if the route out of poverty is seen to lie principally in moving 'up' or 'out' rather than in the transfer of cash, the policy focus will necessarily be upon enhanced *mobility*. In education, but in other social policy areas too – particularly in access to employment – the promotion of social mobility was an overriding imperative for New Labour. I considered some of the general conceptual and measurement problems surrounding this issue in the previous chapter. As I observed there, social mobility is *not* the same as equality of opportunity (even 'real' equality of opportunity, whatever we take that to mean). In looking here at the New Labour record, I again focus on *outcomes*. Social mobility policies are for the long term and the full consequences may not be seen for a generation. But we can consider policy successes (and failures) in a much shorter time frame – even if our more definitive judgements must wait a little longer. Once again, I use the evidence collated by the Social Mobility Commission to assess the New Labour performance.

As we have seen, Labour invested heavily in education and in preschool provision across its time in office. And, as was the case with Sure Start, resources were particularly focused upon improving outcomes for children from disadvantaged backgrounds. As might have been expected, improvements were quite slow to emerge. When reported cognitive performance did eventually improve (after 2007), it improved for *all* children, meaning that the gap between poorer children and the rest remained (see Figure 1.14). While there was some narrowing of pupil attainment in primary schools, at secondary level the attainment gap in public exams between students receiving FSM and the rest remained fairly constant (see Figure 1.15). In higher education, Labour got a long way towards its ambitious target of getting half of the 18-year-old population into university-level institutions by 2010, and substantially raised participation for those from less advantaged backgrounds. But access to the most selective higher education institutions remained very low for these students, at around 2 per cent (see Figure 1.16). Overall, this looks like a record of partial success in raising standards and increasing participation – but not really mobility.

One of the explicit aims of these reforms in education was to increase social mobility in the field of employment – particularly to improve the range of opportunities and outcomes in work for those from poorer households. In fact, a lot of what passes for 'social mobility' upon this account is really a concern to get more people into 'better jobs'. Indeed, much of the material collated by the Social Mobility Commission (2019) concerns more or less effective attempts to get people into the labour market (the New Deals and Working Tax Credits) or to tackle very low pay (the minimum wage). When it turned to actual job mobility – the capacity of people from less-privileged backgrounds to access high-status well-paid jobs – little had been done, and to little effect. Nor was there a lot of traffic moving in the opposite direction. Abigail McKnight's (2015) work for the Social Mobility Commission on upward and downward mobility in access to employment (identified in Chapter 1) dealt with a cohort most of whose working experience would have been under a New Labour government (they would have been 27 in 1997). She found that 'children from advantaged social class backgrounds are four times more likely to be in a high labour income group in adulthood than children from disadvantaged social class backgrounds'. If the route up was (at least partially) blocked, so too was the route down: since 'more advantaged families are able to protect early low attaining children in cognitive tests from downward social mobility' (McKnight, 2015: iii, 19).

In modern Britain, downward social mobility has always been quite limited (see McKnight, 2015). In practice, social mobility in relation to employment has depended upon the number and nature of jobs in the national economy. It really is a matter of the number and nature of career *opportunities*. It was a change in the structure of opportunities that made social mobility possible in the post-war world. Put simply, there were more 'middle-class' jobs for the sons and daughters of working-class parents to enter (Bukodi and Goldthorpe, 2019). But the structure of the contemporary economy (in Britain as elsewhere) looks very different from this. Whether or not one accepts Guy Standing's (2011) contention that up to 25 per cent of the working population now belong to the *precariat* – the fuzzy-edged class of those whose working lives are marked by social and economic *in*security – the supply of 'good' jobs – well-paid, secure, permanent, with a range of social entitlements and decent pensions – seems to have dried up. It is not clear how any government could 'fix' this, but we can be sure that it cannot be sorted simply by improving either educational opportunities or even educational outcomes. As Standing observes, the precariat may be 'the first class in history expected to labour and work at a lower level than the schooling it typically acquires' (Standing, 2016: x). I return to the consequences of these findings for the claim that New Labour forged a 'new' sort of social democracy, later.

Inheritance

We have already seen that the importance of inequalities in *wealth* tends to be underestimated in favour of a focus upon inequalities in *income*, even though – or more maybe because – differences in holdings of wealth are so much larger. In any case, this makes this issue of the *transmission* of wealth increasingly important. Like social mobility, the scale and impact of inheritance is something we would normally expect to observe over the long term. Having said that, there was a really substantial and quite

Figure 2.4: Total real values of estates passing on death and average amount inherited, UK/GB

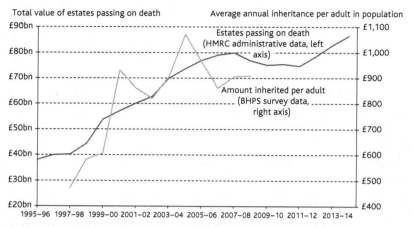

Note: HMRC = HM Revenue and Customs; BHPS = British Household Panel Study
Source: https://www.resolutionfoundation.org/publications/the-million-dollar-be-
question-inheritances-gifts-and-their-implications-for-generational-living-standards/ p 16

rapid change between 1997 and 2010. At its simplest, the total value of estates passing at death and the average amount inherited by individuals came close to doubling (see Figure 2.4). And, as we saw in Chapter 1, inheritance tends to reinforce wealth inequalities between individuals and families.

Much of what I said about the pattern of inheritances in Chapter 1 (for 2010–20) applies to the New Labour years as well. Here I confine myself to plotting how inheritance changed over the period from 1997 to 2010. The first thing is to observe just how much greater inherited wealth became in this period – rising from around £31.7 billion in 1997/8 to £55.4 billion in 2009.[13] The housing component in this total rose still more sharply from £12 billion at the earlier point to £29 billion in 2009/10. Looking back to 1984/85 shows us just how much inheritance values lifted with a period of increase in house prices after 1997.[14] More people had more things of more value – above all, houses – to pass on.

The number of estates passing at death every year remained fairly stable – at somewhere around 250,000 – throughout this period. And those inheriting represented around 2.5 per cent of the population in any year. It was the overall value of the estates that increased (Karagiannaki and Hills, 2013: 94). As we would expect – and as we have seen was the case after 2010 – this inherited wealth is very unevenly distributed. According to British Household Panel Study data, in the decade down to 2005, the top 1 per cent received around 12 per cent of all inherited wealth. The top 10 per cent took around one half. The bottom 50 per cent may have received as little as 7 per cent. As well as the inheritances themselves being so much larger, those towards the top end of the wealth scale were also much more likely to inherit – perhaps twice as likely as those in the bottom fifth of the population (Karagiannaki and Hills, 2013: 101).

Despite this, it is not clear that inheritance really *increased* wealth inequality – at least, in part, because wealth is *so* unequally distributed to start with. And, as we saw in discussing recent trends in wealth more generally, the fact that such a large part of the increment in values after 2000 came from an increase in house prices meant that growth moved some way down the wealth profile (to include many middle-income homeowners, whether outright or mortgaged). Eleni Karagiannaki and John Hills drew the following carefully balanced conclusion (based on the evidence down to 2005):

> Inheritances are … both highly unequal and greater for those with other wealth, widening *absolute* gaps in the wealth distribution. However, because some inheritances go to those with little or no other wealth, their net effect on *relative* wealth inequalities is mildly equalizing. Given the small size of this effect, and uncertainties about how people use inheritance, the fairest conclusion is probably that inheritance *maintains* the inequality of wealth, but did not change it hugely in either direction during the period we can examine. (Karagiannaki and Hills, 2013: 117)

Karagiannaki (2015: 191) observes a broadly similar trend for the period 2006–10 (see Figure 2.5).

The New Labour record

There is a vast literature on New Labour and its domestic political programme and a lot of it is deeply partisan.[15] Much of it was written relatively early on (before 2002). Indeed, some of it was substantially complete *before* New Labour ever came into office and, at least in some instances, it looks as though the judgements were in when the jury should still have been out.[16] Much of this work focused upon the question of how the new Labour Administration related to what had gone before – and sometimes to the shorthand of whether (or not) Blair's governments represented a continuation of Thatcherism. Much of what actually happened to welfare through the New Labour years gets lost in these accounts. Critics tended to focus on the continuity in new public management techniques – contracts and quasi-markets, league tables, greater conditionality, the Private Finance Initiative – and the fact that income inequality had not been reduced by the end of Labour's years in office. Supporters tended to point, in a rather general way, to the increased

Figure 2.5: Increase in asset values, 1984–2008

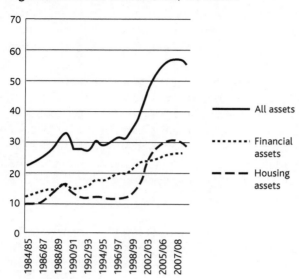

levels of expenditure and reductions in child and pensioner poverty. Almost every political judgement on Labour's reform programme – from abject failure to sparkling success – is available for those who want to read them. There is little point in rehearsing these long-gone disagreements one more time. And I will not do this.

There are just two aspects of this earlier dispute – one nested within the other – that I will explore here. The first, keenly contested at the time but which we can now review with the benefit of a little more hindsight, is the extent to which New Labour really did create a *new* sort of social democratic welfare state. The second issue – sometimes noticed but not very often discussed in any detail at the time – is the extent to which this (as it turns out, rather misleading) prospectus for newness rested upon a misreading or misremembering of what the 'old' social democracy and its welfare state had been. On the basis of this review, I shall suggest a rather more complicated history of social democratic ideas in Britain– certainly more complicated than the New Labour variant, which was synoptic history with a very particular and contemporary intent. Whether or not the New Labour variant of social democracy was very new – I shall suggest that in its essentials the answer is probably 'not really' – it is an approach that is now exhausted. Much of the mainstream of social democracy that preceded it, whether as ideas or as practice, is also more or less finished. But if we hunt around in those earlier ideas (much more than in the practices), we can find something different and at least potentially useful *in the circumstances that we now face.* Even if and as they supported the 'Keynesian Welfare State' settlement, some social democrats recognised that this was an approach that was time-limited or just might not work. Were that true, they were prepared to try something different – perhaps instead, perhaps in addition. This might mean going back to an even older view of social democracy as being about changed means not ends, and using established democratic mechanisms to press for more radical change.

The Third Way and the social investment state

Clearly, what mattered most about 'New' Labour was that it wasn't 'old' Labour. And the most important marker of this 'newness', among its advocates, was the claim that it was following a distinctive 'Third Way'. The idea of a 'Third Way' always met with a good deal of scepticism from those who held that it masked an underlying continuity, whether this was with an 'old Labour' politics (the claim of those on the right) or with Thatcherism (the matching criticism from some of those on the left). And its 'golden age' was rather short: perhaps lasting rather less than a year, from the publication of Blair's eponymous Fabian Tract (in September 1998) to the Blair-Schroeder manifesto (published in June 1999). But it was and is a useful shorthand for what was supposed to be new about the Labour Government that came to office in 1997.

Much of the ballast underpinning the Third Way came from the distinguished sociologist, and then Director of the London School of Economics, Anthony Giddens. Giddens's *The Third Way* (Giddens, 1998) became its definitive statement (and justification). The early texts of Blair and Giddens are full of summary statements both about what the Third Way is and about what it is for. Perhaps the very briefest characterisation is this: the Third Way stands for 'equal opportunity, personal responsibility and the mobilization of citizens and communities ... Public policy has to shift from concentrating on the redistribution of wealth to promoting wealth creation' (Blair, 1998: 7). In relation to social policy, with which it was centrally concerned, upon Tony Giddens's account, it meant moving from a 'traditional' welfare state to a 'social investment state, operating in the context of a positive welfare society' (Giddens, 1998: 117). It required reconfiguring equality as 'inclusion', fostering 'a dynamic, life-chances approach to equality, placing the emphasis upon equality of opportunity' (Giddens, 2000: 86). It mandated a transition from 'what has sometimes been in the past an obsession with inequality', to a new focus upon the 'redistribution of possibilities' (Giddens, 1998: 100–1). The watchword was to be 'investment in *human capital* wherever possible, rather than the direct provision of economic maintenance' (Giddens, 1998: 117). Giddens grounded this need for a new politics in his own long-standing investigation of the transformation of modernity. Most of the key ideas that we find in his discussion of the Third

Way – risk, life politics, generative politics, positive welfare, the politics of second chances – first appear in this earlier work which is all about the ways in which our lives, both individually and collectively, in both their intimate and their public moments, are transformed by the transition from simple to reflexive modernity, in a context of accelerating globalisation. Indeed, the substance of his argument is to be found not so much in *The Third Way* as in *Beyond Left and Right: The Future of Radical Politics* (from 1994), a title and text which more aptly describe his overall approach.

Unsurprisingly, many of the same ideas come through in Blair's own treatment, even if the language is a little less fancy. In the 1999 Beveridge Lecture in which he declared war upon child poverty, Blair identified six features that should characterise 'a modern popular welfare state': (1) tackling social exclusion, (2) offering 'a hand-up not a hand-out', (3) ensuring that 'most help should go to those with most need', (4) eliminating 'fraud and abuse', (5) encouraging the voluntary sector and public/private partnerships, and (6) giving renewed weight to services, as opposed to benefits (Blair, 1999). In a 2004 speech on 'reforming the welfare state', he spoke of 'the vision of a true opportunity society replacing the traditional welfare state'. He identified the need 'to move from a welfare state that relieves poverty and provides basic services to one which offers high quality services and the opportunity for all to fulfil their potential to the full' (Blair, 2004).

Of course, for all of this to succeed in being 'new', something else had contrastingly to be 'old'. In fact, while its function as the Third Way's dysfunctional forerunner is an important part of the story, discussion of 'the old Left' is fairly cursory in both Giddens and Blair. Giddens's engagement is confined to short commentaries on certain key figures: William Beveridge, Tom Marshall, Tony Crosland. More normally, his treatment of 'old-style' social democracy is more generic; as, for example, when he argues that 'until the setbacks of the late 1970s, social democracy everywhere followed a linear model of modernization – the "path of socialism"' (1998: 10). Writers like Marshall and Crosland thought that the problems that had come to plague class-divided societies had been fixed – once and for all – under the regime clumsily summarised by Crosland as 'Keynes-plus-modified-capitalism-plus-welfare-state'. But that was wrong. Marshall's view was 'too passive and too patronizing' and, in the decades since they wrote, 'by and large the economic changes they expected and advocated have not occurred' (Giddens, 1994: 73, 74). Almost all the certainties that the model of 'classical social democracy' took for granted – stable, patriarchal families, stable labour markets, mass production, an elite state with a public-service bureaucracy, national economies amenable to Keynesian economic management – have disappeared. Their solutions are not fit for purpose for the sorts of people we now are, in the sorts of societies that we now inhabit.

If Giddens's view is founded in his sociology of reflexive modernisation, Blair's account is much more firmly grounded in the messy history of the British social democratic tradition and the (relatively few) achievements and (many) failings of past Labour Party politics. There is some ambivalence about what constitute the first and second options to which the Third Way offers an attractive alternative. At the start of his most comprehensive treatment of the topic (in a pamphlet written for the Fabian Society in 1998), he offers at least two alternatives: the 'New Right' versus 'the Old Left' (a little later, 'neo-liberalism' versus 'a highly statist brand of social democracy') and 'a moderate Left' versus 'a fundamentalist Left'. While it is not quite clear how they should fit into this taxonomy, the revisionists are dismissed in one sentence: 'Revisionists periodically tried to change the agenda, but success was limited' (1998: 1, 5). In one sense, none of this matters very much, since Blair insists that the Third Way does not lie *between* but rather *beyond* all of these existing positions. And, in any case, his ambition is (as he sees it) to take a step further back and to bring together (again) the 'two great streams of left-of-centre thought' parted in the early 20th century – 'democratic socialism and liberalism'. In this way, it should be possible to resolve the 'progressive dilemma' (Blair, 1998: 10) which handed over power through most of the 20th century to (minority) conservative opinion. It is to the failures of the subsequent Labourist tradition, as exemplified by the lived experience of the British Labour Party, that Blair addresses himself.

As an astute politician, Blair is careful to begin his survey of Labour's past by praising the achievements of Attlee's iconic post-war Administration – 'the greatest peacetime government of this century' (Blair, 1995: 2) – and the welfare reforms of William Beveridge (himself a Liberal, which is part of Blair's point). But, for Blair, 1945 remains, despite some later achievements, Labour's *one* moment of success. The record of serial underachievement thereafter he attributes to a wrong turn in social democratic thinking and practice: an 'Old Left preoccupied by state control, high taxation and producer interests' or 'old-style collectivism'. The fundamentalist left stood for 'nationalisation and state control as an end in itself' (Blair, 1995: 4). The more moderate left limped along behind, with a watered-down version of what was essentially the same programme. This politics, whether in its full-blown or its scaled-back version, is now exhausted. The only alternative is to go back to a still earlier and value-driven variant: a value-based ethical socialism. The origins of this view lie as much with the New Liberals – Blair names Hobhouse and Hobson, among others – as with Labour's social democrats. Hence, the way should be open to overcome the progressive dilemma and reunite the two branches of left-of-centre opinion in the one project.

New Labour? *Old* Labour?

Just how 'new' was this new social democracy? Among its critics, as we have seen, those on the right often argued that it was just (bad) old Labour in see-through new clothes, while many on the left condemned it as a continuation of Thatcherism (under another name). Neither of these approaches quite does it. Although in 1997, it was a very long time since a Labour Government had had charge of social policy (among others), the policy programme of the new government did look different from what Labour had done in the past. There was a qualitatively different attitude to the paramountcy of employment (for nearly all), a more deregulated labour market, a recalibration of the role of producer interests, greater benefit conditionality, more private-sector involvement in the delivery of services and so on (and as already reported). At the same time, while Labour lived with much of what had been done over the preceding 18 years – and sometimes claimed to have come to like it – there were real discontinuities with what had immediately preceded it. There were some really new things, including Sure Start and a National Minimum Wage and, while the heightened levels of income and wealth inequality created in the 1980s were not reversed, levels of social expenditure were transformed. The impacts upon pensioner and child poverty were real and sustained – and quite unlike what had gone before.

In policy terms then, there was a mix of the old and the new. But at the heart of it all was what remained a classically social democratic strategy: maximising employment and economic growth in a (now rather less) mixed-market economy with a view to increasing overall labour incomes and using a still progressive taxation system to address acute need and to moderate/compensate for income inequality through the provision of widely accessed public services. And ironically, New Labour had the greatest impact when it did traditional social democratic things in a traditional social democratic way – using 'tax and spend' to redistribute – rather than through the much-heralded 'redistribution of opportunities' in the worlds of work and education (as we have seen, social mobility largely stalled through the New Labour years). One could think that this was simply the wrong thing to do, or that it could never be enough – a staple claim of those who reject social democracy, from Rosa Luxemburg onwards (Miliband, 1973; Panitch and Leys, 2001; Luxemburg, 2006 [1899]). But for a long time this strategy seemed to have worked well enough. That is, until the Global Financial Crisis of 2008 struck. For many, it seemed like one of the ironies of the crisis that only states, and indeed only internationally coordinated states, were able to prevent a global economic meltdown (and thus 'save capitalism'). But these states were forced to reset the world economy on terms set by newly powerful and increasingly deregulated global financial actors. The countervailing forces – above all, organised labour – which had, for an earlier generation of social democrats, been one of the background conditions under which their political economy had run, just did not exist in the way and to the extent that they had. Although the least privileged were to some extent protected in the short term (in the UK as elsewhere), there was no way to re-establish the post-crisis economy in a way that made those who were responsible for it pay for it. In the decade that followed, as we have already seen, disparities of wealth and income – particularly at the very top end of the scale – intensified. While austerity failed (where it was tried), even *before* it was overwhelmed by the tsunami of deficit spending triggered by COVID-19, the intent was clear enough.

Seen in this way, in relation to social policy at least, the crucial thing about the Third Way is not so much that it was *new* but rather that it was the *last* social democratic welfare state. In Yanis Varoufakis's somewhat colourful account, social democracy had entered into a sort of 'Faustian pact' with finance capital (2016: 211). Earlier social democrats had relied upon the economic growth delivered by an economy a large part of which was privately owned (whether or not they said this was 'no longer capitalism'). But it was, of course, a mixed economy over which the government had much more effective leverage and in which the owners of industry faced a real-world counterbalance in the form of organised labour. The political economy of the early 21st century looked very different from this. When the banking crisis struck, it seemed that the good times of positive-sum growth – in which everyone could win simultaneously – were over. As Varoufakis says of Faust, his choice was understandable under the circumstances – but still catastrophic.

Of course, *if* this assessment were right it might seem not to matter very much whether New Labour was new or old – since, in either case, it looks like a politics that has reached the end of the line. And that could be right. Social democracy has been in trouble (on or off) for 50 years. Confidence that this is something that could be fixed has waxed and waned but, as it happens in the years *since* New Labour fell apart, social democracy nearly everywhere has performed badly at the polls (Benedetto et al, 2020). We don't have to search very hard or very far to find the judgement that social democracy is finished (see, for example, Guy Standing, 2011, 2016). But the lesson I draw is a rather different one. A part of the story about what made New Labour 'new' involved a misrepresentation of what the 'old' social democracy had been. It isn't that the things that Giddens and Blair saw in the 'old' social democracy weren't there. They certainly were. But they weren't the *only* things that were there. And these other things remain interesting, indeed they are *newly* interesting, precisely because the mainstream forms (and the background conditions) of that older politics (which, ironically, New Labour represented) no longer work.

Social democratic politics is always meliorist. It has always held that incremental improvement is worth having. In a very different world, it looked as though 'Keynes-plus-modified-capitalism-plus-welfare-state' would deliver cumulative and progressive change and, by some criteria, it did. Those who supported it were sometimes unduly optimistic about what it could do. It is unfortunate that this is almost the only bit of Crosland's case (from *The Future of Socialism*, 1956) that everyone remembers. But social democrats – *including* both Crosland *and* the Swedish Social Democrats whom he so admired – also recognised that this might *not* always be the case and that, if it weren't, they would have to do something else.[17] And finding that 'something else' could often mean going back to the sorts of things that social democrats valued *before* the Keynesian Welfare State presented itself as the magic way out of the hard choices that all earlier reformers (including earlier revisionists) had recognised that they faced.

The point here is not to belabour New Labour. As I have already observed, the record was mixed and the judgements are very varied. My much narrower point is this: showing that the Third Way was 'new' and 'different' required the construction of an 'old Labour' other that did not really exist or that, more properly, was just one strand among many in Labour's past. (Indeed, as we shall soon see, it is pretty tricky to fit British revisionism into the Blairite prehistory of the Third Way.) Why *this* matters is that, if we delve into this past, we can find plenty of thinker-practitioners who did not believe that the problems of a class-divided society were definitively resolved in post-war Britain and who thought that the Keynesian welfare state settlement was very likely to run into financial and fiscal difficulties, *unless Labour did something more and other to address systemic inequalities*. They recognised that it was not enough simply to address inequalities of income – or to deal with the dysfunctionalities of advanced capitalism with *redistribution*. It was also necessary, indeed still more important, to address inequalities in *wealth* – and its intergenerational transmission – and to tax it effectively. Things could not be fixed simply by expanding the domain of public ownership, or raising taxation on personal incomes or, very clearly, by growing the welfare state (however good a thing this might be in its own right). They argued for something else because they recognised the likelihood or at least the possibility that we should end up confronting just the sorts of circumstances that now perplex social democratic forces – and which an updated Third Way is more or less powerless to address. It is to some of these thinkers and their recommendations that I turn in Chapter 3.

Back to the future, again

Those who search diligently enough through the dust-covered boxes in the lumber room of old Labour ideas will generally find what they came looking for. Writers of almost every disposition – from hopeful flat-earthers to scheme-mongering crypto-fascists – have at some time or another ventured an essay on 'Labour and the way forward'. Whether these are hidden treasures or well deserving of their long-standing neglect, there is plenty to choose from. As with all Labour Party history, this rather selective searching is almost always undertaken with a very presentist and political intent. This chapter is one more example. I do not pretend that the story I tell is the *true* story of Labour's ideational past, though I would say that the contrasting Blair-Giddens account of 'old Labour' is something of a caricature. I will argue that, for all their failings, many earlier Labour thinkers (and not just those on the fringes of the party) were well aware of the challenges of effecting gradual change in a capitalist economy and society. They often recognised that wealth was more important than income. They saw that there were limits to what a progressive taxation system could do. They did not think that a slowly expanding welfare state could go on indefinitely eroding (class) privilege, *if prevailing patterns of ownership were left untouched*. In government, and for completely understandable reasons, Labour almost always ended up doing, rather messily, what it incrementally could – and tended to tell itself a comforting story about how this made things (at least a little bit) better. In this most unbookish of parties, if it needed a source it might well turn to Crosland's *Future of Socialism* (without looking too closely at the text). But there was much more and else in the Labour backstory and, despite our very changed times, that something else matters as much now as it ever has.

'Old' Labour

The attitude to state ownership and to state welfare that critics advocating a Third Way see as the abiding weakness of an 'old' Labour way can certainly be found. The most (in)famous example is, of course, Part Four of Clause Four of the Party's new Constitution from 1918 with its commitment 'to secure for the workers by hand or by brain the full fruits of their industry … upon the basis of the common ownership of the means of production' (Webb, 1918: 10). While the practical significance of this commitment for Labour Party *policy*, and more particularly for the policy of Labour Party *governments*, has long been questioned, its iconic status for the party's *members* all the way down to Blair's reforms in the 1990s, seems clear enough.[1] It was always a part of Labour's 'Sunday Socialism'.[2] Just as important, certainly for Blair, was Labour's experience with the 'Alternative Economic Strategy' in the 1970s and 1980s. Disappointed by the failure of Labour Governments of the 1960s and 1970s to do *anything* to promote the sorts of policies to which Clause Four seemed to have committed them, the (Bennite) left of the Party made a concerted push for a policy agenda built around public ownership and economic planning. Articulated most effectively in Stuart Holland's *The Socialist Challenge* (1975), the argument was that, since Keynesian social democracy had clearly failed, it was necessary to pursue a more directly socialist alternative built upon public ownership and planning from the centre (plus price and import controls). Correspondingly, Labour's Programme from 1982, for example, insisted that 'our social and economic objectives can be achieved only through an expansion of common ownership substantial enough to give the community decisive power over the commanding heights of the economy' (Labour Party, 1982: 9).

In party statements, this public ownership was resolutely tied to the idea of economic planning. The belief that markets were anarchic and irrational and that (therefore) collective ownership should be planned and rational was long-standing, going all the way back to the Utopian socialists of the 1820s and 1830s. *Signpost for the Sixties* – the major domestic policy statement prepared by the National Executive Committee for the 1961 Labour Party Conference – led on the issue of planning, adding the kudos that came from identifying it with 'the scientific revolution'. Thus, it insisted, 'the enlargement of freedom which we all desire cannot be achieved by opposing State intervention but only by assuring that national resources are wisely allocated and community services humanely planned' (Labour Party, 1961: 7). In this context, an expansion of public ownership was seen as a part of what made a more rational and planned use of national resources possible (Labour Party, 1961: 16–18).

The ideas that Blair and Giddens attribute to 'old' Labour are certainly there then. But these were just one set of options (among many) and in the periods when Labour governed (at least after 1951) they were almost uniformly subservient to ideas that we can usefully (though with some caution) label 'revisionist'.[3] Indeed, as we have just seen, the whole purpose of the Alternative Economic Strategy was to displace a revisionist strategy that, so its critics supposed, had been tried and seen to fail. Despite its importance, this revisionism merits almost no attention from Blair and Giddens. But it was these ideas – if any – that best characterised governing Labour regimes between 1964 and 1979. I return to revisionism, and its own contested place in the recent history of Labour's strategic thinking, a little later in this chapter. But I want first to delve into some even older Labour sources – and to point to some of the ideas in Labour's ideational attic that have often been passed over in the more recent past. It matters that Labour's history was not quite what Blair and Giddens told us it was, not least because understanding these earlier thinkers aright may help us to understand how we got to be where we are – and what we might try to do next.

'Technocratic socialism'

To help to organise what is an admittedly eclectic search, I draw on the classification offered in Nick Ellison's (1994) study *Egalitarian Thought and Labour Politics* – an unusually fair-minded attempt to plot thinking within the Labour Party around the central issue of equality, from the early 1930s to the late 1980s (and just about beyond). Ellison identifies three 'visions' that define these Labour approaches. The first is a technocratic approach, further divided into left-wing and centre-left variants: exemplars of the first include Frank Wise and Harold Laski;[4] of the second, Hugh Dalton and Evan Durbin. A second group – the 'qualitative' socialists – emphasised the value of fellowship and the ethical bases of communal life. Its leading representatives are identified as R.H. Tawney and G.D.H. Cole. The third 'vision' is that of various 'Keynesian socialists'. This group is again divided between those who were more 'liberal'-minded (including Douglas Jay and James Meade) and those whose approach was more explicitly 'socialist' (in particular Tony Crosland). In among these sources, we can certainly find aspects of the views that Blair and Giddens criticised – but very much else besides.

Wise to Dalton

It is among Ellison's left-wing technocrats that we come closest to the approach that Blair and Giddens depict as 'old' Labour. An exemplary case was Frank Wise, first chair of the Socialist League, who argued unambiguously, in the wake of the debacle of MacDonald's Second Labour Government, in favour of wholesale and immediate socialisation of the economy, and the redirection of economic life according to a 'National Plan':

> The first objective of a Socialist Government, as soon as it attains office should be the capture of administrative and economic power ... it should proceed methodically and rapidly to eliminate private ownership from the leading industries and services of the country. It should transfer them to communal ownership in such a manner that there can be no return to private ownership ... The second objective will be the bringing into operation of a National Plan for economic development. (Wise, 1933: 68–9)

Other 'technocrats' also emphasised public ownership and planning but their views were less straightforward and their immediate ambitions more modest. Prominent among these was Hugh Dalton, an influential economic thinker in the 1930s and Chancellor of the Exchequer in the first two years of the Attlee Government (1945–47). Dalton certainly stood for nationalisation and planning – being one of very few Labour chancellors ever to oversee the transition of an industry into public ownership – but his views were much closer to what was the mainstream in more influential parts of the party. His *Practical Socialism for Britain* (Dalton, 1936) was a compendium of what he took to be the current Labour Party position. His book contained a commitment to *gradual* socialisation – identifying the key industries to which this was to be applied (plus the banks) much as they were for the Labour Government that took office in 1945. He insisted (contra-Wise) that 'socialism is a quantitative thing. It is a question not of all or nothing, but of less or more'. He favoured economic planning, which for him included the creation of National Parks and an enhanced role for the eminently respectable National Trust, which he described as 'an example of practical Socialism in action' (Dalton, 1936: 26, 243–51, 284–98: 292).

His views on equality sound like something straight out of the Third Way handbook. Thus: 'educational advance is one of the main roads towards the abolition of class privilege'. Even more New Labour was this: 'equality of opportunity means variety of opportunity'. Perhaps echoing Tawney, he insisted that 'socialism aims at a vast increase in private property' (for those who currently have almost none). And he foresaw significant barriers to redistribution through taxation: 'there are limits to the practical possibilities of the reduction of wealth based on high taxation within the framework of capitalism'. Nonetheless, he insisted that there was still considerable scope for increased tax revenues, to come not from earned incomes but from inherited wealth (see Dalton, 1936: 322–9). He also personally favoured a one-off capital levy that would effectively represent a confiscation of part of the wealth of the very rich. (He later described this as creating 'socialism in an afternoon'; Dalton, cited in Jackson, 2005: 426, n.23.) On property in land he was very clear: 'to permit land to become private property is one of the greatest historical errors committed by governments'. The 'unearned private increments of the past' taken from the land could and should be restored to the public through the application of Death Duties (Dalton, 1936: 322–7, 149, 153). All of this followed from his observation (nearly a hundred years before Atkinson and Piketty!) that 'the inequality of incomes from property is generally even greater than the inequality of incomes from work' (Dalton, 1920: 271).

Dalton always favoured the measures that we would come to call social security and associate with the welfare state. As Chancellor of the Exchequer in 1946, he is said to have signed off the cash to fund the introduction of family allowances 'with a song in my heart' (as reported in Griffiths, 1969: 81). In 1947, he even introduced 'tobacco tokens' for pensioners, so that they could avoid paying an increase in the duty on cigarettes![5] In an early text (Dalton, 1920) he had interestingly described these social measures (including the old-age pension) as 'civil rights' (which, of course, they were never to become). But he shared with Wise the view that poverty could not be eliminated in a capitalist society. In a socialist society, such provision would be more deliverable but also, of course, less necessary.

Overall, Dalton presents an interesting and mixed view. He supported increases in social security and in the availability and quality of the public housing stock. He saw education as the single most important route towards 'real' equality of opportunity. He called for a National Minimum Wage and for savings incentives for small savers (Dalton, 1936: 19, 271). He described socialism (as we have seen) as increasing (not abolishing) private property. But, at the same time, he still gave priority to socialisation and planning because he believed that without them, all the other reforms that he recommended would be undeliverable.

Evan Durbin

An even more interesting and instructive case is that of Evan Durbin. Like Dalton, Durbin was trained as an economist, but he was born some 20 years later and, while Dalton's formative views were essentially pre-Keynesian, Durbin was trained in an age in which Keynes's ideas were already becoming influential. He held many of the same views about the changing character of contemporary Britain as did those of his peers who went on to be the leading 'Keynesian social democrats' of the 1950s and 1960s (Durbin himself died in a drowning accident in 1948 at the age of 42). But his judgement on the ideas of the great economist was always more ambivalent than theirs – and he did not draw the same conclusions as they did. It is interesting to consider why.

Although his major text on *The Politics of Democratic Socialism* was written in the late 1930s and published in 1940, Durbin had many of the markings of a classical post-war social democrat (Durbin, 1940). He was unreservedly hostile to Marxism (and to the Russian regime that ruled in its name) and unshakably wedded to the idea of a 'parliamentary road to socialism'. He repeatedly emphasised the need to seek out the political middle ground. And he insisted that while it was still the problem, British capitalism had changed significantly. The 'state organized private property monopoly capitalism' of the 1930s was quite different from its 19th-century forerunner: 'The capitalist economy is ossified, restrictionist and unjust; but it is expanding and stable. The society based upon the capitalist economy is unequal and restless; but it is democratic, middle class and conservative' (Durbin, 1940: 146).

Echoing the German Social Democrat Eduard Bernstein, he argued that 'small property' was expanding, not least in the working class (who now had something other than their chains to lose). He even claimed to have coined an ugly new word to describe this process: *embourgeoisement* (1940: 113). But the class structure of the *haute bourgeoisie* had also changed. The growing division between formal ownership and effective managerial control meant that the structure of interests, organisation and power within private industry had been fundamentally transformed. It was now the *rentier* who was the real villain of the piece. Private property in the means of production had lost its function, that which alone could have justified it: 'the property holder … has become wholly parasitic' (1940: 127).

And yet in the face of all these social changes, Durbin remained firmly committed to public ownership of a significant part of the economy – and planning.[6] In a speech to his local constituency party in 1947, the year before he died, he declared that 'socialism means two things – the substitution of a planned economy and the public ownership of the basic industries for private enterprise, and the rise of the growing economic power of the state to bring about a more equal distribution of income and property' (cited in Brooke, 1996: 690). In the dispute that broke out within the Labour Party towards the end of the 1940s about whether or not to press for further nationalisations, Durbin was among those who argued the case for more (see Durbin in Brooke, 1996: 50, n.111). More than this, Durbin *always* gave priority to a programme of social ownership over what he called the politics of 'social amelioration' – by which he meant the formative measures of the welfare state – even though he recognised that this would be unpopular: '[reformers] should be willing to reduce their social service proposals to the minimum consistent with the retention of political power in order to pursue more actively the transfer of industrial ownership' (Durbin, 1940: 298).

He set out this agenda and this order of priorities (which he recognised to be politically difficult) precisely because he thought that who owned (the means of production) still mattered: '[The problem with] purely ameliorative legislation is that it deals with the consequences of inequality, and brings about a substantial redistribution of income without changing the basic principle of administration in the capitalist system, or the distribution of executive power between the classes in it' (Durbin, 1940: 293).

To press for further social amelioration funded out of taxation *without* changing the structure of the ownership of industry would undermine investment and curtail future growth (Durbin, 1940: 293–4). In other words, a political strategy that relied upon the welfare state to do all the work of reducing inequality, while leaving ownership largely unchanged, would fail. Durbin anticipated much of the sociological approach of later Keynesian social democrats and, like them, he recognised change in the structure of contemporary capitalism, including a division between ownership and control. But he drew precisely the opposite conclusions about what this meant for the politics of socialisation and the welfare state. I will return to the Keynesian social democrats. First, I consider the distinctive vision of Labour's 'qualitative' socialists.

'Qualitative socialism'

'Qualitative' or 'ethical' socialism has a special place in Tony Blair's story. As we have seen, he appealed to his party to go back before the 'big mistake' represented by state socialism to embrace the enduring ethical values that key figures in the Labour Party (including Cole and Tawney) shared with 'social liberals', like Hobhouse and Hobson (Blair, 1994). This would open up the way for a reintegration of a progressive alliance in British politics that had been suppressed for the best part of a century. Before turning to Labour's own ethical socialists, it is worth reporting that Blair's is a deeply misleading characterisation of the 'other half' of the progressive alliance. While the New Liberals certainly cared about ethics, their views on property and taxation were both profoundly radical and resolutely statist. Their brand of liberalism involved a recognition that the creation of all wealth is social, that property is 'a trust for the common good' and that the state may legitimately regulate the property regime and interfere in the 'private' property rights of individuals to secure the common good. Thus Hobson (1896: 198): 'In recognition of the co-operation of society in all production of wealth, the community claims the rights to impose such conditions upon the individual as may secure for it a share in that social value it has by its presence and activity assisted to create.'

Similarly, Hobhouse insists that 'if property is of value ... to the fulfilment of personality, common property is equally of value for the expression and development of social life'. We have, he writes, 'to restore to society a direct ownership of some things but an eminent ownership of all things material to the production of wealth, securing "property for use" to the individual, and retaining "property for power" for the democratic state' (Hobhouse, 1913: 31).

G.D.H. Cole

Cole is 'a bit of a puzzle'. According to one contemporary wit, 'a Bolshevik soul in a Fabian muzzle' (cited in Wright, 1979: 262). While this aphorism doesn't quite capture Cole's motile political affiliations, he certainly moved around a bit. He said that he came to socialism through reading Morris's *News from Nowhere* – and, towards the end of his life, claimed that this was an influence that stayed with him always (Cole, 1949; 1960). If this heritage makes him a 'qualitative' socialist – which at times he clearly was – he was also much else besides. In the period down to 1920 – and a little beyond – he was a leading advocate of Guild Socialism, a movement deeply sceptical about the role of the state and which wanted to see socialism built and delivered by self-managing workers in their own workplaces (Cole, 1917, 1920). In the late 1920s and the 1930s, he spoke up for a kind of state-delivered socialism that brought him much closer to the current Labour orthodoxy, though he was always critical of what Labour achieved in practice (especially in the disastrous experience of 1931; Cole, 1929, 1932). While some saw him, in the period after 1945, as a mainstream Labour social democrat, he always insisted that he had never lost his passion for guild socialism – or Morris. He praised the initiative-taking of Attlee's Government down to 1948, but questioned its 'consolidation' thereafter. While never in the frontline of (Labour) party politics, Cole was a decisive influence upon many who were – and a source of ideas for the Labour Party across a period of nearly 50 years. He was a 'loyal grouser', with an approach he called 'sensible extremism' (Cole, 1929: 18). Both paradoxes capture something of his equivocal position and contribution.

Given this trajectory, it is unsurprising that Cole's views on nationalisation and planning (and taxation) changed across time. In his guild socialist period, he was generally hostile to collectivism and a state-managed economy, though, of course, he favoured the transfer of ownership to workers (Cole, 1920: 123). With guild socialism defeated, in the 1920s he came to reassess his view of what the party could and should do (for example, Cole, 1929). He anticipated Durbin and Crosland in arguing that the class structure of Britain had changed decisively and that (most) workers had something more than their chains to lose. There was no revolutionary road to socialism in Britain and those who advocated a *collapse* of capitalism (as the prelude to socialism) were wrong and would simply frighten potential allies into the opposing camp. Gradualism was necessary, but reformism was not. The mistake that Labour had made prior to the disaster of 1931, and stood to make again, was to prioritise tax-funded increases in social services over a change in control of investment decisions. It was impossible just to go on 'squeezing the capitalist orange' (Cole, 1932: 7). This was electorally popular – but economically unsustainable. If investment decisions were left in private hands, the consequences of increasing the tax take to fund improved social services would lead to a downturn in economic activity – lowered growth and increasing unemployment:

> The sort of 'Socialist' legislation that aims only at developing the social services and so adding to the effective incomes of the poor, without altering the structure of the productive system itself, therefore speedily reaches its limit. For more money cannot be found through taxation without discouragement to

profit-making enterprise; and, if private enterprise is discouraged, unemployment increases; and the State has to assume new burdens. Affairs get into a vicious circle, from which the capitalist structure of industry allows no escape.[7] (Cole, 1932: 10–11)

The solution was 'not to take one or two industries into public ownership but to socialise the investment function – and introduce the planned use of resources' (Cole, 1932: 12). In relation to nationalisation, this meant that he showed little interest in the party game of drawing up a list of 'strategic industries' to be brought into public ownership. He focused instead upon the socialisation of investment and taking control of both the Bank of England and the joint-stock banks. And in the mid-1930s he did everything that he could to substantiate what 'planning' might mean in practice, not least in his attempts to popularise the work of the Belgian socialist, Henrik de Man (1935). In his own *Principles of Economic Planning* (1935), Cole anticipated an economy in which both production *and* consumption were planned. In such an economy, wages would be much less important. The greater part of people's incomes (perhaps amounting to two thirds of the overall national income) would come to take the form of a 'social dividend' paid on the basis of people's citizenship (Cole, 1935: 234–6). Cole called himself a 'reluctant gradualist'. Very radical changes were needed, he thought, but British institutions and British society afforded no mechanisms for immediate and revolutionary change. Labour had to find ways to make capitalism work in the interests of a wide community outside the investing classes (and not just the working class) while not undermining the investment upon which a growing social increment depended, and simultaneously achieving movement towards a 'more socialist' society. That was a tough assignment – but it was the only game in town.

R.H. Tawney

Just how tough an assignment this was is captured in an essay on 'The Choice before the Labour Party', in which R.H. Tawney (1932) reflected on the defeat of Labour in 1931. Tawney has been described as 'arguably the most influential thinker on the British left from the First World War down at least to the publication of Crosland's *Future of Socialism* in 1956' (Clift and Tomlinson, 2002: 315). And he was quite unambiguously an 'ethical socialist' – indeed, for the British Labour Party, given his importance, perhaps *the* ethical socialist. His Christian socialism was clearly heartfelt. And yet, at the same time, Tawney was resolutely this-worldly and practical when he considered the challenges that faced the Labour Party – and what it could do about them. The idea that Blair canvasses in his own 1994 pamphlet on *Socialism* (Blair, 1994) – that there is a sort of ethical socialism out there grounded in 'eternal values' that can somehow be contrasted with a (time-bound) socialism concerned with who owns what and how to change that – is poorly vindicated by a reading of Tawney. Tawney certainly cared about fellowship and the common good – and he probably thought that there were 'eternal values' – but what needed to change was not just the way people thought and what they believed but also, and perhaps most importantly, the mechanisms through which profound inequality was instantiated in Britain's capitalist society. Effecting that change was what the Labour Party was for.

This is clear in the obituary he wrote barely a year after the fall of MacDonald's Second Labour Government (Tawney, 1932). Tawney's judgements are severe – and they are economically and politically grounded, rather than ethical. Labour failed because it did not know what it wanted. It did not stand its ground because it did not know on what ground it wanted to be stood. As a minority Administration, it should have pressed forward with a clear and socialist programme – and gone down to defeat. Instead of which, it vacillated to keep itself in power – and was hopelessly lost. For the party, 'socialism' did not express a clear idea and consequent programme. It was a 'glamourous' word behind which to shelter. For Tawney it was clear that socialism had to mean a classless society (adding that 'it is absurd that at this time of day the statement should be necessary'; Tawney, 1932: 333). In pursuit of this, the principal objective of the Labour Party had to be the removal of class privilege. The key mechanism in delivering this goal was 'the transference of economic power to public hands', alongside a policy of wholesale improvement in the public provision of education and health services. Inevitably, this meant class war with those who stood to lose: 'The plutocracy consists of agreeable, astute, forcible, self-confident, and, when hard-pressed, unscrupulous people, who know pretty well which side their bread is buttered, and intend that the supply of butter shall not run out' (Tawney, 1932: 337).

This battle would be difficult and hard-fought. The easy days for socialists (and the Labour Party) were over. In the most-cited passage from Tawney's essay, he argues 'onions can be eaten leaf by leaf; but you cannot skin a live tiger paw by paw; vivisection is its trade, and it does the skinning first'. He insisted that the party should be girding the loins of it supporters for a fight, not promising them 'beer and sunshine' (Tawney, 1932: 340).

While Tawney's essay from 1932 is particularly direct and polemical, it is consistent with his more considered views about what socialism was and about how to achieve it. These views are well represented in *The Acquisitive Society*, written more than a decade earlier. Here, Tawney's core values could be said to be 'ethical' rather than 'economic'. Social life exists to secure the common good. Liberty is important, but it is often trumped by duty. Providing service to the community is the core value in our collective life. A good society is a 'functional' society. To serve a function is to fulfil a social purpose; to realise a social purpose is to secure the common good. Economic rewards should follow not our market power but our capacity and willingness to be of service to our fellow citizens.

We live now in acquisitive societies which are profoundly unequal – and what socialists recognise to be wrong in societies like ours is the gross misallocation of property. This has led some of them to the mistaken conclusion that all private property is 'wrong' and that everything should be in the hands of the community or the state. But, Tawney insists, the real problem is 'functionless property' (or 'passive property' or 'property for exploitation' or 'improperty'): that is, property that does not serve a social purpose and which does not secure the common good. Many small-scale property holdings – the plot of land worked by a smallholder or the savings put aside by workers for a 'rainy day' – are functional (or 'active property'). They give individuals security and they contribute to human well-being. This property we should defend. The mistake is to think that *all* property is 'functional' or 'active' – and therefore to be protected in the same way. For the most part, privately owned capital is not functional. Nor is the large-scale private ownership of the land:

> The institution of private property in land and capital [creates privilege and inequality]: on this inequality is erected the whole apparatus of class institutions, which make not only the income, but the housing, education, health and manners, indeed the very physical appearance, of different classes of Englishmen almost as different from each other as though the minority were alien settlers established amid the rude civilization of a race of impoverished aborigines. (Tawney, 1920: 81–2)

In failing to discriminate between different forms of property, socialists have made a profound and strategic political mistake. When, like their opponents, they treat all private property as if it were the same thing, they needlessly drive all the small property-holders into the arms of the grandees. 'Functionless property' should be reclaimed by the community. 'Nationalisation' is just one name and one form for that act of reclamation – municipal ownership and cooperatives are alternative forms – but often it will be appropriate, and in these cases it is fully justified.

Tawney's *Equality*, first published in 1931, expands on this theme (Tawney, 1964 [1931]). The centrepiece of the book is widely taken to be the fourth chapter on 'The Strategy of Equality', which has been seen as anticipating Labour's post-war ambition of using the welfare state as an agency of redistribution and social change. In the recent past, the English have, so Tawney reports, 'stumbled into' a series of reforms that have cumulatively made significant inroads into long-entrenched patterns of class inequality. These changes are of three types: provision of social services and progressive taxation; the development of effective trades unionism and employment legislation; and the emergence of 'not-for-(private)profit' public or cooperative production. The chapter focuses largely upon the first of these reforms and the possibilities for its further development. Tawney discusses reforms in three key areas: health, education and social welfare (old-age pensions, maternity benefits, FSM, unemployment insurance, sickness benefits and so on). At present, the redistributive consequences of these measures are 'minute', but they do generate for most ordinary citizens a sort of 'social income', which sits valuably alongside whatever they are able to earn in the marketplace. They lessen the most extreme forms of inequality and mitigate the life-determining consequences of social class. Above all, they provide social *security*. They can and should be expanded.

The wealthy will always argue that the progressive taxation needed to fund these services has a depressing effect upon economic growth, as well as representing an attack on personal liberty. But Tawney rejects both claims – and insists that, rather than choose between welfare and investment, we should socialise the latter. If capitalists will not invest, then the investment function should be transferred to the state. Tawney fully recognises that his is really a strategy for equalisation, not for equality. Even when more fully developed, significant inequalities of income and of wealth would remain, but '*capricious* inequalities of circumstances and opportunity ... perpetuated from generation to generation by the institution of inheritance' would be removed: 'Differences of remuneration between different individuals might remain; contrasts between the civilization of different classes would vanish' (Tawney, 1964 [1931]: 150; emphasis added). This is not so much a strategy for the abolition of all inequality as a strategy for the abolition of class-based inherited inequality.

For Tawney, it was important to defend this 'strategy of equality', against both those who regarded it as a terrible assault on personal freedom and (quite as much) those who thought it a 'mere palliative'. But, pursued on its own, it would fail. It is a policy that 'till a radical change has been effected in the balance of economic power [by changes in the ownership of productive capital] will at every point be thwarted and checked' (Tawney, 1964 [1931]: 120). Improving healthcare and educational provision, and providing social security, had a real and equalising effect. We were very far from the economic limits of viable progressive taxation. But Tawney insisted that unless inequalities of power in economic life were addressed, these social reforms would be undermined. Addressing these was the purpose of the fifth chapter of *Equality*: 'The Conditions of Economic Freedom' (Tawney, 1964 [1931]: 158–88) This did not mean that *every* business had to be brought into public ownership. But for the larger and strategic concerns, generally it did. For smaller and more marginal enterprises, regulation might suffice – but, overall, the state needed to take a more directive role in economic investment (Tawney, 1964 [1931]: 186).

In an essay from 2002, Clift and Tomlinson argue that Tawney spoke for 'an ethical socialism at odds with powerful statist and mechanistic traditions in British socialist thinking' and was, to this extent, 'an important antecedent to third way thinking' (Clift and Tomlinson, 2002: 315).[8] As it stands, this seems misleading. Tawney was certainly an ethical socialist. He took an unusual interest in forms of corporate governance (hoping that the management of private industry might become more 'professional', and hence 'functional'). But, at the same time, he argued for a much enhanced role for the state and for a large-scale expansion of public ownership (some of which would be 'nationalisation'). A part of that change of ownership was necessary because national economic life needed to be planned. He advocated a welfare state that instantiated the rights of citizens; for which he applauded Dalton's term 'civil rights' (see the section on Dalton; Tawney, 1964 [1931]: 147). The welfare state was there to redistribute wealth and to reduce the transmission of class inequalities. He was certainly fearful about the possible consequences of unemployment benefit – not because of a few 'statistically unimportant' work-dodgers, but because he thought it would allow employers and governments to neglect the requirement to make sure that there was appropriate work for everyone who wanted and needed it. Tawney did not anticipate that (any time soon) the welfare state would become 'too expensive'. In every circumstance, we had to choose what we wanted: costs had to be set against benefits, not just for those who received social security but also for those who had to pay for it (Tawney, 1964 [1931]: 153–7). At the same time, he did believe that to rely exclusively upon the welfare state without addressing questions of economic power (and who owned) was unsustainable. You had to address, and change, who owned the nation's productive assets (Tawney, 1964 [1931]: 120). All of this makes Tawney an unlikely ancestor of the Third Way.

The Keynesian case for socialism

Keynes has a tiny walk-on part in Tawney's story (Tawney, 1964 [1931]: 104). But from the mid-1930s on, it is possible to detect an increasing impact for Keynes's thought in the more general shape of social democratic thinking, especially among those working behind the scenes in or close to the Labour Party (in the New Fabian Research Bureau and the XYZ Club, for example; see Brooke, 1989). This influence was always at one remove, since Keynes was not a socialist (nor even really a new liberal after the fashion of Hobhouse), but still it was only *just* at one remove, since he was a critic of many of the things that social democrats most disliked about capitalism (including the *rentier*, unemployment and *excessively* unequal incomes). The key components for this social democratic appropriation come in the final chapter of the *General Theory*: 'Concluding Notes on the Social Philosophy Towards Which the General Theory Might Lead' (Keynes, 1936). Here Keynes identifies two key problems with the contemporary capitalist economy: the failure to secure full employment and the 'arbitrary and inequitable distribution of wealth and incomes' (Keynes, 1936: 372). To address the second of these, it would be necessary to press further the redistributive effects of direct taxation, but happily, and in the face of much orthodox opinion, this would tend to increase rather than diminish the availability of capital: 'measures for the redistribution of incomes in a way likely to raise the propensity to consume may prove positively favourable to the growth of capital' (Keynes, 1936: 373). And over a period of time, Keynes's advocacy of the lowest-possible rates of interest would lead to 'the euthanasia of the rentier, of the functionless investor' and with it, so he thought, 'the euthanasia of the cumulative oppressive power of the capitalist to exploit the scarcity-value of capital' (Keynes, 1936: 376). Keynes anticipated a 'somewhat comprehensive socialisation of investment' but he resisted the call for a broader 'State Socialism', on these grounds:

> It is not the ownership of the instruments of production which it is important for the state to assume. If the state is able to determine the aggregate amount of resources devoted to augmenting the instruments and the basic rate of reward to those who own them, *it will have accomplished all that is necessary* [emphasis added]. (Keynes, 1936: 378)

He concludes: 'the necessary measures of socialisation can be introduced gradually and without a break in the general traditions of society' (Keynes, 1936: 378).

Douglas Jay

One of the first texts clearly to reflect this influence of Keynesian ideas on social democratic thinking is Douglas Jay's *The Socialist Case*, first published in 1937 (Jay, 1946 [1937]). Here Jay maintains a pretty traditional definition of what socialism is: that is, 'collective ownership and collective control' (Jay, 1946 [1937]: xiv). And he retains a place for both nationalisation and planning. But of the first, he insists that it is not the key component: 'we must define socialism as the abolition of private unearned or inherited incomes rather than of the private ownership of the means of production' (Jay, 1946 [1937]: 196). And of compensated nationalisation (which Jay believed to be the only form in which it could be contemplated in a democratic society), he maintains that it would do almost nothing to redistribute either economic wealth or economic power (Jay, 1946 [1937]: 199–200). Planning had a rather larger place in the second edition of his book (published in 1946), as he reflected upon its successes in wartime Britain, but he did not opt for a 'planned economy' and still preferred to see what he called 'the price scramble' prevail across large areas of the economy, especially in relation to consumer goods (Jay, 1946 [1937]: 115).

But these are not the key elements of Jay's argument. He is centrally concerned with questions of wealth and income, and their redistribution. It is just that he thinks that most of the work of change can and should be done through the taxation system. He recommends some increase in the (differential) taxation of earned incomes but believes that most of the work has to be done by redistributing the wealth tied up in land and inherited property. These have, upon his account, no merit and no justification and he argues that, across time, they could and should be taxed out of existence, leaving the State as the 'universal landowner' (Jay, 1946 [1937]: 193, 251). Taxation, being a system of 'slow confiscation' can do the work of redistribution which nationalisation will not.

> There is no form of socialism more desirable than the ownership of land, factories, and houses, and so of rent, by the State. And the enforcement of really effective inheritance-taxation, payable in land and real property, as well as securities and cash, is the most practical and equitable way to achieve it. (Jay, 1946 [1937]: 224)

> What is more: The abolition of unearned incomes and the consequent social ownership of property must be the centre and heart of socialism. The traditional socialist belief that unearned incomes are the main removable cause of poverty and inequality is supremely important and supremely true. (Jay, 1946 [1937]: 194)

But this does not mean the wholesale elimination of private property, of capital or profit: echoing Keynes, he writes that 'it is not the ownership of the means of production as such but ownership of large inherited incomes, which ought to be eliminated' (Jay, 1946[1937], 195). Within limits, wages should be established by collective bargaining and the range of free choice in consumer goods maximised. Planning must stop at the point that it infringes on personal as opposed to economic freedom: 'personal freedom means the right of the individual to do what he likes with himself, to work for whom, for what, when and where he chooses' (Jay, 1946[1937], 273). State expenditures should be focused upon narrowing wealth differentials, in some cases through the direct supply of essential goods, but more generally through the provision of social services and through cash transfers (for example, pensions and family allowances) (see Jay, 1946 [1937]: 240–1).

When he returned to these questions some 15 years later, in *Socialism in the New Society* (Jay, 1962), he maintained a very similar line. There was a place for public ownership and planning but at the heart of the socialist enterprise was not a change of ownership but the redistribution of wealth and income. An economy that secured long-term economic growth and full employment was likely to *exacerbate* rather than reduce inequality. The rewards generated by such an economy required 'massive redistribution ... if political freedom and other civilized values are to be preserved'. Under these circumstances, 'it should be the aim of the democratic State to reshare out these rewards – to socialize the national income, if you like to call it that, on socially just principles' (Jay, 1962: 178). The way to do this was through a mixture of progressive taxation and extensive public services. Since wealth was more unequal than incomes – and since some differences in earned incomes were justifiable and necessary – taxation should so far as was possible be raised upon capital gains ('the Windfall State'), company profits and (especially) inheritances (Jay, 1962: 207). Social ownership still had an important place – but traditional forms of nationalisation were close to their limits. They did very little to redistribute wealth. They were unpopular (in ways which their mixed economic record alone could not justify). Rather, the state needed to take a stake in the successes of the market economy: through establishing investment funds which would hold the equities of private companies. It should encourage its worker-citizens to have a stake in that success too, promoting personal savings and participation in unit trusts. Indeed, Labour should steal (back) from the Conservatives the claim to be promoting a 'property-owning democracy' (Jay, 1962: 259, 290–4).

James Meade

Even more innovative, and heterodox – perhaps in part because of his greater distance from the party – were the views of the Nobel Prize–winning economist, James Meade. Although his Nobel Prize was for his work on international trade, Meade had a lifelong interest in what he called 'the just economy' (Meade, 1976). For him, the challenge was to secure an order that could reconcile two desirable but conflicting outcomes: economic efficiency and distributional justice (Meade, 1964: 11). The solution was likely to be some sort of hybrid (and a compromise): a 'Mixed Society-Mixed Economy', embedding what he called a 'Liberal-Socialist Solution' (Meade, 1948). In his last substantial published work, Meade imagined how this might look in the economy of 'Agathotopia', a good, rather than a perfect place. He even called it a 'Third Way' (Meade, 1990, 1993).

From very early on, Meade argued that 'very extensive measures of State planning, ownership, control and intervention' were justified – sometimes on efficiency grounds – but wholesale nationalisation and the quantitative planning of production were not (Meade, 1948: 11). Markets and the price mechanism (including labour markets) served an indispensable function in relation to allocative efficiency: 'A first basic lesson is that wherever competition is possible a free-price mechanism market is a better method than a centrally designed and controlled plan for obtaining an efficient system of production in a free society' (Meade, 1990: 5).

But such a free-market economy could not guarantee full employment (paid work for everyone who wanted and needed it) and its allocative outcomes were profoundly unjust. Indeed, left to itself, 'efficient' wage-setting might intensify existing and large inequalities of income and wealth. And the automation that Meade thought was an inevitable part of our further economic development would just make this problem worse. Such a change would be likely further to empower the holders of capital against those with (only) their labour-power to sell, thus intensifying already unacceptable levels of inequality. The danger was that we would create a 'Brave New Capitalists' Paradise', with a few super-wealthy owners, a small cohort of highly qualified and well-paid workers running largely automated industrial processes – and a large lump of poorly paid surplus labourers providing personal services to the super-rich. Meade (1964: 33) called this a 'hideous outlook'.

Since 1945, the creation of a welfare state and the expansion of public education had had a real impact on these inequalities. But, as a strategy of equality, it faced two debilitating weaknesses: first, a really substantial equalisation of incomes effected through a progressive income tax would have serious implications for economic efficiency – and the greater the redistribution, the greater the (potential) inefficiency; and second, it would do almost nothing to alter the very unequal ownership of property (rather than income). For Meade, wealth was much more important than income as a source of unequal power and status (Meade, 1948: 40, 1964: 38–9).

A strategy of redistribution through the welfare state could not be sustained. Instead, Meade argued, it was necessary to change directly the ownership of capital. This did not mean that the state should simply 'take over' the role of capital (through wholesale nationalisation) but rather that those who presently relied upon their power to labour should be given a really substantial claim upon capital. In 1964, Meade called this prospective regime a 'Property-Owning Democracy' (1964: 40–65). One route into this desirable outcome was to recast businesses as capital–labour partnerships, with a part of workers' income being tied to the profitability of the individual businesses within which they worked. The other was to give every citizen an income independent of their employment or other status, an income which would give them a stake in the overall social wealth of the community – and which would largely replace the patchwork of benefits and payments associated with the welfare state. In his first substantive discussion (in 1948), Meade calls this a 'social dividend' (Meade, 1948: 43). In 1990, he called it a 'Basic Income'. At the same time, Meade suggested that governments should bolster the capital holdings of small savers, by giving them generous tax allowances. His hope was that, under such a regime, 'a shift of national income from pay for work to profits on capital would have no adverse redistributive effects. What the citizen lost on the swings of pay he or she would gain on the roundabouts of profit' (Meade, 1990: 10).

Funding an adequate Basic Income for all citizens is expensive – 'hideously expensive', according to Meade (1990: 11). He proposed two ways of meeting these costs. One was to increase substantially progressive taxes on wealth (rather than income), especially upon 'unearned wealth'. This meant introducing a Wealth Tax and a Capital Transfer Tax and ratcheting up the effective taxation of inherited wealth. At times, he recommended a (one-off) capital levy (for example, Meade, 1948: 49). He also proposed substantial environmental taxes which would raise revenue and ensure that 'the polluter pays' (1990: 11). All of these new taxes would substantially increase revenues to the state (out of which a Basic Income could be paid), and reduce inequalities of property ownership among the population directly, without having the economically irrational effects of a heavy progressive income tax. There was one more key measure that Meade recommended: that, using the income from its capital taxes, the state should itself become a substantial owner of equities traded on the Stock Exchange – perhaps aiming to own as much as 50 per cent of the nation's total wealth in this way (1990: 15). When Labour had nationalised certain key industries after 1945, it had paid full compensation to the previous owners and took on responsibility for managing these concerns. This had effectively done no work of redistribution – and had left the state with a set of new managerial responsibilities. The alternative was for the state to own shares in private companies: '[Under this] Topsy Turvy Nationalisation the State obtains the beneficial ownership of the income earned on certain capital assets without undertaking any responsibility for the management of the business concerns which is left to the private market' (Meade, 1990: 13). It might even make sense for the state to sell off some of its existing industrial concerns, provided only that it secured the maximum possible price and devoted the monies raised to paying off debt, indirectly releasing funds for Basic Income payments (Meade, 1990: 14).

Meade mingled among those left-of-centre economists in Oxford (and sometimes Cambridge) in the 1930s who went on to be leading figures in British revisionism. He was a key adviser to Labour, as a civil servant, in the period after 1945. But he was always at some distance from the party, eventually serving as an economic adviser to the much-despised breakaway Social Democratic Party, the SDP. His views were difficult to reconcile with Labour's 'tradition'. His argument that trades unions needed to reform themselves to become something other than the defenders of their members' immediate workplace interests was bound to be unpopular, as was his scepticism about nationalisation. His calls for the abolition of rent controls and the selling-off of public housing were, taken out of their immediate context, unsaleable to the party membership. His views about eugenics were also controversial (as he recognised; Meade, 1964). But he was extraordinarily prescient. He foresaw the core problem of the welfare state as a strategy for equality almost a decade ahead of the New Right and the neo-Marxist left. He presented unequal wealth rather than unequal income as the key problem and, correspondingly, called for tax policy to focus on inheritance and capital gains (that is, wealth), rather than income. He divined that addressing inequalities in societies like ours required that labourers be somehow enabled to participate in capital, rather than simply pressing a policy of (sectional) wage maximisation. He recognised very early that changes in the character of our economy – including automation – meant that citizens needed to have a secure income that was not tied to their employment status. If there are problems with his analysis they are more political than economic.

Tony Crosland

If Meade was an outsider, Crosland definitely belonged to the Labour Party. He was and is the best-known of all the British revisionists – 'the revisionist *par excellence*' – and his *Future of Socialism* has been called 'the bible of Labour revisionism' – albeit by one of his fiercest critics (Miliband, 1973; Diamond, 2016: 2). When the former Labour minister Peter Hain chose to undertake a wholesale review of Labour's future prospects (in 2015), he called his book *Back to the Future of Socialism* (Hain, 2015), evoking the memory of the best-known defence of democratic socialism in Labour's (rather modest) canon. *The Future of Socialism* was written in the early to mid-1950s at a time when the British people, and British workers, had 'never had it so good' and when the successes (and the privations) of the post-war Attlee Government were still fresh in the memory. Crosland was something of an iconoclast. He begins his book by observing how different is his case from pre-war socialist arguments. And he explicitly invokes the memory of Eduard Bernstein – Germany's 'great socialist "revisionist"' (Crosland, 1956: 98). Although Crosland joined Bernstein in arguing that Marx was 'wrong' – though not in quite the same ways nor in quite the same places – his is principally a revision not of Marxism but of pre-war Labour thinking. Nationalisation and planning certainly feature in this list of revisions, but the most important theme in Crosland's book – indeed, its leitmotif – is that the core problems of pre-war capitalism are 'sorted'. In his review of the five aspirations that he takes to define the contemporary case for socialism, he argues that there are two which need no longer concern us: primary poverty and (un)employment (Crosland, 1956: 104).

Crucially, in the context of settling his accounts with Marx, Crosland insisted upon 'the growing irrelevance of the ownership of the means of production'. Britain had been a capitalist society between the 1830s and the 1930s. But by 1956, according to Crosland (1956: 68, 76), it was not. And these changes had succeeded in 'rendering academic most of the traditional socialist analysis' (Crosland, 1952: 35). But if Britain was now 'post-capitalist', it was not yet (quite) socialist. It was a transitional form that Crosland described as 'Keynes-plus-modified-capitalism-plus-Welfare State'. At its simplest, the state could now set the parameters of the economy (particularly in terms of fiscal and monetary policy) in a way that could *induce* private owners of capital to do what, in the aggregate, governments wanted them to do (substantively, to support growth and full employment).

Other components of the modification of capitalism were also crucial. One of these was the growing complexity of the class structure. Crosland always argued, in the face of those who wanted their working class to do something more noble, that ordinary people should be enabled to *consume*, in a way which had once been reserved for their social superiors (see, for example, Crosland, 1974: 78–9). And in 1950s Britain, this was already happening. Equally central for Crosland was the functional division between capitalist ownership and control. A part of what made Britain in 1956 so different from what it had been in the 19th century was the fact that those who managed private industry were (increasingly) a class apart from those who owned it. The people who ran industry were not profit-maximisers but professional managers – 'a largely non-owning class of salaried executives' (Crosland, 1956: 63). It was crucial for Crosland that (with the help of Keynes) this was an economy that could be run more or less permanently at full employment. This was important not only because mass unemployment had been the scourge of interwar labour but also because it raised working-class incomes and security. Just as crucially, it empowered trades unions. For Crosland, powerful trades unions were a *necessary* part of this new political economy. One reason for abandoning the concern with social ownership was that trades unions were now an effective real-world counter to the power of private capital; 'whoever governs at Westminster, the organised workers will remain the effective power in industry' (Crosland, 1956: 32–3, 61).

The third component in Crosland's definition of this new social order was the 'Welfare State'. It was, for Crosland, part of what made Britain in 1956 'not capitalist': 'primary poverty has been largely eliminated; the "Beveridge revolution" has been carried though; and Britain now boasts the widest range of social services in the world, and, as a result, the appellation "Welfare State" '. There was still much relievable distress to be dealt with, and a good deal of 'secondary poverty' to be removed, but that was 'a new and different question' (Crosland, 1956: 113).

It followed from all of this that Crosland placed a much reduced weight upon public ownership as either a necessary or even a desirable policy for social democratic parties. He was not opposed to the selective extension of state ownership but, where it was necessary or useful, it should not consist in the public appropriation of a whole sector but rather in the state acquiring a (leading and guiding) stake in a given sector through owning a 'competitive public enterprise'. On planning, he argued that, while it had loomed large in Labour strategies of the 1930s, it was now a 'diminishing area of controversy'. No one really believed that the state could plan an entire economy from the centre; but, conversely, no one (including the Conservatives) thought that the state should never intervene to push investment or innovation in particular directions (on a case-by-case basis) (Crosland, 1956: 482, 487–90, 498–511; see Jackson, 2005). Although his comments on nationalisation and planning loomed large for later revisionists – for whom these were signature issues – for Crosland, they just don't seem that important. He only discusses them in any depth towards the end of a very long book (starting at p 462 in the unabridged version). Given that ownership was 'an irrelevance', public or private was a matter of some indifference.

Of course, since this was not socialism, Crosland believed there was still plenty of work to do. He was passionate about the necessity of reforming the education system so that it could deliver really equal opportunities for all. Of education, he wrote, that 'the school system in Britain remains the most divisive, unjust, and wasteful of all the aspects of inequality' (Crosland, 1956: 258). His reforming intent was nicely captured in his most famous policy statement: 'If it's the last thing I do, I'm going to destroy every fucking Grammar School in England. And Wales. And Northern Ireland' (Crosland, 1982: 148). On taxation, his views were similarly radical. Despite all the changes that had taken place, Crosland called the distribution of wealth in Britain in the 1950s 'flagrantly unjust' (1962: 37). He recommended that we should use progressive taxation to address this inequality: both reducing differences in ownership but also enhancing the quality of tax-funded public services, so that the rich could no longer buy themselves (and their children) a better quality of life. Significantly, he thought that this work could not be done by the heavier taxation of *incomes*. As early as 1951, he argued that income tax was approaching its effective limits. The real target had to be unearned wealth: capital gains, the *inter vivos* gifts of the rich to their children and especially inheritance. He was sympathetic to some sort of ongoing wealth tax (though not to a capital levy). As for Tawney and for Meade, for Crosland the problem was not too much private property, but too little in the right hands. With appropriate reforms in place, property could be rehabilitated as a positive principle: 'if the property is well distributed, a property-owning democracy is a socialist rather than a conservative ideal' (Crosland, 1962: 39).

To his credit, when Crosland returned to these issues some 20 years later in *Socialism Now* (1974), severely chastened by experiences in and out of government in the intervening years, he recognised that the 'relative optimism' of the *Future of Socialism* had been misplaced. He defended the subsequent record of the revisionists, as constituting 'sound progress', but conceded that, in the core area of its economic policy, the 1964–70 Labour Government had failed. Overall, he judged, 'extreme class inequalities remain, poverty is far from eliminated, the economy is in a state of semi-permanent crisis and inflation is rampant'. If anything, these disappointments made Crosland *more* radical. On public ownership, he argued that 'in the light of the improved performance of the public sector, [it] can now be more freely used' (Crosland, 1974: 26). His priorities for public ownership were land ('overwhelmingly first'), private rented housing, parts of the construction and insurance industries, plus a state oil company for the North Sea. He floated the idea of state ownership in the form of 'competitive public enterprises' and of the state owning equities, through some sort of public holding company, reviving an earlier suggestion that one avenue for redistribution was for the state to have a financial stake in private companies and their growth (Crosland, 1974: 43–8).[9]

Conclusion

As I suggested in the introduction to this chapter, my intention in rifling through Labour's ideational back catalogue is quite specific. There is, for example, a very good case, of broadly Marxist lineage, that argues that social democracy will always and necessarily fail because it simply misunderstands the nature of capitalism and of the politics that is required to replace it (Rosa Luxemburg's argument identified in Chapter 2).[10] This may be right. But I have not discussed it, because for now I am interested in a debate *within* social democracy – and this Marxist position is not really what Blair and Giddens had in mind when they mounted their assault on 'old' Labour. The problem, for them, was that earlier social democrats, for the most part quite happy to see themselves as social democrats, had got it wrong. And they had got it wrong, above all, by subscribing to a 'simple' model of socialism and modernisation, at the heart of which was a commitment to state ownership and a planned economy. I have confined my attention to a number of the most distinguished representatives of Labour's past who might be held to represent this view.

I finished with a discussion of Tony Crosland. Though he died in 1977, this seems appropriate enough. In Britain, Crosland continues to be the most widely cited social democrat and *The Future of Socialism* the most widely cited text. Every attempt to breathe new life into these ideas seems to start here (see, for example, Hain, 2015; Diamond, 2016). In fact, Crosland was one of the most optimistic of the social democrats and *The Future of Socialism* perhaps his most optimistic text. At the core of his vision is the judgement that for all that was wrong with Britain in the mid-1950s (or mid-1960s), it was no longer a capitalist society and it had (more or less) solved the core problems of running a permanently growing, privately owned economy in the interests of all of its citizens. Even in this most benign of social democratic moments, Crosland reminds us that there is plenty that is still wrong – wealth inequality that is 'grotesque' and an education system that embeds 'flagrant inequality of opportunity' – and he argues for the more effective taxation of unearned wealth: inheritance and capital gains (Crosland, 1956: 261, 1962: 37). But, in the light of our subsequent history, his looks like a wildly optimistic judgement. Of course, this sort of hindsight is easy enough – and in the 1970s Crosland was one of the first to admit that things had not worked out as he had both hoped and expected. But the real problem is not that Crosland was 'wrong'; it is that his political judgement has so little to say to our current circumstances. (Consider, for example, his belief that the status of trades unions as co-determinants of what happened in industry was a once-and-for-all change or that the 'full-employment Welfare State' was a non-negotiable political achievement; Crosland, 1956: 61.)

Writing even earlier than Crosland, Douglas Jay had come to some very similar conclusions. He also argued that state ownership and economy-wide planning were of limited importance. Most of the necessary work of redistribution had to be done through the taxation system (a process he described as 'slow confiscation') and a welfare state focused upon delivering high-quality services (and some transfers). But taxation of incomes was already close to its limits. Tax revenues needed to be raised on capital gains and inheritance. The state should seek to reclaim the ownership of land that had passed into private hands. In the face of a widespread assumption that 'a rising tide would raise all boats', Jay argued that a growing economy would tend to generate *increasing* inequality, unless countermeasures were taken. Among these countermeasures, Jay argued for the state to take a stake in the private-sector economy through buying equities and to encourage private savings among its working-class constituents. Like Crosland, he thought that the idea of a 'property-owning democracy' could and should be reclaimed from the Conservatives.

If we go still further back in Labour's history (into the 1930s), it is easier to find defences of nationalisation and planning as core requirements of a social democratic strategy – though, somewhat inconveniently for Blair's argument, we find these defences as much among 'ethical' socialists as anyone else. Dalton is a good example. His *Practical Socialism for Britain* (published in 1936) had a central place for both socialisation and centralised planning. He also favoured increases in taxation and further development of social services and public education. But he identified real limits to the further taxation of incomes, preferring to see revenues raised on inheritances and capital gains. He thought that the state should be moving to reclaim the ownership of land (through a rigorous application of Death Duties). Like others, he thought that the problem was not too much property, but too little property for those who had none. The state should be encouraging small savers to accumulate a little property of their own. Tawney told a similar story. He distinguished between property that was and was not 'functional' and accused those socialists who condemned *all* private property as guilty of 'a piece of scholastic pedantry' (1964 [1931]: 110). Ownership needed to be *spread* not eliminated or focused solely in the state. But he still accepted the case for widespread socialisation. (He had a hand in writing *For Socialism and Peace* (1934) in which the Labour Party provided a lengthy list of industries it aimed to nationalise; Clift and Tomlinson, 2002.) And he was an early advocate of the state providing a *social* income, which would provide *social* security. Given his status as a foundational figure for Labour's post-war welfare state, it is important to report that he thought that this 'strategy for equality' could not be sustained without changes in who owned industry. And, if the owners of private capital said the welfare state was 'too costly', we should not retrench on welfare but socialise the investment function. The same strategic point was made by Cole. You could not just go on indefinitely 'squeezing the capitalist orange'.

If we are prepared (somewhat dangerously) to summarise the position of pre-war Labour thinkers on this issue, we find support for state ownership (and planning) grounded in arguments that go back to the foundational moments of social democracy in the 19th century – whether with Louis Blanc in 1848 or Ferdinand Lassalle in 1875 – and which have everything to do with the consequences of expanding democracy to include the (male) industrial working class. But a consistent secondary theme is that, *however difficult it may be*, changing who owns is necessary because, without it, all the other things that social democrats want to do – including providing social citizenship and a framework for social security – will be thwarted by the minority who would still hold effective economic power. In the long run, they more or less all thought, a capitalist welfare state would not work.

In the transition towards the world described by Tony Crosland, Evan Durbin is a revealing transitional figure. Durbin saw (or foresaw) many of the same changes that Crosland (and Jay) identified – including the impactful division of ownership and control within private industry and the *embourgeoisement* of the working class. Durbin was no great enthusiast for the owning role of the state. And yet, he insisted that socialisation remained necessary. Indeed, he recommended that Labour should prioritise nationalisation *over* social welfare – even though he thought it would be electorally unpopular. His reason was that, without these prior changes in ownership, social amelioration would (in the longer term) fail.

As we have seen, Keynes was, albeit indirectly, quite crucial to the way in which Labour strategy was reformed after 1945. Among those closest to the great economist – and a great economist himself – was James Meade. For reasons we have already identified, Meade has not (at least until very recently) featured so strongly in the Labour story. And yet he is in many ways the most interesting and, for us, the most relevant of all the post-war revisionists. There was, for Meade, a (limited) place for state ownership and (macroeconomic) planning, particularly because left to itself a free-market economy could not guarantee full employment and would have allocative outcomes that we would regard as unjust and unwelcome. In practice, it was best to stick with what Jay had called 'the price scramble'. But, given this, it was absolutely necessary to change who had a claim upon capital – especially as the tendency of automation would be to increase the returns to capital and reduce the saleability of labour-power (with a consequent effect on its price and security). There was a range of ways of doing this. Within industry, Meade favoured (somewhat unfashionably) capital–labour partnerships, in which a part of workers' income would be directly tied to profitability of the particular concern within which they worked. Given the vulnerabilities to which labour would be increasingly liable, Meade also argued that a growing part of citizens' income should take the form of a 'social dividend' or 'Basic Income' provided by the state. The Basic Income should replace most of the transfer elements in the welfare state – leaving more space/resource for public services (including health and education). On the revenue side, Meade believed that further increases in income tax were generally unsustainable. It was important to shift away from taxing income to taxing *wealth*, especially unearned wealth: a Wealth Tax, a Capital Transfer Tax and much more effective taxation of inheritance and *inter vivos* gifts. The state should also improve its financial position by investing in private equities.

The rather partial story of Labour's past that I have reconstructed in this chapter looks very different from that which forms the 'other' of the Third Way. There is plenty of support for nationalisation and planning – but this is motivated less by a fixation with 'socialism' than a concern to address the power that remains with those who control the key levers of industrial production and investment. There is plenty of advocacy of the welfare state – but this is almost always tempered by the qualification that, if things elsewhere in the economic equation are not changed, as a 'strategy of equality', it will not work. In a changing economy, citizens will increasingly need an income that is dependent upon neither wages nor benefits. There is a widespread call for increases in taxation – but rarely on incomes and almost always on unearned wealth. This goes alongside a recognition that automation will increase the earning power of capital over against labour. *Somehow*, labour has to be able to share more effectively in the wealth of capital. Making the welfare state do all the work of redistribution in an economy whose underlying structure has not been changed just will not work.

Ironically, it is this 'old' Labour thinking that now seems much more relevant to our current challenges than does the logic of a revived Third Way. We cannot afford to be relaxed about wealth, because wealth is where most of the action is. We need to shift our taxing attention away from (earned) incomes and towards wealth, land and inheritance. We have to find *new* ways in which labour can participate in the gains made by capital. Of course, upon one account, *all* of the social democrats failed. And in some ways, the prospects look even worse now than they did in the past. Almost every thinker I have considered here thought that trades unions were an effective counterforce to capital in the workplace that was here to stay – and that a party like Labour could and would mobilise widespread support among an industrial working class which, however *embourgeoisified*, knew on which side *its* bread was buttered – and would vote accordingly. More than this, almost every social democratic strategy that I have considered here failed even to address Tawney's key conundrum: how do you skin a tiger paw by paw? As I turn in Chapter 4 to our prospects now, this remains, as it always has been, the most difficult (and rarely posed) question of all.

4

Future imperfect

At last, we have reached the future! In this chapter, I think about possible welfare futures in the light of everything that has gone before and in the shadow of the challenges that lie ahead. I should begin by reiterating this key point: unless we experience a catastrophe that makes our present way of life unsustainable (and in which all bets are off), the welfare state is not going to disappear. Into the foreseeable future, whoever governs, we shall have a large state that uses the dynamics of taxing and spending to redirect resources to services and benefits for (especially its older) citizens. Here I am concerned with the much narrower, but also much more difficult, question of what a welfare regime that constituted some sort of 'strategy for equality' could look like. I begin by looking at three of the biggest challenges that we currently face. I then turn briefly to some of the most widely canvassed 'solutions' that are already out there. Finally, I raise some more radical alternatives which have the virtue, for me, of squaring up resolutely to the difficult but unavoidable question of who owns what – and of how we might change that. How all of this might be impacted by COVID-19 is the topic of a separate chapter.

It is now some 25 years since Paul Pierson alerted us to the coming age of 'permanent austerity' in developed welfare states (Pierson, 1998). For him, this had three key components: slowed economic growth (associated with the expansion of the service sector of the economy); a sort of 'growth to limits' in existing governmental commitments to welfare; and the ageing of the population. All three of these developments have had an impact upon the kind of social democratic strategies we considered in Chapter 3, not least because virtually *all* social democrats came to believe that economic growth could and should be used to finesse the distributional conflicts associated with growth in the generosity of welfare states. It is a serious problem if this is no longer an option. I begin here with the third element singled out by Paul Pierson: the (continuing) demographic challenge.

The demographic challenge

We have already established that welfare states are, above all else, systems of transfers and services directed towards older people (and, to a much lesser extent, children). At its very simplest, if the numbers of older people in the population increase, the costs of providing the welfare state will also increase.

Britain is an ageing society – though it has the advantage of starting out pretty 'aged' – and this creates pressure on welfare budgets. When the modern welfare state was created in the UK (in the late 1940s), life expectancy at birth was 66 for men and 72 for women. In 2019, the corresponding figures were 79 for men and 83 for women. In the period between 1950 and 2020, the numbers of those at or beyond retirement age more than doubled (from around 5,300,000 to 11,900,000).[1] In fact, growth in life expectancy (at birth) has faltered since 2011 and the numbers entitled to pensions has actually fallen a little in recent years (as the age of eligibility for women has rapidly increased). But, if existing policy commitments are sustained – not just on pensions but also in relation to health and social care – at some point over the next decade, the upward pressure of numbers on costs will re-emerge (see Figure 4.1).

For many observers, the key problem here is not the sheer growth in numbers of older people (whose longevity everybody is careful to point out is a 'good thing') but rather the relationship between these older beneficiaries of the welfare state and those required to fund it – often taken to be those whose age makes them potentially 'economically active' (by convention, the population aged 16–64). The proportionate relationship between these two groups is described as the 'old-age dependency ratio' (OADR). One of the key concerns for those who perceive a coming crisis is that the size of the working cohorts who will have to pay for welfare is getting smaller. This reflects the existence of a 'baby boom' (between 1946 and 1966) among those now at or near retirement age and a (less clearly defined) 'baby slump' in the period that has followed. In 2019, the total fertility rate in the UK was 1.63. It last reached the level necessary to replace the population (2.1)

Figure 4.1: Historic and project welfare spend as a proportion of GDP, UK

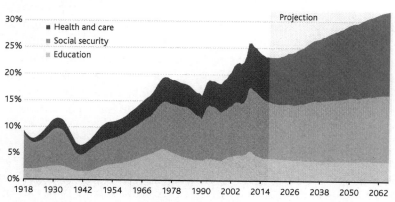

Source: https://www.resolutionfoundation.org/publications/an-intergenerational-audit-for-the-uk/, Figure 56, p 97

in 1972.[2] The challenge follows from the fact that *societal* ageing (rather than changes in individuals' longevity) depends upon both length of life *and* fertility. It matters that the cohorts coming up behind are much smaller. In the UK, this challenge is still more anticipated than real. The OADR is currently around 3.3:1 (rather more than three people of working age for every one older person). It has been at this level since the mid-1970s. It also very much matters that the proportion of those in the relevant 'active' age group (16–64) who are employed has risen significantly (from 65.6 per cent in 1983 to 76.3 per cent in 2019), almost entirely due to the increased labour force participation of women. Nonetheless, the OADR does look set to increase significantly from around 2030.[3]

Plenty of statisticians and policy makers have expressed their dissatisfaction with the OADR, especially as a guide to action. There are certainly more older people around – and they are living longer. But many of them are in much better health than were people of a comparable age one or two generations ago. Many more of them are working past the 'standard' retirement age (which has become more flexible, as well as being moved later). Many of them are not so 'dependent', enabling others to work (by providing childcare) or delivering informal care (in particular to spouses or even older parents). And pensioners do pay taxes (on their private pension incomes, as well as on goods and services)! The ONS has suggested that, under these changed circumstances, we might want to think less in terms of 'chronological' age than of 'prospective' age. This would mean focusing less upon an (arbitrary) fixed age threshold and rather more on projected years of life remaining (or remaining life expectancy). This is the basis of the ONS claim that 'age 70 [may be] the new age 65'.[4]

With all of these qualifications in place, it remains the case that there will be significant new costs associated with an ageing population. Pensions as a percentage of GDP have risen by a modest but significant 1 percentage point since 1997 (from 3.5 to 4.6 per cent) but the NHS budget (disproportionately spent on the elderly) has risen rapidly in the same period, from 4.6 per cent in 1997 to 7.4 per cent GDP in 2019/20 (pre-COVID).[5] Social care is a nettle that for now remains ungrasped – in essence because the politics of allocating the costs is so difficult to manage. Old age may start a little later but it will still be associated (eventually) with morbidity, dependency and mortality. The number of those over 85 is set to double by the middle of the century and they are perhaps always likely to be 'old' (in policy-relevant ways).[6]

The threat posed by an ageing population has been a commonplace in the critical literature calling for welfare state retrenchment for a very long time. In 1954, the Phillips Committee on the Economic and Financial Problems of Provision for Old Age recommended adding three years to the retirement age (to 63 for women, to 68 for men) because of the fear that funding the state pension would become unsustainable by 1979 (Phillips, 1954). One of the first to draw attention to the 'time bomb' that pension spending represented was Margaret Thatcher (reported in *New York Times*, 22 January 1984). By the end of the 1990s, the idea had become so widespread that Phil Mullan (2000) felt it necessary to write a corrective counterblast (in *The Imaginary Time Bomb*). A little bit more measured has been the widely heard assertion that the practical dynamics of ageing, within mature welfare states, has given rise to a profound and intensifying intergenerational conflict. The originating source is David Thomson's *Selfish Generations?* (Thomson, 1991). A more recent restatement is David Willetts's *The Pinch* (Willetts, 2020).

Willetts's book is a carefully researched interrogation of the changing economic fortunes of succeeding generations in the UK over the past hundred years, with an especial emphasis on the relationship between the Baby Boomers and Millennials. But the book's provocative subtitle – *How the Baby Boomers Took Their Children's Future – and Why They Should Give it Back* – reveals Willetts's polemical purpose. He sees our problem as a breakdown in an intergenerational contract through which, in varying institutional and financial forms, succeeding generations look out for each other. In the very briefest version of his story, the Baby Boomers have been all take and no give.

Willetts is clearly onto something. He reports many of the same trends that we saw in Chapters 1 and 2. Wealth is increasingly more important than income and it has grown much faster over the past 25 years. Wealth in housing assets and pensions is increasingly significant, and it is disproportionately held by older people. Wealth has grown rapidly and most of that growth has been 'passive': for the most part, the value of houses and pensions has 'just grown', without their beneficiaries doing anything. Younger people are much less likely to be homeowners (at the same age as an earlier generation). They are much more likely to be living in private sector rented accommodation in buy-to-let second homes, providing an income to older and richer landlords. They will not receive the Defined Benefit pension wealth that many of their parents did. At the same time, in terms of welfare provision, states have prioritised pensioners – above all, through a decade of the 'triple lock' – at the expense of other (often poorer) claimants. Inheritance is newly (or renewedly) important.

Intergenerational inequality certainly is a problem and it is growing. But it is just part of a much wider problem. There is plenty of evidence that *intra*-generational inequalities are also growing – among younger cohorts *and* among older people themselves.[7] (While the Gini inequality coefficient was generally pretty flat in the decade after 2010, it *rose* for those above retirement age.[8]) Over the past 30 years, we have seen a wholesale change in the wealth status of older people. While it was never true that most older people were poor, it was once true that poor people were likely to be old (Boyer and Schmidle, 2009). Relieving pensioner poverty was a great achievement (much of which has to be down to the New Labour governments after 1997). The fact that pensioner poverty has continued to be low in the decade after 2010 while child poverty has been allowed to soar may be disgraceful – but the responsibility does not really lie with older people (as older people). Cohorts don't act politically, even in the truncated sense in which states or parties can be said to act. The key problem is not that the old have so much more (wealth) than the young but that the rich have so much more (wealth) than the poor.

The work challenge

Long before it was associated with guaranteeing the welfare of its citizens, the state was centrally concerned with regulating the world of paid work, and its workers. As far back as Elizabeth I's Statute of Artificers (1563) and throughout the golden age of the workhouse and beyond, the state governed who had to work and where they could do it, fixed wages and terms of employment – and disciplined those who broke the rules.[9] Upon one famous definition, the purpose of the welfare state (for social democrats at least) is to *decommodify* workers – that is to protect them against the consequences of being the sellers of their own labour-power (Esping-Andersen, 1990). But even social democrats have been centrally concerned with waged work – which, for most adults of working age, has been both their principal source of income and their ticket to many of the welfare services provided by the state (including a pension). Thus, work and welfare have always been intimately related. But there is a real question about whether and how this relationship can be sustained given the coming changes in the world of work and employment. What we need may be not more of the same – say, more jobs and greater welfare conditionality – but something quite different, perhaps the opposite.

Nearly 100 years ago, Keynes wrote a brilliant but, as it turned out, not very prescient essay about what the grandchildren of his generation might expect of their economy (Keynes, 1963 [1930]). He thought then that we faced a future of 'technological unemployment' (Keynes, 1963: 364). Technical innovation would increasingly eliminate the need for humans to work. This was basically a benign development – even if it was a bit of a shock. We might choose to labour for a few hours a day (Keynes suggested three!) but we should be doing this primarily to scratch the itch – the work ethic – which thousands of generations of struggling to survive had embedded in all of us. With another hundred years of technical innovation and incremental economic growth, 'the economic problem may be solved' (Keynes, 1963: 366). What we would then have would not be societies of abundance, but they would be societies that had overcome scarcity, in a way that no human society before us had been able to do. In this new economy, we should all have more than enough. And we would then have to face up to the *real* problem of human existence: what to do to make our lives worth living (Keynes, 1963 [1930]).

It hasn't turned out this way – perhaps we should add, not yet! – and over the last 50 years, as we have continued, as societies, to grow richer, most of the policy traffic has been travelling in precisely the opposite direction. Before COVID struck, there were more people employed in the UK economy than ever before. There was a greater number of people beyond the standard retirement age (then 65) in paid work. There has been a sustained campaign over 30 years to move more of those classified as disabled into work (sometimes represented as extending 'the right to work' to a previously excluded community). Welfare conditionality – the policing of the entitlement to receive benefits – has repeatedly intensified (Dwyer, 2018). Tax credits of varying kinds, designed to enable both parents in a family to work, now dwarf expenditure on the unemployed (or 'jobseekers' as they have been for the past 25 years).[10] At the same time (as we saw in Chapter 1), wages largely stagnated after 2010. Before COVID struck, nearly 1,000,000 workers were on zero-hours contracts, and nearly 10 per cent of the jobs of those under 25 were zero-hours.[11] Across time, the relationship between welfare and employment has been repeatedly tightened even if, as has often been the case, the price has been degrading those jobs (increasing insecurity, limiting wage growth, reducing workplace benefits, reducing the value of pension entitlements).

COVID-19 will surely intensify the challenge of reconciling work and welfare (and is discussed in Chapter 5). But there is another pre-existing and, potentially, longer-lasting threat to the existing settlement (in line with Keynes's expectations): that is, automation. In the most widely cited survey of the employment consequences of automation, Frey and Osborne (2013) estimated that nearly half (47 per cent) of all jobs in the US would be very vulnerable to automation in an unspecified but not very distant future (maybe over the next 20 years). A part of the story here is that automation and/or computerisation – while once confined to certain simple or repetitive and mechanical tasks – are now capable of replacing much more sophisticated forms of human labour. Tied to new information technologies, automation can replace all sorts of (middle-class) jobs that once looked invulnerable. If jobs really are disappearing in large numbers, it is difficult to see how we can sustain a welfare state that relies upon getting more and more people into the paid workforce. Or perhaps we shall face an alternative future in which, for very many people, low-paid, low-prospect jobs become the norm – and in which poverty becomes further entrenched for those at the bottom end of the job market and the wages scale (and their children). (This, it will be recalled, was Meade's great fear of an automated future in which a privileged few would be waited on by an excluded mass; see Chapter 3.)

Of course, such large-scale technological unemployment may never happen. Doubters point to the long and pessimistic (and mistaken) tradition of Ned Ludd – and the replacement of farriers and lamplighters by car mechanics and electricians. And it is just too early now to know how great a change we will experience – and/or what its knock-on consequences will be.[12] To take just one example, close to the top of the list of occupations which Frey and Osborne see as most vulnerable to technological redundancy is truck-driving (given the prospect of driverless vehicles). But in the last decade the number of van drivers in the UK has increased by nearly a third (from 200,000 to 276,000) directly as a result of changes brought on by technological change (the rise of online shopping).[13]

At this point, it may be worth recalling that technological unemployment was not the only – perhaps not even the principal – theme of Keynes's futuristic essay. Underlying everything, for Keynes, was the sheer growth in output that he foresaw in the economy of 2030. This part of his prediction was remarkably accurate. The UK economy in 2018 was around eight times what it had been in 1930 (when Keynes wrote his essay).[14] It was *this* development which led Keynes to believe that we should be living now, not in abundance but *beyond scarcity*. That this does not well describe our present circumstances is due mainly to the way in which that extra wealth has been *distributed*. Inequality of wealth was very much higher in 1930 than in 2020 but Keynes might well have anticipated that a much wealthier society would at least have overcome the problem of poverty (if not of inequality). Indeed, he does make precisely this supposition. In the society of 2030, everyone would have sufficient (in terms of the socially prevailing values). Inequalities of wealth and income (at the top) would largely reflect the vanity of those who wanted to be seen to have more. But, as we observed in Chapter 2, the UK is a rich society with a lot of poor people.

Keynes's strange mixture of insight and oversight points us towards a still more fundamental question. Do we want and need to live in a 'work-based society'? Keynes's point is that for most of human history, we had no choice. But now we do. Or at least, we *should* do. One more challenge for the welfare state (or for us) is to try to imagine a world in which we can (either individually or collectively) make just that choice.[15] We may even wonder if we can any longer *afford* to live in societies that continue to require that everyone works. Both classical social democratic strategies of equality *and* more recent work-first approaches to welfare reform relied upon economic growth to finesse distributional issues. But this is a luxury we may no longer be able to indulge. And if we can't do this, we may have to think again about how work, welfare and well-being intersect. It looks as though something has to give – but deciding what and how is, as we shall see a little later in this chapter, not easy.

The climate change challenge

In its most basic form, the general nature of the third challenge is by now mind-numbingly familiar. The planet on which we live, and on which we rely for *everything*, is warming with consequences which, if not arrested, will make civilised life on earth virtually impossible within a foreseeable time frame (say, 100 years). The informed scientific consensus is that this process is real and any disagreement is about the pace and severity of change. To deny that this is true has become the contemporary equivalent of saying that the earth is flat – and in what follows I will just take it that the scientific consensus is right. A key resource for these judgements is the International Panel on Climate Change (IPCC) which argues that:

> Continued emission of greenhouse gases will cause further warming and long-lasting changes in all components of the climate system, increasing the likelihood of severe, pervasive and irreversible impacts for people and ecosystems.
>
> … There are multiple mitigation pathways that are likely to limit warming to below 2°C relative to pre-industrial levels. These pathways would require substantial emissions reductions over the next few decades and near zero emissions of CO_2 and other long-lived greenhouse gases by the end of the century. (IPCC, 2014: 8, 20)

They conclude, with considerable understatement, that 'implementing such reductions poses substantial technological, economic, social and institutional challenges'. They also note that this challenge is the more acute because the risks associated with climate change 'are unevenly distributed and are generally greater for disadvantaged people and communities in countries at all levels of development' (IPCC, 2014: 20, 13).

In 1973, Horst Rittel and Melvin Webber published a very widely cited paper in which they identified (for planners) the phenomenon of the 'wicked problem': a problem which is hard to specify, difficult to operationalise, with no 'right' answer and no permanent solution – and highly consequential (Rittel and Webber, 1973). In 2012, Kelly Levin and her co-authors identified climate change as a 'super wicked' problem. In addition to the features attaching to an 'ordinary' wicked problem, they identified four additional characteristics: 'time is running out; those who cause the problem also seek to provide a solution; the central authority needed to address them is weak or non-existent; and irrational discounting occurs that pushes responses into the future' (Levin et al, 2012: 124). For all sorts of reasons, fixing climate change is a deeply intractable problem. I confine myself here to a brief consideration of some of the ways in which climate change and, above all, possible policy responses to it may impact upon the future shape of the welfare state, focusing on the British case.

There is a huge literature on the problem of climate change, just as there is for the future (problems) of the welfare state. The literature which addresses the interrelationship between the two – 'eco-social policy' or an 'eco-social political economy' – is very much smaller.[16] This is perhaps understandable. These are two domains in which the leading actors, both professionally and politically, have been rather different. It is not immediately clear how and where they 'connect'. And while climate change is definitively a global issue, welfare state politics has remained resolutely nation-state based. As it happens, countries with more developed welfare states (especially those within Western and Northern Europe, including Britain) are among those that will be less immediately and directly impacted by rising global temperatures. But, given their critical position within the global economic order, the challenge here is still acute.

The future of the welfare state and the global climate are intertwined in several ways. These are likely to become ever more salient as time passes, and the climate challenge intensifies. In some instances, this challenge may be very *direct*. It may, for example, jeopardise secure sources of (cheap) food. It could make certain geographical locations uninhabitable – or make certain housing locations (on coasts or flood plains) unviable. At the same time, it may increase forced migration, a trend which has already posed problems for the legitimacy of national welfare states – and encouraged forms of welfare chauvinism (in which welfare is regarded as something we owe only to a 'native' population; see Greve, 2019). These problems are real enough – and likely to increase. But here I will focus on a range of still more systemic challenges, which put in question whether anything like our existing political economy of welfare can be sustained into the medium term.

The key problem here is that addressing the threat of climate change – whether by adaptation or mitigation – requires that we drastically reduce global gas emissions, particularly of carbon dioxide (among other changes which would include transforming our use of water). Under these circumstances, it may be that the only way to mitigate the (further) damage that we do to our environment is to constrain our economic activity and learn to live within the limits that arise from our occupying a finite space with finite natural resources (for a detailed account, see Jackson, 2009). If this is right, then it also seems that those who consume the most and are responsible for the greater part of global emissions – which would certainly include the citizens of the more developed welfare states, not least Britain – will have to take the biggest hit in constraining growth.

What this means in terms of how our economies must come to look is wildly contested terrain. Some proffer a technological fix. Aaron Bastani (2019: 94–116), for example, argues that even now we have the capacity to produce almost limitless, free, non-polluting (solar-sourced) energy; certainly enough both to meet the climate challenge and carry us into a world that is 'post-scarcity'. Others have more modestly supposed that we could retool for an economy of 'green growth' or 'ecological modernisation', combining continued (if slower) growth with reductions in energy use and gas emissions. This sounds promising – but such empirical evidence as we have suggests that it is extremely difficult to achieve any 'absolute' (rather than 'relative') decoupling of GDP growth from growth in emissions (see Jackson, 2009; Hirvilammi and Koch, 2020). The alternative to this is some sort of 'post-growth' or 'degrowth' economy. An influential source here has been Tim Jackson's (2009) *Prosperity Without Growth?* Jackson is quite explicit. The idea that everyone – that is all 9 billion members of the earth's human population – could come to enjoy an income comparable to the average citizen of a wealthy developed country (like the UK) is unimaginable. We have to find ways of stopping growth. But if we do that, in a world in which maybe as many as 2 billion people are still abjectly poor, we also have to find ways of *redistributing* the wealth that we do have, so that everyone can enjoy (at least) sufficiency.

It is here that we can locate the general challenge to the way that welfare states (like Britain's) work. As we have already seen (successful) welfare states were premised upon economic growth. This generated the resources to fund expanding budgets – in pensions, education and healthcare, for example – while also making it possible to fudge the difficult politics of redistribution that this seemed to require. When public expenditure and private incomes can both expand at the same time, difficult questions about which to prioritise can be avoided. It is not entirely clear when this benign regime stopped working (if ever it did). Wolfgang Streeck's *Buying Time* (2017) is premised on the idea that for the last 40 years (or more) this regime has been built upon an unsustainable political economy of debt – first public, then private, then public again – which cannot go on indefinitely. Committing to economic degrowth would bring this unsustainability into the sharpest possible focus.

Of course newer technologies *can* help us. We could produce electricity without the emission of greenhouse gases and we can drive around in electrically powered cars. And, as Aaron Bastani (2019) and Paul Mason (2015) both argue, information technologies really do make some goods almost infinitely and costlessly replicable. (We can *all* enjoy *The Marriage of Figaro* simultaneously online, even if very few us can afford to go to Glyndebourne.) But there is no general technological fix for the hard distributional choices we need to make. If we have to reduce our consumption, some will have to reduce more than others. Those who have most will have to give up most. This is a logic with both a global and a national dimension. Globally, while those of us in the most affluent parts of the world, with the biggest carbon footprints, will have to reduce our consumption, billions of others will need to *increase* their consumption in order to live minimally good lives. A similar logic applies at the nation-state level. And it is a sad paradox that those who consume the most are proportionately less polluting. Every pound spent by a poor person will have a bigger carbon imprint than a pound spent by someone who is more affluent – because poor people spend more of their income on essentials (such as heating and food) which have a higher carbon component (see Gough, 2017: 150–2).[17] Almost every version of the reduced consumption story assumes that we will be working less. But if that is so, we shall need to rethink drastically the ways in which we manage the relationship between work and income. Welfare states – perhaps especially Britain – have spent the last 30 years *intensifying* the connection between work and income and driving more and more people into paid work (of almost *any* kind). The climate change challenge implies that we need to throw this process into reverse.

Overall, the climate change challenge means that welfare states – in Britain, as elsewhere – will need to do *more* work of redistribution with a *smaller* resource base. If we combine this with what we have already seen are the demographic and work challenges we may feel that we need to create a new category: the hyper-super-wicked problem. What we can do about all of this is the subject matter of the rest of this chapter.

Social investment and asset-based welfare

I begin with 'social investment'. This is an idea that has attracted a good deal of attention in recent years; so much so that, in the eyes of its keenest advocates, it has come to constitute a 'third paradigm' for the welfare state, replacing the now defunct models of Keynes-Beveridge and its neoliberal opponents (see Hemerijck, 2017, 2018). Promoted as a model for European welfare states, it emerged in the UK principally through the advocacy of Giddens in *The Third Way* (Giddens, 1998; see also, Esping-Andersen, 2002). Some saw it manifested in the brief life of Labour's Child Trust Fund (for example, Sherraden, 2018). Once the New Labour chapter was over, it re-emerged, somewhat reconfigured, under the adjacent logic of 'predistribution', an idea briefly anticipated in Jacob Hacker's short essay on 'the institutional foundations of middle class democracy' and then re-presented as 'a new governing prospectus for the centre-left' (Hacker, 2011; Chwalisz and Diamond, 2015).

At its simplest, 'social investment' means recasting welfare expenditure as a down payment on future productivity (and well-being) and building a regime of 'inclusive growth'. In Anton Hemerijck's version, it has four core features: (1) a shift from (backward-looking) redistribution and compensation towards (future-oriented) investment and preventive policies; (2) growing the 'carrying capacity' of the welfare state, for example by taking steps to maximise involvement in paid work; (3) refocusing upon the dynamics of 'the work-family life course', with an accompanying reorientation of policy around the lives of women and children; and (4) promoting 'institutional complementarity'; ensuring that the parts of the new welfare deal work together. In summary, 'social investment is an encompassing strategy of developing, employing, and protecting human capital over the life course for the good of citizens, families, societies, and economies' (Hemerijck, 2018). Hacker's core idea is rather more straightforward – and more immediately political. To avoid the (increasing) difficulties of prosecuting a politics of *re*distribution, progressives 'need to focus on market reforms that encourage a more equal distribution of economic power and rewards even before the government collects taxes or pays out benefits': that is, *pre*distribution (Hacker, 2011: 35).

There is much about the idea of social investment which seems unobjectionable – if also rather unexceptional. Who is it who would not want to invest in our children's future? But getting beyond its immediate rhetorical appeal, there are a number of doubts. Some – Ruth Lister (2003) for example – have queried whether we should value our children as future wage-earners or as people of value in their own right (which might, for example, alter what we think it is valuable to teach them). Brian Nolan (2013, 2017) questions whether we can really operationalise a sharp distinction between social spending that constitutes 'investment' and 'consumption'. In practice, the relationship between 'social investment' and economic growth is radically underdetermined. Similarly, predistribution seems to make sense – especially in what is a cold climate for more traditional policies of redistribution. But we must wonder if it is ever likely to be enough. The protection of employment, for example – whether through legislation or trades union action – is something which has been repeatedly undermined in labour market policy of the last 30 years (under New Labour among others). In any case, none of this is really all that new. Recall this passage from Tawney's *Equality*: 'the greater part of the expenditure upon the social services in not a liability but an investment' (Tawney, 1964: 156). Overall, this looks like adjusting to a welfare state–unfriendly political economy, rather than the positive forging of a new paradigm.

Social investment is sometimes tied to the case for more 'asset-based' welfare (see, for example, Sherraden, 2018). Asset-based welfare takes a number of (anticipated) institutional forms but the core insight around which its advocacy is built is that those who are the beneficiaries of welfare state expenditure need to receive not just short-term *income* streams but (also) *assets* that they hold in the longer term and over which they have more discretion. This is based, in its turn, upon a still more primitive insight: that, for everyone, well-being relies upon wealth. One of the key expectations of proponents of asset-based welfare is this: that it would (in time) change both the attitudes and the behaviour of the poor – enabling them to take a longer-term view of their lives (and welfare) that would in the end redound to the benefit of everyone.[18]

Among the earliest and most influential interventions (in the US) was Michael Sherraden's *Assets and the Poor* (Sherraden, 1991). According to Sherraden, it was important that the poor should have access not just to *income* but also to *assets* (however modest these might be). Holding assets changes the mindset and makes it possible to think ahead. They allow for positive forms of *investment* – in the self and in the future – which were previously unthinkable. Sherraden's substantive proposal was to create Individual Development Accounts (IDAs) in which savings made by poorer people would receive matching funding (from government or charities), provided the funds were then spent on certain 'good' things (education or housing, for example). The slightly later, but similarly influential model proposed for the US in Ackerman and Alstott's (1999) *The Stakeholding Society* was rather more radical in its redistributive intent. The authors recommended that a grant of $80,000 should be made to every US citizen upon reaching adulthood. This would represent 'her fair share of the nation's patrimony': and 'Americans who begin life with greater opportunities cannot complain when their tax dollars go toward expanding the life-options of the less privileged' (Ackerman and Alstott, 1999: 3–4). Although the recycling of funds (with recipients returning their share when they died) might eventually make the scheme self-financing, in the early generations these grants would be funded by a 2 per cent wealth tax. Ackerman and Alstott placed no limits on the ways in which these funds might be used. It was for the beneficiaries to decide how their money should be spent.

There is a key insight in this asset-oriented literature that we should endorse: wealth matters. And it is also right that we need to think much harder about taxing wealth and its inheritance. More than this, we can also find here a welcome recognition that asset-based welfare matters for *everybody*, and not just for those who don't have very much. Sherraden, for example, argued that current government welfare spending is strongly skewed towards the 'haves' rather than the 'have-nots'. Overall, he calculated that only 16 per cent of welfare expenditure goes to the poor; the remaining 84 per cent is directed towards the nonpoor (1991: 69). But, despite their undoubted strengths, proposals for asset-based welfare just do not look up to the scale of the tasks that we know that we now face (in terms of the three challenges outlined earlier in this chapter). More assets would certainly help the people who don't have any, but it is quite unrealistic to think that they could transform their situation. Ackerman and Alstott's $80,000 would make a *real* difference to poorer young adults – but coming at 18, it is already too late! Educational inequality will have been embedded before these individuals even got to school and a (self-funded) tertiary education is not going to reverse this.

We may get a clearer sense of these limitations by looking briefly at the recent record of what is the single most important form of actually existing asset-based welfare in the UK (for those lucky enough to have it): housing.[19] Alongside implicit future pensions claims – though it is much more fungible than these – for those outside the top 10 per cent, housing is the most important repository of wealth in Britain. It also makes up a very substantial part of that wealth which is passed on from generation to generation. As we saw in Chapters 1 and 2, patterns of ownership in relation to housing have changed very substantially over the past 20 years. Overall, owner-occupation has declined (since 2003) and, correspondingly, the rental sector (and more especially the private rented sector) has increased. This has both an intergenerational and an intra-generational component. In relation to both, the ownership of housing (and its value) has become more unequal (see Arundel, 2017; Christophers, 2018, 2019). In general, it has become harder for younger generations to get a foot on the property ladder but – as the growing salience of the Bank of Mum and Dad shows – those with their own housing assets have been much better placed to assist their children in making a start. If housing is a welfare asset, it is one that is available to a decreasing proportion of the adult population. It is an asset that is distributed *more unequally* than it was a generation ago.

There is a second telling *welfare* aspect to this change. We can see this in the much-augmented private rental sector. The numbers of tenants in the private rental sector in the UK has doubled since the turn of the century (to around 20 per cent in 2020).[20] By 2019, the number of landlords had also risen to stand at around 2,500,000.[21] On the one hand, this means that a decreasing proportion of the population holds assets in housing – and they have to pay rent to provide themselves with somewhere to live. But, at the same time, renting *out* a property has become an important source of income and security (that is, welfare) for (especially one-property) landlords (Kemp, 2015: 608). Soaita et al (2017) identify landlords engaged in a range of 'property-based welfare strategies'. Some were interested both in rental incomes and capital gains but some, rather more, were principally interested in capital gains. These landlords undertook their role precisely to take advantage of the increase in house prices which was forcing tenants into a position where they had to rent (because house prices and associated deposits were too high). One interviewee described his rental income as 'my pension'. In the judgement of Montgomerie and Büdenbender: 'housing-based welfare strategies reinforce existing wealth inequalities because house price inflation will concentrate wealth gains at the top end of the distribution and serve to make housing more unaffordable for those lower down the distribution' (Montgomerie and Büdenbender, 2015: 391).

The idea of asset-based welfare, and in particular the demogrant to those coming of age, is often retraced to the case made by Tom Paine in his 'Agrarian Justice' (Paine, 1899 [1797]). But it is less frequently recalled that for Paine this was as part of a wholesale attack on the existing maldistribution of property (which was then held primarily in land). As we have already observed, and just seen again, *everybody's* welfare is asset-based. However worthwhile it may be in itself, we are not going to change anything much by giving everyone a (comparatively small) one-off payment on their entry to adulthood. And the general direction of travel (in housing, for example) is towards the *more unequal* ownership of wealth. In addressing our three challenges, this is the reality we have to confront.

Universal Basic Income

Paine's 'Agrarian Justice' is also frequently cited as an inspirational source for what is, by some way, the most widely canvassed radical alternative on welfare of the past 25 years – that is the case for a Universal Basic Income (UBI).[22] The core idea is simple enough. UBI is 'a regular cash payment income paid to all, on an individual basis, without means test or work requirement' (van Parijs and Vanderborght, 2017: 1). The underlying intuition which makes it so popular (for those who support it) is probably this: in societies that are as rich as ours no one needs to be poor or, a little less succinctly, no one should lack the material means to live an adequate life. Providing this secure base was, more or less, what the post-war welfare state was supposed to do. It was the 'first marriage of justice and efficiency'. But for all sorts of reasons, most of which have been identified somewhere in this book, that solution no longer works. UBI is 'the second marriage of justice and efficiency' (according to van Parijs, 1990: 1).

Although many have argued for UBI in the intervening period, the key intellectual source remains Phillipe van Parijs's 1995 text *Real Freedom for All: What (If Anything) Can Justify Capitalism?* Van Parijs has spent the last 25 years tirelessly defending his argument and pressing the case for policy reforms to match. Although, from time to time, advocates argue that Basic Income is 'an idea whose time has come', and there have been plenty of 'experiments', the on-the-ground record of innovation is disappointingly thin. One thing that we can very certainly say about the advocacy of UBI is that it explicitly addresses at least two of the key challenges I identified in the opening part of this chapter. (It has nothing very special to say about ageing.) To this extent, it very definitely commands our careful attention.

The critical literature for and against UBI is vast, and useful guides include Standing, 2017; and the comprehensive Widerquist et al, 2013. Among many others, two criticisms are especially prominent. One is that unconditionality means that those who choose to live on their Basic Income – and elect not to work – are exploiting those who do work and (thus) fund the incomes taken by others. The other is that, for two reasons, it is not feasible. First, while UBI may be popular with much (though certainly not all) of the social policy community, unconditionality is not popular with the demos (which has been led in precisely the opposite direction for the last 40 years). Second, an adequate UBI cannot be funded. I will not discuss these claims any further here, beyond saying that it is not clear that the opponents of UBI have it all their own way. I focus instead upon the ways in which UBI is said to confront the challenges of work and climate change.

In relation to the changing world of work, the seemingly endless arguments about whether 'surfers should be fed' (following the provocative title of van Parijs's 1991 paper) may miss the most important point about what it is that has changed. Such evidence as we have suggests that a Basic Income would not lead to a mass exodus from the world of work and all previously existing societies have found a way to cope with the fact that some of their number – whether indolent surfers or aspirant artists – would rather get by on a little and do what they want.[23] As supporters of UBI have pointed out, we could do with rather more people who want to do something other than consume scarce resources. But the real problem here is that the nature of work has changed – to become less secure, often less well paid and (if the prophets of artificial intelligence – AI – are right) increasingly scarce. The share of wages in the economy has been falling for 30 years, at least. The sorts of working lives on which the traditional welfare state was built – not least in the accumulation of pension rights – no longer exist. We persist in driving more and more people into paid work – often in roles which we don't need. Hence the exponential growth in so-called 'bullshit jobs' (jobs for which no one, including their holders, can see any real point; Graeber, 2019).

UBI certainly changes the jobs calculus. In providing a baseline below which an individual's income shall not fall, it militates against an obligation to work for an inadequate wage. This security should also enable potential employees to be more choosy about what work they will (and will not) take. It should give them the time to retrain (where necessary) and allow them to wait for the right job to come along. It should strengthen their position when negotiating with employers. It would eliminate the various 'poverty traps' and 'employment traps' that make the transition into work difficult for those with low earning capacity. It would enable people to do socially useful things which are typically not in the realm of paid work (say, providing informal care to friends or relations) (on all of which, see Standing, 2017).

A further perceived advantage of UBI is that it should encourage and enable us to do what we *really* want to do – and, for many of us, that may be to work less. It is here that UBI arguments in relation to work elide with those that relate to climate change. UBI has long been popular with Greens. (In the UK, the Green Party is the only party to have consistently argued for a

Basic Income.)[24] UBI is perhaps seen as an anti-poverty measure – seeking to establish a floor beneath which incomes may not fall – but it may also constitute a step away from an employment-focused economy (and society). Were our well-being less closely tied to our employment status, we could choose how much we wanted to work (perhaps reducing our hours or years of employment) and do more of the other things we value (more). If we really want to stop growth and reduce consumption (in already wealthy societies), we need to produce less and buy less, and that probably means that we need to work less. Loosening the tie between employment and income makes that change (more) possible. And if and when AI makes more jobs redundant, we can avoid the imperative to create new jobs to 'soak up' the displaced workers if we do not require them to work. More broadly, we can only imagine moving towards a less productivist (and consumption-focused) economy and society if and when we de-emphasise the need to work (as Keynes had thought we would nearly 100 years ago). All of this needs somehow to be done without worsening the position of those who are worst off and don't have enough (even when 'enough' has been recalibrated downwards). According to Jan Oto Andersson: 'A solution that curbs excessive consumption patterns and enhances the life chances of the poor at the same time is superior to a scheme that is either purely redistributive or purely eco-efficient without regard to distributive justice' (2009: 5). 'Work less, consume less, play more' may be a fitting message for a society which cannot afford to grow its way out of its distributional challenges.[25]

There is a great deal to recommend a UBI – perhaps now more than ever. But it is still not clear that 'it's time (really) has come'.[26] COVID might change that – but maybe not. As its supporters rightly point out, we do not need to move straight to a 'gold standard' full UBI. But some of the potential partial schemes appear to have perverse effects in terms of social inequality and fiscal efficiency. Martinelli's modelling of some of these schemes showed that the poorest households might lose out significantly under a UBI if existing (targeted) benefits were withdrawn (Martinelli, 2017: 42–50). If they were not withdrawn, the distributional outcomes would be less perverse. But this opens the door to those who argue that our tax pounds would be better spent on refurbishing our existing welfare state (for example, Häusermann and Gingrich, 2020) – or opting for a different alternative (for example, universal basic *services* as recommended by Coote and Percy, 2020). Overall the fear remains that 'an affordable UBI would be inadequate, and an adequate UBI would be unaffordable' (Martinelli, 2017: 43).

This argument rumbles on. In concluding my discussion, I want to draw attention to a different issue. Many have been drawn to arguments for a Basic Income because they think that contemporary capitalism has failed: generating unacceptable levels of economic inequality (*within* affluent societies) in an economy that is ecologically unsustainable. But it is important to note that the current advocacy of UBI is also rooted in an argument about the historical failures of *socialism*. Ten years before the publication of *Real Freedom for All*, van Parijs co-authored 'A Capitalist Road to Communism', plotting the only route left to us given the twin failures of actually existing socialism (in the East) and actually existing social democracy (in the West) (Van der Veen and Van Parijs, 1986). Van Parijs was not unsympathetic to what socialists wanted – in so far as this was to maximin real freedom for all – but socialism could not deliver this. UBI was the 'what (if anything)' that could justify capitalism. I don't want to discuss whether or not van Parijs was right. (Right on socialism, wrong on capitalism is one possible if rather depressing answer.) I simply observe that one consequence of arguing in this way is that attention tends to drift away from wealth towards incomes. Some do recognise (with Paine) that grants to citizens rest upon the misappropriation of shared resources ('land' in Henry George's extended sense) and that this requires that we focus upon the taxation of *wealth* (and especially inherited wealth).[27] But too often the UBI discussion focuses upon the redistribution of *incomes*. *No one* can believe that a sustainable Basic Income is going to be grounded in extraordinarily high levels of taxation of earned incomes. It is time to turn to those who respond to our three challenges by taking wealth seriously.

Milanovic

Branko Milanovic, formerly lead economist at the World Bank, queries the end of jobs as we have known them, thinks that the limited carrying capacity of the earth is a delusion which we use to give ourselves a scary thrill and doubts the value of UBI (Milanovic, 2019: 199–205). For him, both the problems and the solutions are to be found elsewhere. In *Capitalism, Alone*, he argues that capitalism is all we have and will ever have. It currently takes two forms: 'state-led political, or authoritarian capitalism' (of which the modal example is China) and 'liberal meritocratic capitalism' (which is what we have in the US and the rest of the West).[28] Liberal meritocratic capitalism has dominated for the last 40 years, ever since it came to eclipse its briefly dominant (1945–80) social democratic capitalist forerunner. It has shifted resources (and power) decisively in favour of the holders of capital with wealth and income increasingly concentrated in the top 10 per cent of the population. These societies run the danger of becoming democratic in name only, as a self-replicating upper-class elite comes to control the political process, as much as the economic one, through the overwhelming force of its money.

If we want to change this, which Milanovic thinks we should, we need radical reform. We cannot hope to achieve this through traditional welfare state policies. Rather, we need somehow to achieve 'approximately equal endowments of both capital and skills across the population'. And to get there, we need to alter the system of taxing capital to encourage small and medium shareholders, to promote more worker-owned enterprises and to beef up the taxation of wealth, especially of inherited wealth. On the labour and skills side, we need 'to equalize teaching standards among schools'. We also need to clean up the funding of political campaigns (to restore democratic accountability) and introduce a new denizen status for economic migrants (to overcome welfare chauvinism) (Milanovic, 2019: 46, 50, 217).

On this basis, Milanovic offers two possible – and, for him, attractive – alternative capitalist futures. Under what he calls *popular capitalism*, 'everyone has approximately equal *shares* of both capital and labor income [though] people's incomes still differ'. Under the more radical *egalitarian capitalism*: 'Everyone has approximately equal amounts of both capital and labor income, such that a large increase in the capital share does not translate into greater inequality. Interpersonal inequality is low. The role of the state in redistribution is limited to social insurance. Relative equality of incomes ensures equality of opportunity.' In this way, Milanovic argues, 'libertarianism, capitalism, and socialism come close to each other' (Milanovic, 2019: 216–17).

Piketty

Thomas Piketty is well known for his globe-spanning meta-history of economic inequality, originally just of the three most recent centuries of capitalist development but now stretching all the way back into the ancient world (Piketty, 2014, 2020). His overall account, and his periodisation of the development of capitalist societies in the West shares much with Milanovic. The proprietarian (property-based) societies that came to dominate before 1914 were extraordinarily unequal because of the hyperconcentrated private ownership of wealth. In the aftermath of two world wars, and the special circumstances that these triggered, this gave way to a social democratic episode in which economic inequality was substantially reduced. In the period since 1980, we have seen the (re-)emergence of (neo-)proprietarian societies which have at times (most notably in the US) come close to the levels of inequality that prevailed before 1914. For Piketty, the underlying dynamic which has driven this extended historical process is that returns to capital tend to increase faster than overall economic growth (r>g), so that across time and open-endedly returns to capital will generally outstrip returns to labour (Piketty, 2014: 25–7). Unless we make systemic changes (above all, to our property regime), inequality will continue to intensify.

Piketty is not so much concerned with the 'new' challenges I identified in the opening part of this chapter – largely, because he thinks the problems of the future are already with us. (We do not, for example, need the destruction of jobs by AI to give us intensifying returns to capital.) He does give some space to climate change – indeed, he writes that 'along with rising inequality, global warming is the greatest challenge the planet faces today' – and he does call for a progressive carbon emissions tax. He also supports the idea of some sort of substantial citizen's grant – in wealthy Western societies, he suggests a sum around 60 per cent of average adult wealth could be given to every citizen at age 25 – but he has reservations about whether a UBI could be made to work. In terms of predistribution (like Milanovic), he places overwhelmingly emphasis upon the need to *equalise* the educational experience of *all* children, in a way that would make social mobility meaningful. He has an especial concern with the dynamics of tertiary education (Piketty, 2020: 1004–5, 669, n.42, 981, 534–48).

But in many ways, Piketty's concerns – and his remedies – are (perhaps surprisingly) quite old-fashioned. *The* problem is (extreme and unmerited) economic inequality and its transmission across generations. *The* answer is to redistribute that wealth, repeatedly – for example through the taxation system.[29] He favours (the return to) a much more progressive tax on income (at 'confiscatory' levels for 'excessive' incomes). He also argues for (the return to) a much more progressive and effective taxation of inherited wealth, more innovatively, to a progressive global tax on carbon emissions and, most significantly, to an international annual progressive wealth tax. His focus is on property relationships. He evokes a very ancient idea (of 'usufruct') in talking about the need to move towards 'temporary ownership' (property as a 'social relation' rather than as 'natural right'). To do good, property needs to be circulating, not concentrating (Piketty, 2020: 971–9).

Piketty is brave enough to call this agenda for reform 'participatory socialism' and to say explicitly that we need 'to transcend capitalism and private property' (Piketty, 2020: 862, 972). He complains that 'social democrats never really considered the issue of just ownership after the collapse of communism' and that 'in the end social democrats almost entirely gave up even thinking about moving beyond private property' (Piketty, 2020: 41, 495). To this extent, Piketty echoes the arguments of an earlier generation of social democrats (including the British social democrats we considered in Chapter 3) from *before* the revisionist turn. Although the circumstances were very different – not least because there really was a labour movement at the time – these earlier writers persisted in thinking that who owned really mattered and that property relationships had to be changed if a social democratic politics was to be advanced. I have argued earlier that abandoning this view was a strategic (if understandable) mistake. To the extent that Piketty shares this view, I think that he is right.

Gough

In this survey of alternative views, I turn finally to someone who takes the challenge of climate change *extremely* seriously. Ian Gough's (2017) *Heat, Greed and Human Need* is an attempt to rethink what sort of a welfare order we should be working towards within an overall framework that really does what we need to do to address the crisis of climate change: 'the most encompassing and threatening of all the planetary limits' that we collectively face. The changes we need to make if (above all, carbon) emissions are to be reduced to levels that are consistent with tolerable living conditions around the globe now and in the future cannot be achieved incrementally. And 'growth alone, even green growth, cannot eliminate poverty without laying waste to the planet'. Our ambition must be to secure 'wellbeing and social justice within planetary boundaries'. To do this, we need 'a radical redistribution of carbon, time and wealth' (Gough, 2017: 1, 64, 37, 14).

In the second half of his book, Gough considers what this might mean for the developed (welfare) states of the global North. He identifies three possible routes towards decarbonisation. Policies for the mitigation of carbon *production* would include carbon pricing, the increased regulation of emissions and strategic investment in 'green' (energy) alternatives. A second and more radical approach involves the attempt to decarbonise *consumption*; by reducing absolute levels of personal consumption of (especially high-emission) goods. Since Gough is committed to guaranteeing the poorest people a minimum level of consumption and, given that their 'bundle of goods' will include a substantial proportion of high-emitting goods (for example, food and fuel for heating), this would require very significant reductions in 'non-essential' consumption among those who are better off. This persuades Gough that we should think in terms not only of *minimum* but also of *maximum* levels of consumption, allowing us to establish a 'consumption corridor' whose limits all citizens should respect. Getting there would require high taxation of high-emission goods, more social production/consumption (in transport, for example) and (probably) personal carbon allowances. Gough also identifies a number of necessary 'upstream' social policy interventions, including (drawing on Michael Marmot's work) 'fair employment and good work, a healthy standard of living for all, and healthy and sustainable places and communities'. In this way, social policy involves 'changing patterns of consumption as well as redistributing incomes' (Gough, 2017: 166, 170).

But even these changes are unlikely to be enough – especially as it is the richer global North (and especially its richer citizens) that must do most of the required carbon-shedding. And Gough finally lays out what it would take to build an equitable no-growth economy – which is what it may take. As well as calling for a stabilisation of population and a growth in the social commons, Gough insists that we need radically to reduce (paid) working time and to expand the collective ownership of wealth and capital: 'A reallocation of property rights would give everyone a stake in capital and a non-labour source of income. This would require on the one hand steep taxation of inheritance, land, and capital transfers and on the other hand building up the state's store of public capital' (Gough, 2017: 180). It seems highly unlikely that any of this could take place within the structures of 'carboniferous capitalism' (Gough, 2017: 8).

Conclusion

I have covered a lot of ground in this chapter. It is time to take stock. As we saw in Chapters 1 and 2, welfare state budgets and institutions have been under intense pressure for at least the last 25 years. Although sustained economic growth gave New Labour some scope to increase spending during the first decade of the new millennium, in the second decade (under 'austerity') budgets were squeezed hard – substantially increasing child poverty, for example – but without achieving a really significant *reduction* in the scale of welfare spending. The three challenges I have identified in this chapter – around ageing, work and climate change – make the social policy context even more difficult. The challenge of ageing is already pretty well known to us but, though it has been around for a while, most of the difficult decisions are still to come. The future of work is more uncertain but, for a number of reasons, greater conditionality and the aspiration to tie welfare still more tightly to work look increasingly unsustainable – unless we are willing to force increasing numbers of our fellow citizens into poorly paid, insecure work, with no welfare protection. (Since this is what we *have* done over the last decade or two, this is not a possibility we can easily dismiss.) The work issue easily elides into the climate challenge. Unless and until we discover some radically other way of producing and consuming (with minimal emissions), it looks as though the best (perhaps the only) way to decarbonise the economy is to produce less, to consume less – and, correspondingly, to work less. If this is not to result in still higher levels of inequality, we should need to redistribute more, probably *much* more.

It is perhaps not surprising that in the face of challenges on this scale, most of the policy alternatives on offer look either inadequate or unachievable – or both. Social investment is a good idea but, on its own, it is unlikely to make a difference on the scale that we need. Asset-based welfare is certainly very important (for the 'haves' as much as for the 'have-nots') but even the most radical reforms, for example, Ackerman and Alstott's wealth tax–funded citizen's grant, don't really look up to the task. And, of course, the greater its redistributive potential, the less is the chance that a reform will be implemented. The attractions of a UBI are obvious enough – and this is an approach that really does engage with questions of work reduction and climate change – but it is very unclear that a sufficient UBI can be delivered, or that it is an *efficient* way of meeting our needs (Ian Gough describes UBI as 'a powerful new tax engine … pull[ing] along a tiny cart'[30]). More than this, it is a mistake to focus too exclusively upon *incomes* (rather than assets). In *Real Freedom*, van Parijs judges that there is just not enough asset-based wealth to fund a UBI – which is why he characterises jobs as 'assets', which we can then tax. But if we take a more capacious view – like that of Henry George – we can surely see much more wealth out there whose taxation can give us resources we can then redistribute.[31]

It is these considerations that brought me to Milanovic, Piketty and Gough. In their different ways, all three recognise that we can only begin to address our welfare challenges by refocusing attention on property – who owns what, and how we might change that. (This is, of course, precisely the question raised by the first social democrats.) Milanovic insists that capitalism is all we (can) have. And yet his egalitarian capitalism (indeed, even his popular capitalism) looks quite unlike anything we have ever seen in the real world. He rejects UBI at least in part because it is unrealistic – and yet his insistence that we need an educational system that delivers the same quality of experience for every child looks to be at least as fanciful as any other reform we have considered here. Piketty places changing the unequal ownership of wealth right at the heart of his agenda for reform – but concludes that his call for a global progressive tax on capital remains, for now, a 'useful utopia' (Piketty, 2014: 530). Gough is careful to consider the alternatives to a post-growth political economy before insisting that this is the only option that will really work. Of course, for him, this would require 'a major reallocation of property rights'.

In politics, the first question is always this: what is to be done (now)? I return to this most difficult challenge in the book's conclusion. First, I ask briefly (and provisionally) how is any of this changed by the coronavirus pandemic?

5

COVID-19 and after

Nothing changes *everything*. Given the scale of the disruption and desolation that the pandemic has wrought – from the truly global to the irreducibly intimate – it is tempting to think that COVID-19 is the exception. But it isn't. Other pandemics have been and gone.[1] We will not be living in a siege economy and society for ever. And a combination of herd immunity, vaccine and collective boredom will allow some sort of everyday to re-emerge. But we shall not be returning to the world just as it was, nor any time soon.[2] The Global Financial Crisis (of 2008) now looks quite modest by comparison to COVID-19 but when the pandemic struck we were still in the process of recovering from that earlier disaster. As we saw in Chapter 1, the financial crisis ushered in an economic 'lost decade' and, as we also saw, the associated economic costs and losses were very unevenly distributed. The Global Financial Crisis was a 'temporary shock' with 'persistent effects' (Hanlon, 2017) – and this is one useful way to think about the COVID experience. Of course, in the latter case the 'temporary' is pretty long-standing and the 'persistent effects' are still extremely unclear, but certain to be profound – and to persist for at least a decade, probably much longer. What we also know is that, as after 2008, these consequences will be differentiated by class, gender, ethnicity, location and perhaps by age.[3]

'Scarring', both social and economic, is something which always has its origins in present injuries. Although the world after COVID is clouded in uncertainty – not least knowing when it will 'end' and what that would mean – there is plenty that we *do* know. And a significant part of our still quite uncertain future is determined by what has happened already – not just the pathway of the disease but also, for example, the scale of public indebtedness. The challenge of the public debt is, of course, principally a threat – but it is also an opportunity (to do things differently). In this chapter, I concentrate on what is happening to our welfare regime (broadly conceived) in the wider context of an ongoing recession. I focus first on the recent past and the near-present. A little later, I turn to what may happen in the near-future. The rather more distant future is something I return to in the concluding chapter.

COVID: the first year

This is the bit of the story of which we were all a part and which we all lived through. It makes our pre-COVID lives look and feel a world away. At its very briefest that story is this. Late in 2019, scientists in the Chinese city of Wuhan identified a new virus which had triggered Severe Acute Respiratory Syndrome (SARS) in a number of vulnerable patients. This was SARS-CoronaVirus-2 and the disease with which it was associated came to be labelled by the WHO (World Health Organization) COVID-19. Although less virulent than the virus which had caused the global outbreak of SARS in 2003, the new coronavirus was highly transmissible, and many of its carriers were asymptomatic. The first confirmed cases in the UK were identified at the end of January 2020. By the end of February, there were 23 confirmed cases in the UK. Numbers accelerated in early March and the first COVID-related death was reported on 5 March. On 11 March, the WHO designated COVID-19 a pandemic.[4]

On 23 March 2020, in response to the rising incidence of the disease, the government instituted a first nationwide lockdown, with stringent limits on all travel and social contacts, the closure of schools and colleges and a ban on many business activities.[5] In the UK, the numbers of those hospitalised with the condition rose steeply to peak at around 21,000 in the first two weeks of April 2020. Associated deaths peaked at just above 1,000 per day on 10 April.[6] Alongside the lockdown, the other key element in the government's response was a system to 'test and trace' those who had the disease, and their close contacts. Announced by the Health Secretary Matt Hancock on 23 April, mass testing did not really get under way until the autumn of 2020. Tests conducted only consistently exceeded 100,000 per day at the end of June; they routinely exceeded 200,000 from 7 September. The test and trace system struggled to contact up to a third of those who were identified as needing to self-isolate to prevent the spread of the infection.[7] A report by the House of Commons Public Accounts Committee in March 2021 concluded that the 'unimaginable' sums spent on test and trace (around £37 billion over a two year period) had made 'no measurable difference' to the management of the pandemic.[8]

As hospitalisations fell through May, June and July 2020, there was a gradual loosening of regulations. Having levelled off through the summer, a second wave of infections starting in early September took daily hospital admissions close to 2,000 by mid-November. New restrictions were introduced (with a three-tiered system) on 14 October and this was followed by the reimposition of a full lockdown (though this time excluding schools and universities) on 5 November. On 3 December, there was a return to a (more severe) form of tiered restrictions. This second wave accelerated through Christmas and into 2021, amid reports of new and more virulent variants of the virus.[9] An

England-wide lockdown was reimposed on 6 January 2021. For the following three weeks, COVID-related deaths exceeded 1,000 per day, peaking at 1,359 on 19 January. At the height of this second wave, the number of patients in hospital was almost twice what it had been at the peak of the first wave (at 39,000 and 22,000 respectively).[10]

The really big change at the start of 2021 was the development of a programme of mass vaccination against COVID-19 across the UK. This had been heralded by the announcement by Pfizer-BioNTech on 9 November 2020, that they had trialled a vaccine that was 90 per cent effective against coronavirus. This was closely followed on 23 November by news of successful Phase III trials of a vaccine created by Oxford/AstraZeneca. These were the first in a series of 'success stories' from other potential vaccine producers.[11] The vaccination programme, delivered by the NHS, began, in December 2020, with the elderly and the clinically vulnerable. By 23 March 2021, a year on from the announcement of the first lockdown, nearly 30,000,000 people in the UK had received a first dose of a vaccine. At this point, the number of patients hospitalised with COVID-19 had fallen rapidly to be just around 5,000. Under these circumstances, the government announced on 23 February a 'roadmap' for the gradual lifting of coronavirus restrictions, with much of the apparatus of lockdown to be lifted by 21 June 2021, provided the vaccination programme continued to be successful in moderating the incidence and severity of the disease.[12]

COVID: economy and welfare

The government was very widely criticised for the slowness and inconsistency of its response to the COVID crisis.[13] I will not consider those claims here. Rather I will concentrate upon one area in which the government was widely seen to have performed relatively well in the context of the crisis – that is in their emergency measures to limit the economic damage of the virus for both businesses and individuals, and its welfare consequences.

The scale of the hit to the economy in March and April 2020 was unprecedented. GDP fell by a quarter in these months, recovering to be 8 per cent lower by September. In its March 2021 Report, the OBR reported the overall decline in GDP across the preceding year to be around 10 per cent.[14] The hit to the labour market was substantially moderated by government interventions, with unemployment rising (pretty modestly) to be around 5 per cent in the last quarter of 2020.[15] Announcing £330 billion of guarantees to businesses on 17 March, six days before the first lockdown was introduced, Rishi Sunak insisted that the government would do 'whatever it takes' to get through the crisis. Three days later, the government introduced a raft of job support measures. Of these the most important (and expensive) were the Coronavirus Job Retention Scheme (CJRS) and a little later the

Self-Employment Income Support Scheme (SEISS). At its peak, close to 9,000,000 jobs were furloughed under CJRS (with the government paying 80 per cent of employees' wages up to £2,500 per month), representing close to a third of all employees.[16] Both schemes were extended in the March 2021 Budget to run to the end of September 2021. The OBR estimated the combined net cost of the two schemes (after tax) to be close to £100 billion.[17] The government also sought to support businesses with a range of tax 'holidays' or deferrals – and a reduction of VAT in the worst-affected industries.[18]

Many of these economic measures have a substantial 'welfare' component, as the OBR recognised.[19] Supporting the jobs of those who were not working or who were working substantially reduced hours kept these individuals off the unemployment register, with its attendant penalties and rewards. Nonetheless, there was a substantial growth in the size of the welfare state as more traditionally conceived in the wake of the pandemic. The OBR estimates the increase in the welfare spend in 2020/21 to be nearly 9 per cent (an increase of 1.6 per cent as a proportion of GDP).[20] Most of this increase is down to the increased cost of working-age benefits, above all UC, where the number of claimants leapt from around 3,000,000 in March 2020 to more than 5,500,000 in July.[21] On 20 March 2020, the government announced a flat-rate, one-year 'bonus' to UC payments of £20 per week (later extended to September 2021). At the same time, it increased the generosity of the basis upon which Housing Benefit claims were met. It also changed the rules to facilitate the receipt of UC by those who were self-employed. The UC 'bonus' (plus an equivalent uplift in Working Tax Credits) increased the welfare budget by around £6 billion for the year. Overall, the non-pensioner welfare budget was projected to increase to 5.7 per cent of GDP in 2020/21, a record only equalled in the immediate aftermath of the Global Financial Crisis of 2008. For 2020/21, the overall welfare budget was around £246 billion.[22] Spending on public health is generally included in wider measures of welfare state effort and this also increased very substantially in what was first and foremost a health crisis. In November, the Health Foundation estimated the government's additional healthcare spend for 2020/21 to be around £47 billion, including £12 billion for test and trace and £15 billion for PPE (personal protective equipment). This came on top of a projected NHS budget for 2020/21 of around £150 billion.[23]

Although everyone was touched by COVID-19, its impact across the population was uneven. Unsurprisingly, it was the old and those with existing serious health conditions who were most vulnerable to the disease and this is reflected especially in data on deaths. In the first six months of the pandemic in the UK, for example, those aged 70–9 were about 20 times more likely to die from COVID as those under 65. But there were also other ways in which the incidence of morbidity and mortality was unevenly distributed.

Men were significantly more likely to die than women, perhaps as much as twice as likely. Rates were strikingly high (for both men and women) in ethnic minority populations, with black men being especially vulnerable (at least twice as likely to die as white men). Levels of mortality in the most deprived English locations were higher than those in the least deprived areas; in March and April, more than twice as high. And there is also evidence (down to the end of the first lockdown) that those in manual occupations (and generally less likely to be able to work from home) experienced a higher incidence of the disease.[24]

The immediate economic impact of COVID – and the government's countermeasures – was also uneven. As has been very widely observed, it was the leisure and hospitality sectors that were most impacted both directly by the spread of the virus and by the government's countermeasures (social distancing, curfews and lockdowns).[25] Along with arts and entertainment, these were the sectors that fell the furthest and were the slowest to recover. Workers in these areas were disproportionately female, young and low-paid. The ability to work from home – and therefore maintain a 'normal' employment relationship while working in a safe environment – was inversely related to both income and level of education (Blundell et al, 2020). Furloughing protected many jobs after March 2020. But as unemployment began to rise (slowly) towards the end of 2020, it was disproportionately young people who lost their jobs. While the overall unemployment rate rose by less than 1 per cent, for the 18–24 age group it rose by 3 per cent (to 13.6 per cent in September 2020).[26]

One further consequence, especially of the countermeasures taken to control the spread of the disease, was a disruption across the educational sector at primary, secondary and tertiary levels. Interruption to learning is likely to have a long-term (perhaps a lifelong) effect on those whose schooling and further education has been disrupted. The evidence indicates that the out-of-school learning experience varied significantly, by parental income within the state sector, and, more substantially, in the contrast between state- and private-sector education.[27] Evidence from the aftermath of the Global Financial Crisis suggests that those entering the labour market in a period of recession struggle not just to get (decently paid) jobs at the time but also in terms of career progression over an extended period.[28]

Given all of this, it is unsurprising that the *distributional* outcomes of the early months of pandemic were also quite uneven. Some of the very poorest families – those relying upon benefits *before* the pandemic kicked in – actually saw a *rise* in their incomes (because of the increased generosity in UC and Housing Benefit). But many of those who were in work but low-paid were more vulnerable to short-time working or unemployment and saw their incomes fall. There was a reported fall in expenditure across most households but there is evidence that, in poorer families, this often reflected a lack of income, and the lowered expenditure related to foregone 'essentials', while in more affluent households the missing expenditure related to opportunities to spend that did not exist (eating out or taking foreign holidays, for example). While some affluent households were 'forced' into additional savings (because of a lack of opportunity to spend), many poorer families had to draw upon their (much more limited) savings to cover everyday needs.[29]

For a modern government in peacetime, the scale of public expenditure involved in the response to the pandemic was unprecedented. Conservative-led governments after 2010 had triggered a decade of austerity, arguing for the absolute necessity of driving down the government's deficit. By 2020, through a mixture of spending cuts and tax rises, the deficit had returned to around 2.5 per cent of GDP (similar to pre-crisis levels in 2008).[30] Public sector net debt had remained broadly flat (at around 80 per cent of GDP) for around five years. By the end of 2020, the deficit had risen to around £355 billion (19 per cent of GDP). Although it was anticipated that the scale of deficit would fall back sharply in 2021/22 (as recovery kicked in), the elevated level of public debt – rising above 100 per cent of GDP in 2020 – looked set to persist to 2025/26 and beyond.[31]

Longer COVID

In the year following the first lockdown, things changed very fast. The process of infection management and what turned out to be three lockdowns were chaotic at times. The roll-out of a vaccine programme seemed to promise substantial change – though nothing so straightforward as an 'end' to the crisis. But, a year in, *actual* outcomes – and their timing – were still shrouded in uncertainty. Despite this general uncertainty, there are some things, in relation to welfare and the public finances at least, that we do know. First, we have already entered a sphere of public indebtedness that has no equivalent in peacetime Britain. Second, and following on from this, provision has to be made to deal with the public debt and this will involve some 'fiscal tightening' (the polite name for increasing taxes and/or cutting public expenditure). Third, the costs of the pandemic, in terms of health and well-being – now and in the longer term – have been unevenly distributed. And fourth, when the dust has settled, we shall still be left with all of the long-term (welfare) challenges that were there before COVID – principally the challenge of what to do about an ageing population in a context of global climate change.

Under these uncertain circumstances, it was the statutory duty of the OBR to try to make projections for the economy and public spending down to 2024/25 (though not to make recommendations about taxation) and I construct my own survey of what might happen over the next five years around their account (from November 2020, updated in March 2021).[32]

The first task of the OBR's *Economic and Fiscal Outlook* was to record the unprecedented scale of the recession triggered by COVID in March and April 2020 – and the extraordinarily high levels of public spending to which it gave rise as a response. Its second task was to attempt to predict what would happen next. Given the acute uncertainty, it offered a range of possible outcomes: an upside, a downside and a central forecast. These outlooks were loosely tied to the progress of the pandemic (and its containment) in the year that followed. Understandably, for the present, the central forecast looks closest to where we are at (both with the disease and with the government's countermeasures) and I shall generally focus on this model. On this central forecast, GDP would return to its January 2020 level in the second quarter of 2022. However permanent 'scarring' leaves the economy 3 per cent smaller in 2025 than it would have been given the growth anticipated before the crisis. Given the extension of CJRS (furloughing) until the end of September 2021, the OBR anticipated that unemployment would rise to a peak of 2,200,000 (6.5 per cent) in the final quarter of 2021, falling steadily to a little over 4 per cent in 2024/25. After a brief decline in 2020, the OBR predicted that average earnings will be 10 per cent higher by 2025. CPI inflation is anticipated to reach its 2 per cent target in 2025.[33]

One of the things that made the recession of 2020 'special' is that it was largely induced by the government forbidding what would otherwise have been normal economic acts (among others) between consenting adults. This is one of the things that leads the OBR to hope and expect that the bounce back from recession may be unusually quick. This recession was also marked, as we have seen, by quite exceptional levels of spending on the part of government. While these expenditures turned out be anything but one-off, they were intended to be temporary – and this is reflected in OBR predictions about the public finances down to 2025. Much of the 'emergency' welfare state that was created to deal with the virus was meant to disappear within a couple of years. Temporary employment and income support measures plus the steps taken to support businesses cost around £165 billion in 2020/21. The government intended that these should fall away in 2021/22 (although there will be higher welfare costs associated with substantially higher unemployment). Additional funding for public services (much of it in healthcare) in 2020/21 amounted to £158 billion. Although the Chancellor budgeted around £50 billion of additional money for coronavirus-related healthcare costs in 2021/22, there is no additional resource identified for later years. The Spending Review also included a reduction of around £10 billion in departmental non-coronavirus budgets – and a commitment to freeze the pay of public sector workers outside the NHS (earning above £24,000).[34] A further £4 billion-worth of savings were identified in the March 2021 Budget.[35] Overall, public spending is predicted to fall from its extraordinarily high level in 2020/21 (54.4 per cent of GDP) and its unusually high level in 2021/22 (46.5 per cent) to be around 42 per cent in 2022/23. This is still fully 2 percentage points above the 2019/20 figure (39.8 per cent). The OBR envisaged that the public sector deficit will fall away steeply to be around £106 billion (close to 4 per cent of GDP) in 2022/23; public sector net debt will be around 104 per cent of GDP.[36]

If we look at the more traditional welfare budget (still the single largest item of government expenditure) in this period, we see a substantial increase of around 13.7 per cent between 2019/20 and 2025/26. The UC spend is reduced as the £20 bonus is withdrawn (in September 2021) but it still remains above it pre-pandemic level. The cost of disability benefits is projected to rise significantly. Still, around three quarters of the growth in this budget down to 2025/26 is explained by increases in pension expenditures (despite a discernible 'saving', of as much as £0.9 billion, from excess COVID deaths).[37]

Overall, the OBR judgement looks like this. We are experiencing an economic crisis and recession of unique severity. But it is a crisis that has not arisen from some malfunction in the economy itself but because of a fully justified government intervention to shut down substantial areas of social and economic life in order to contain a virulent and lethal virus-borne disease. The induced recession was severe – with GDP falling by 25 per cent in March and April 2020 – but the government took extraordinary steps to preserve people's incomes, and jobs, through the downturn, and we can hope and expect that recovery will be more rapid than in earlier recessions. Except in the circumstances of the OBR's extremely optimistic 'upside' scenario (which we can probably already say has not happened), there will be lasting damage to the economy ('scarring'). This may leave the economy 3 per cent smaller in 2025 than it would otherwise have been – though, of course, the accompanying pain is not evenly spread across the population.

Under these uncertain circumstances, the OBR is understandably *extremely* cautious about the robustness of its forecasts. The range of their predictions for growth in GDP down to 2025, for example, varies by a full 6 percentage points.[38] But we may still wonder how compelling these numbers – in particular, those in the central and most likely projection – really are. A number of commentators – Paul Johnson at the IFS and Andrew Harrop and Howard Reed of the Fabian Society, for example – suggest that scarring will be deeper and longer-lasting than the OBR supposes.[39] The uncertainty is inevitable but one way to approach this question is to compare the projected recovery this time around with what the OBR predicted and what actually happened after the earlier crisis in 2010.

This comparison is not encouraging. Predicting the recovery from the Global Financial Crisis was one of the first tasks undertaken by the OBR after its creation in May 2010. In retrospect, its expectations look way out of line with what actually happened, grossly overestimating both the scale and the speed of recovery. Across the decade from 2010 to 2020, the OBR consistently predicted growth in excess of 2 per cent but this was achieved in fewer than a third of the relevant years. In four years (out of ten), growth was below 1.5 per cent. Contrastingly, in terms of growth in employment, by 2019 there were nearly 1,000,000 *more* people in work than the OBR had anticipated (close to 33,000,000 rather than 32,000,000). But perhaps the gravest error related to the growth in average earnings from employment. While this was anticipated to be above 3 per cent in six out of the ten years, in fact average real wage growth was *negative* in several years and it took fully 11 years for (real) wages to return to the levels reached before the crisis in 2008. And it is worth remembering that these disappointing averages conceal a much worse experience for certain disadvantaged sections of the relevant population. The experience of low pay, for example, differed by gender, ethnicity, region and, perhaps especially, by age (with the youngest cohorts faring much worse than those over 55).[40] The OBR's predictions were not out of line with other major forecasting agencies, either in 2010 or later in the decade. Nonetheless, this material does give us reason to think that our experience down to 2025 may prove to be somewhat worse than the OBR expected – not least in relation to wage growth. All of this will have an impact on both the 'temporary' welfare state and the 'permanent' welfare state that will be left behind.

Finally, we should note that one of the more extraordinary consequences of this 'special' recession is that it appears that, after a short-term hit in the opening months of the pandemic, overall wealth *increased substantially* in 2020 and 2021 – perhaps by as much as £890 billion. Most of this increase was accounted for by increases in asset prices, and most of this increase in asset prices was focused upon the housing stock. As the bottom 30 per cent of the population own very few assets, this development further widened income inequality, though it was those in the middle of the income distribution (whose principal asset holding is their own home) who benefitted most.[41]

COVID: paying for it

Everyone seems to agree that at some point, but definitely not now, the government's colossal borrowing will have to be paid for (at least, in part). As we have seen, 2020/21 is truly exceptional in scale – but governments will continue to run augmented deficits down to 2025 (at least). The leap in the national debt should not be repeated – but this still leaves it above 100 per cent of GDP in 2025. Speaking to the Conservative Party Conference (virtually) in October 2020, Rishi Sunak insisted that 'we will protect the public finances. Over the medium term getting our borrowing and debt back under control'. He added: 'We have a sacred responsibility to future generations to leave the public finances strong, and through careful management of our economy, this Conservative government will always balance the books'. As the OBR pointed out, very politely, even upon the most lenient understanding of what is required, it would be a struggle for the government to 'balance the books' within a foreseeable horizon.[42]

One happy irony of the general economic underperformance of the last decade – plus the fact that the Bank of England has committed to nearly £900 billion of quantitative easing in the current crisis – is that it has become much easier for governments to service their debt. Rather quaintly, the costs of servicing the public debt *fall* after the crisis (from 1.7 per cent GDP in 2019/20 to 1.1 per cent in 2025/26), although the vulnerability of government borrowing to an (unexpected) upturn in inflation may have doubled. Still, a substantial payback is coming. The OBR suggested that 'fiscal adjustment' in the period down to 2025 would need to be somewhere in the range £21 billion to £46 billion (0.8–1.8 per cent GDP). The number was widely said to be around £40 billion.[43]

'Fiscal adjustment' after the crisis in 2010 fell more or less evenly across tax rises, benefit cuts and reductions in day-to-day government spending. After a decade of austerity – which was real enough, if not very successful – it was not clear that much scope remained for reducing expenditure. In the wake of the crisis, the government renewed its commitment to increase spending in certain 'protected' areas: including, unsurprisingly, health and education. It also retained its commitment to increase 'investment' expenditure. But it did take £14 billion out of the budgets of 'non-protected' departments. This reduction included a selective freeze on public sector wages and a cut in subventions to local councils – the latter to be covered by allowing local councils to raise their own Council Tax. The coronavirus bonus of £20 per week to UC and Working Tax Credits recipients was scheduled to disappear in September 2021, representing an annual saving of around £6 billion to the government and a potential loss of £1,000 per year for around 6,000,000 claimants.[44] Modelling by the Fabian Society suggested that these benefit cuts would push a further 1,000,000 people – and around 400,000 children – into poverty.[45]

Even with these benefits cuts and budget reductions in place, the government still faced a large hole in the public finances. It could save itself quite a lot of money by abandoning its commitment to the pension 'triple lock'. Introduced by the Coalition Government after the 2010 election, the uprating of pensions was (by 2020) around 10 per cent higher than it would have been if uprated in line with either earnings or the rate of inflation over the preceding decade. In April 2021, as most benefits were raised by 0.5 per cent, pensions were increased by 2.5 per cent. And as earnings 'bounced back' in the aftermath of the crisis, pensioners could expect to benefit from matching a significant improvement in the level of wages.[46] At one point, the OBR supposed that this might add up to £6 billion to the cost of pensions in 2025 (though this figure was later revised downwards). In 2015, the House of Commons Select Committee on Work and Pensions maintained that 'the triple lock is inherently unsustainable'.[47] It may be unsustainable but any government that is brave enough to change it is likely to fudge the reform (say, opting for a less generous 'double lock').

Given the size of the fiscal challenge, one might have hoped that the government would see this as an opportunity to do something to begin to reform a tax system that is, in many ways, irrational and inadequate. Just such a more radical change appeared to be on the cards when, in July 2020, the Chancellor of the Exchequer, Rishi Sunak, commissioned the government's Office of Tax Simplification (OTS) to prepare a report on possible reforms to Capital Gains Tax (CGT). The OTS report disclosed a wide range of irrationalities and anomalies in the existing capital gains taxation regime. They recommended removing a number of 'reliefs' and bringing rates more in line with those applied to income tax (roughly doubling the rates for CGT). They also recommended reforms that would broaden the tax base from its present low of around 265,000 taxpayers. This might notionally raise up to £14 billion annually (though the OTS expected the actual revenue to be very much lower, given the changes in behaviour which a change in the tax regime would bring).[48] This would be a very radical tax reform, not least because it would represent a charge on capital not labour. It would also seem to point towards an accompanying reform of Inheritance Tax (to which CGT is closely related), again a way of taxing wealth (rather than labour). It was always difficult to see how the politics of this could be made to work for a Conservative administration – and the Chancellor omitted to make any such reforms.

Instead, Rishi Sunak opted for some (comparatively) 'easy wins': freezing the personal allowance and higher rate threshold in income tax and raising Corporation Tax very substantially from 19 to 25 per cent (from 2023). The first reform should yield around £8.2 billion per annum by 2025, and the Corporation Tax reform around £17.2 billion. We might expect significant political support for a post-coronavirus 'windfall tax' – for those few businesses which have done extremely well out of the strange circumstances of lockdown – but this would not raise much money, and it would be a one-off. Overall, fiscal tightening should amount to around £32 billion by 2025/26.[49] I will argue in the concluding chapter that further incremental change to our tax regime is unlikely to generate the resources we need. In its November 2020 report, the OBR draws attention to the contrast between 'tax-rich labour income' and 'relatively lightly taxed profits'.[50] We urgently need to find a way to tax wealth effectively – and, in so doing, to redistribute it.

Conclusion: after COVID

It would be tempting to say that, in terms of fundamentals, COVID has changed *nothing*. But that would be wrong. A much more accurate summary judgement would be to say that all the long-term problems we had before the pandemic struck are still with us – they have just become very much harder to solve. In the earliest days of the first lockdown – and as the number of UC clients nearly doubled – there was talk of a 'step-change' in public attitudes to welfare and well-being. One 'bottom-up' indicator of this was a widespread growth in support for food banks, whose levels of activity (for both users and contributors) were transformed in the early months of the pandemic.[51] A little later in the year, Marcus Rashford's campaign to extend the free school meals programme attracted very widespread popular support. This public backing was real enough but there is evidence that levels of volunteering and donations to food banks peaked in the early summer of 2020 – even though the *need* was continuing to rise – and it is easier to mobilise support for poor and hungry children than for many (less attractive) others in need.[52] The fact that the government chose to take on a leading black footballer with an underprivileged family background on the issue of child poverty, only to lose, *twice*, is perhaps, above all, a sign of catastrophic political maladroitness. We would perhaps need to see something more and more sustained to say that we had seen a real and lasting shift in public attitudes.

A second possible token of changing public opinion came with evidence of increasing popular support for the idea of a UBI. In April 2020, YouGov undertook a survey of public attitudes to a UBI in the UK. Its respondents declared 2:1 in favour of a UBI (51 per cent for, 24 per cent against). A similar survey in Scotland in May also revealed a substantial majority in favour of UBI (67 per cent for, 11 per cent against) and the Scottish National Party has declared itself broadly in favour of a UBI for an independent Scotland.[53] The YouGov question was explicitly set in the context of the pandemic and it contained no qualification about potential costs. The same survey also found much larger majorities in favour of a government employment guarantee (72/6) and rent controls (74/8)![54] It is surely clear why the uncertainty and disruption surrounding COVID might make the case for a universally guaranteed Basic Income more attractive, and some pressed the case for an 'emergency' UBI to get us through the pandemic. But it is less obvious that this really changes the underlying arguments of a reform agenda – both for and against. Globally, UBI has made some incremental advances over the past 30 years. And the mundane failings of the present system of income maintenance are highlighted by the crisis, making any alternative seem more attractive. At the same time, and despite the polling evidence from the UK and elsewhere, it is very far from certain that there exists a decided and stable public majority in favour of moves towards a UBI.[55]

At what is more or less the other end of the spectrum, an alternative anticipation is that we are headed towards some sort of Austerity Two – reproducing the response of the Conservative–Liberal Democrat government after 2010. Since the incoming Conservative Government in 2019 seemed to be committed to an 'end to austerity' plus 'levelling up', this might seem unlikely. In the pre-crisis March 2020 budget, the government committed to a 2.8 per cent increase in public expenditure down to 2025, growing the state beyond its dimensions under pre-crisis New Labour. In the Spending Review of November 2020 and again in the Budget of March 2021, while under acute fiscal pressure, Rishi Sunak retained the commitment to (ambitious) levels of public investment in infrastructure that had been made before the pandemic took hold. He also announced a £4 billion 'Levelling Up Fund'.[56] But, at the same time, he did reveal (just) a £10 billion reduction in spending in non-protected government departments (later extended to £14 billion) plus a wage freeze in the public sector. The sanctioning and conditionality of some benefits, which were suspended at the start of the pandemic, were reintroduced. The government remains committed to the welfare cap and to uprating benefits only in line with CPI inflation. This meant that benefits in 2021/22 would be uprated by 0.5 per cent: 37p a week for a single jobseeker, 30p for those under 25. By 2025, the basic jobseeker's allowance should have advanced by a total of £4.93 (to £79.65). The newly upgraded Housing Benefit provision was (indefinitely) frozen at its new level.[57] All of this took place in the context of benefit values which had been systematically eroded over the preceding ten years.[58] Overall, the government seemed to retain its commitment to additional public expenditure – on healthcare, on public infrastructure and, probably, on pensions – but appeared largely unconcerned about the rising incidence of poverty, including child poverty (the two tend to go together). It is only necessary not to undo austerity for its consequences to persist. This is a policy towards welfare that is perhaps best characterised as 'austerity by neglect'.

Overall, we know that COVID will have a serious impact on our future well-being. Levels of economic growth will be lower, with 3 per cent looking like an optimistic forecast (and not forgetting the additional 3–4 per cent decline associated with Brexit). The scarring will be more acute for some than for others – difficult perhaps for the low-skilled and those coming through the education system or entering the labour market in the period of most acute disruption. Budget deficits will not fall in the short term (after they have dropped away from the 'emergency' levels of 2020/21 and 2021/ 22). We shall be living (whether comfortably or not) with a much-increased public debt for a long time to come. At the same time, COVID-19 is only making more difficult deep-seated problems that we already have or that we know are heading rapidly towards us: including the great triumvirate of ageing, climate change and the transformation of work. At present, it seems unlikely that the COVID crisis will make us (collectively) rethink where we are going. The emphasis is likely to be upon restoration (of what we had) rather than transformation (into a world with different values in which we live and work differently). All of this will make it much harder to argue successfully for increased resources to be directed towards those who have the least. But while it will matter very much to them whether we commit a little bit less or a little bit more, that is not what we need. What we *need* is something completely different.

Conclusion

Perhaps the most basic of all the lessons to be learned from our experience of COVID-19 is that we can't get by without the state. We may not like it. And it may have shown itself repeatedly to be unfit for purpose. But it is hard to see how we could hope to navigate our way through this crisis – or indeed the next one – without it. And this state remains, first and foremost, a *welfare* state. In practice, modern states spend most of their time and energy (and resources) funding and organising welfare. *All* states tax and spend. They are huge engines of revenue generation and distribution. And even the 'meanest' of welfare states reduce market-generated inequalities significantly. In Britain, for example, the reduction in the Gini coefficient before and after taxes and transfers is close to 25 per cent.[1] But states do this now in societies that have become much more unequal – socially and economically – and in which those inequalities seem to be ever more firmly entrenched. The task I set myself in this book was to consider if and how we could devise (or, in the first place, begin to imagine) a new welfare regime that might embody a 'strategy of equality' for these changed circumstances. To do this, we had first to look backwards to make sense of what had happened, before thinking about how we could do something different in the future.

In Chapter 1, I looked at the welfare state as it was at the cusp of the COVID-19 pandemic, and after ten years of Conservative management. Austerity was certainly a key theme in this period – but so were conditionality, dependency and paid work (at almost any price). In the shorthand that we use to describe these processes, this might be called a strategy of inequality. While inequality did not quite take off in the ways that some people feared and/or supposed, almost nothing was done to address historically high levels of unequal access to income, wealth, health and opportunity. Significant sections of the population were made poorer and child poverty – which is a good barometer of a society's intention to look after its disadvantaged – was allowed to grow by at least 500,000 across the decade. In Chapter 5, I looked at what had happened to this regime under the impact of COVID-19. In fact, the welfare state grew at this time as it had never grown before – so that many millions of workers were made directly dependent upon the state for an income. And this growth was funded by a similarly spectacular leap in public expenditure and public debt. This was all supposed to be for the short term, but it was a commitment that just kept on growing. Paying for it, at whatever point that happens, will require some sort of innovation in terms of revenue generation (a threat which also represents an opportunity). But while the long-term consequences of the COVID crisis remain very uncertain, and the 'scarring' is likely to be counted in decades or generations rather than years, it is clear that the underlying problems and challenges discussed earlier in this book will not have gone away. At the end of it all, we shall still be a very unequal society in which many millions of our fellow citizens are living in poverty.

My search for alternatives began with a return visit to the New Labour years. I looked briefly – if carefully – at outcomes across this 13-year period. New Labour did more good things than its critics are willing to give it credit for. But there were some important underlying changes in economy and society – many of them neither initiated, nor countermanded, by government – which meant that inequality (especially of wealth) changed very little – perhaps becoming a little worse directly ahead of the Global Financial Crisis. Several of these big societal changes went under the wire, at least partially unrecognised at the time – changes in patterns of homeownership and inheritance, for example – but cumulatively they further skewed the uneven ownership of wealth. In so far as New Labour derived a premium from its policy of economic deregulation, this might be reckoned a one-off boost – and one that looked a bit less golden after 2008. Overall, I judged that what was most important about New Labour in this period was that (perhaps ironically) it pursued a classically social democratic strategy – that is, encouraging socially managed but market-led growth, and then redistributing some of the product in socially progressive ways. In retrospect what perhaps looks most important about its talk of navigating a Third Way is that it misrepresented Labour's past. In so doing, it concealed a rich seam of thinking differently about what social democrats could and should do, in particular about who owns what and how to change it. These are ideas whose time was deemed to have passed, but that now look much more relevant for us than the 'new' social democracy.

It was the task of my third chapter to explore some of this forgotten history. As we saw, 'Old Labour' ideas about nationalisation and state planning could certainly be found back there. For an important section of the party, this was, and it remained, absolutely central. But it was just part of a much wider political sensibility that ownership really mattered. The policy alternatives on offer varied a good deal, but the idea that you could just leave the owners of capital in charge of the economy and then redistribute a part of the economic product through the welfare state in order to promote social equality was one that nearly all of these earlier social democrats rejected. 'Squeezing the capitalist orange' just was not a strategy for the long term. Even in the medium term, such a politics of social amelioration (even where trades unions were a real force) was probably unsustainable. And these earlier social democrats were also very clear that such a politics would always be fiercely opposed. As Tawney observed, there was 'a lion in the path' – and those whose interests (and wealth) would be the price of a social state would avoid paying in any way they could. These thinkers could be quite creative about the alternatives that might be put in place. James Meade, for example, favoured the state owning shares (rather than industries) and the securing of a 'social dividend' or 'Basic Income' as a guarantee for all citizens. One way or another those who laboured had to have a way of participating in the profitability of capital – either in the businesses within which they worked or through tax-favoured savings – which went beyond the wage. And *all* of these social democrats (down to and including Tony Crosland) thought it was absolutely necessary to tax *wealth* and not (just) income. The one-line lesson was this: any strategy for equality had to confront inequalities of wealth – and change them.

In Chapter 4, I began the work of thinking about the future. Since I spent some time looking backwards, it is really important to be clear about the limits of what we can learn from the past. While some old truths persist, the circumstances under which the welfare state might be refurbished now are wholly different from those that prevailed half a century ago. I identified three new challenges for any future welfare order. The first was societal ageing. This is familiar enough but it is worth recalling the sheer *scale* of the changes that (everybody recognises) are ahead of us and the fact that our existing institutional arrangements are completely inadequate to the task. We cannot just do more of the same, without degrading everything else that we want the social state to achieve. The second challenge was the changing nature of work. This might turn out to be not just the disappearance of 'proper' jobs under the impact of automation (as Meade had anticipated) but rather the disarticulation of a whole complex of work-income-security-housing-pensions on which we have come to rely. If paid work can't secure all of these things for us (which for many it has), we need to rethink and retool not just employment, but all these ancillary areas as well. Third, climate change presents a series of new and quite radical challenges. Perhaps the most salient for the world of welfare is a recognition that we cannot just *grow* our way out of our distributional conflicts. As societies or communities or states, we have to make some hard choices.

The shape of things to come

At the end of Chapter 4, I recalled that in politics the first question is always this: 'what is to be done (now)?' In turning to that question it is as well to recall the wry comment with which Rousseau prefaced his *Social Contract*: 'if I were a prince or a legislator, I should not waste time in saying what wants doing; I should do it'. What I have to offer here are not programmatic recommendations but rather some well-intentioned heuristics. These are the sorts of things we would need to do, if we wanted things to change for the better.

I start out from the ideas I introduced in the second half of the fourth chapter. As I said there, there is nothing wrong with the idea of social investment. It is just difficult to see how this could possibly be enough given the scale of the challenges that we face. In relation to asset-based welfare, the key question is always going to be: just how big are the assets? If all we aim to do is to teach the poor how to budget with very little – seemingly one of the ambitions of UC – not much will have been achieved. Ackerman and Alstott's recommendation of a capital grant of $80,000 (1999) would certainly make a difference – though perhaps not enough to overturn two preceding decades of inequality (not least in access to high-quality education). Piketty's recommendation for a capital grant of around 60 per cent of average adult wealth, funded out of a charge on property and inheritances – a figure of around £90,000 in 2018 – and to be given to each individual citizen at the age of 25, would also make a real difference (not least in relation to who could afford to buy a house). But, of course, the bigger the number, the tougher does the politics become.

Two other areas look ripe for reform. *Every* social democrat in this book – from Hugh Dalton to Thomas Piketty, and taking in Tony Crosland and Tony Blair – has called for reforms that would *equalise* children's educational experience. It was high on Branko Milanovic's list too. If we want to build an 'egalitarian capitalism', he argued, we will need 'to equalize teaching standards among schools' by 'leveling the playing field between private and public schools' (Milanovic, 2019: 50). Here again, the politics looks very tough. Since buying your child a privileged education has very real material consequences, resistance to changing it – probably in the name of the 'individual's right to choose' – will be extraordinarily difficult to overcome (as all of these social democratic figures have found). Another area where reform would make a real difference but where resistance is likely to be (correspondingly) severe is housing. In the UK, as we saw in Chapters 1 and 2, the promise of a homeowning democracy has been and gone. Homeownership peaked around 2003. The size of the private rental sector has increased throughout the 21st century. The 'windfall' gains of house price increases have fallen to a declining but still large (and generationally specific) community of interest. As we have seen, below the top 10 per cent, housing is (alongside private pension entitlements) the principal repository of unequal wealth. There have been some recent changes in the tax status and mortgageability of *second* homes, but the really tough challenge is to change the taxable status of *first* homes. Such changes might include lessened exemptions (from CGT) or the charging of taxes on imputed rents, a move recommended by James Meade (1972). Brett Christophers (2019) argues that we should be aiming for 'tenure equality': broadly speaking, a circumstance in which households would be indifferent, in both economic and wider social terms, about whether they owned or rented. At present, however 'good' these reforms might be, they are probably politically infeasible.

This brings me to what must be the core issue in any reform agenda: who owns? – the very question that social democrats had largely chosen to give up when they happily followed Tony Crosland's lead in claiming that this was now 'irrelevant'. This was a mistake. The truth is that it is impossible to think of a sustainable future for the well-being of the mass of the population without a real and substantial change in the distribution of wealth. Here I will address this question, however briefly, in two broad contexts: first, the reallocation of the ownership of capital and then, the more effective taxation of wealth.

The idea that workers should own and control both their own means of production and the product of their labours has a very long history. In Britain, we can trace it back emblematically to the life and work of the Diggers in the 17th century– though all they actually asked for was the right to work the common land in community (Pierson, 2013–20, Vol. 1: 202–6). And the idea of cooperative production has a history at least as old as the labour movement itself. But worker-owned production makes up less than 8 per cent of what is itself a very small cooperative sector of the domestic economy.[2] It is very difficult to imagine this coming to constitute a route into the large-scale redistribution of wealth (however desirable it might be for other reasons). 'Nationalisation' is another and very particular form of the aspiration to shared ownership. However prominent it was in Labour's ethos and its 'Sunday socialism' – and however large it loomed among critics on the Third Way – it was a secondary idea for most of the social democrats we considered in Chapter 3 (with the notable exception of Frank Wise). Some even older social democrats – like Karl Kautsky (1910 [1892]: 110) in the German social democratic party, the Sozialdemokratische Partei Deutschlands – were deeply sceptical about what nationalisation could do for ordinary workers. And, for all the talk of 'putting people before profits', nationalisation was not generally seen as an effective mechanism for redistributing wealth. Where we have seen it applied in the 21st century (though not often daring to use its real name), it has been to bail out private-sector enterprises that were too big and too strategic to fail (notably, banks and railways).[3] These nationalisations have been at a large net *cost* to the public exchequer. Even if some (re)nationalisations are made to happen, they are unlikely to do the work of addressing income inequality.

In the work of the more recent advocates of reform that I considered in the closing pages of Chapter 4, the idea of transferring the ownership of capital to workers is certainly seen as important – but the options identified are mostly rather modest and long-established. Piketty, for example, favours increasing worker representation on the boards of larger companies (building on German and Nordic co-determination) and experimenting with not-for-profit forms of organisation which have no shareholders, like universities (Piketty, 2020: 972–5). Milanovic (2019: 48) looks to a growth of employee stock ownership plans (ESOPs) within existing corporations – a long-established but largely ineffective option – though even he seems to think that this is a second- or even third-best route towards more diversified ownership. By contrast, Ian Gough is *really* radical, insisting that we need to 'partially dismantle a defining feature of capitalism – the private ownership of the means of production' (Gough, 2017: 181). The institutional forms this might take remain unclear, though it would clearly require a much enhanced role for the state as owner.

At this point, it might be useful to reflect briefly on the chastening experience of what was probably the single most bold initiative to transfer ownership to the workers *within* an established capitalist economy: that is, Sweden's experiment with *löntagarfonder*. Sweden built the most powerful and effective social democratic movement that the world has ever seen. The initiative to introduce wage-earners' funds (*löntagarfonder*) came when its powers were at their peak (in the early 1970s), but as its strategists foresaw an emerging problem with its existing welfare state framework (encouraging dynamic capitalist growth and then diverting much of the product into social spending). In short, the team put together by the Social Democratic Party, under the economist Rudolf Meidner, judged that in the longer term (which was now arriving) it was not possible to avoid the question of transferring ownership to workers. Meidner proposed that each year a proportion of a business's annual profits (he recommended 20 per cent) while remaining in the business would be allocated to a fund owned (collectively) by the business's employees. Across time, ownership of the business would be gradually transferred to those who worked within it.

In short, this initiative failed. It is not clear that the leadership of Sweden's Social Democratic Party were ever fully signed up to the policy. The party lost power in 1976 (though probably not over this issue) and on its return to office implemented a much watered-down version of Meidner's original proposal. The scheme effectively lapsed during the 1990s (see Pierson, 2013–20, Vol. 3: 152–5). One lesson is that it is extraordinarily difficult to do the political work of transferring ownership, even where the background conditions are much more favourable than we could ever hope that they would be in the UK.

Taxing wealth

This combination of modest proposals and disappointing outcomes suggests that we will have to look elsewhere for the mechanisms that might achieve a different distribution of wealth. And that means thinking about taxation. Unfortunately, taxation is, like pensions, a bit technical and rather dull. But, just like pensions, it is also hugely consequential for the distribution of wealth over the long term. And, like economics, it is too important to be left to those who have a professional expertise – and a particular world view. Taxing wealth, and especially introducing *new* taxes, is extremely difficult, as every reviewer points out, but it looks as though it may be the only place we have left to go.

On the plus side, there is some evidence of a shift in public opinion in favour of targeting wealth, although everyone seems to think that the wealthy are the people who own just a bit more than they do.[4] We also have a significant body of new work on the wealth tax, including the recent reports of the Wealth Tax Commission (2020) and the Institute for Public Policy Research (2019), upon which to draw (Advani et al, 2020; Nanda and Parkes, 2019). This research itself builds on previous work (largely ignored in practice) that dates back through the Mirrlees report of 2011 to (at least) the Meade Review for the IFS in 1978. COVID-19 has presented us with an opportunity to be politically imaginative. Finding an additional £40 billion of annual revenue to pay for the very exceptional spending of 2020 and 2021 from existing sources will prove extremely difficult. As we saw in Chapter 5, the OTS, which is pretty close to the decision-making machinery of the state, suggested that radically 'rationalising' the rates of CGT could raise annual yields by up to £14 billion. (As we also saw in Chapter 5, the Chancellor Rishi Sunak chose rather predictably to ignore these more radical and interesting options.)

We have already observed several times that inequalities of wealth are much greater than inequalities of income. And yet the weight of taxation falls (disproportionately) upon incomes and, within that category, more especially upon incomes from labour. Between them, income tax and National Insurance contributions make up more than 40 per cent of the UK tax take. The third large component (at around 16 per cent) is VAT, which could be loosely classified as a sort of wealth tax. Income tax is strongly progressive, with around 60 per cent of all tax paid by the top 10 per cent of earners (and around a half of this by the top 1 per cent); National Insurance rather less so. There is some disagreement about whether VAT is actually regressive, but its distributional effects are neutral at best.[5] The next most substantial tax on (property) wealth is Council Tax (around 4.5 per cent of the total), a tax which *is* regressive, is based on house price evaluations that are 30 years out of date and which no one seems willing to defend as a rational and reasonable way of paying for local services.[6] Between them, all other taxes on wealth (CGT, Stamp Duty and Inheritance Tax) contribute around 3.5 per cent of revenues.[7] In 1991, Fritz Scharpf (1991: 261), wrote about 'socialism in one class': the idea that social democrats would have to secure the incomes and well-being of poorer workers out of the earnings of those who were better paid. What we have now is very largely a 'welfare state in one class'. The welfare state is not funded out of our combined wealth, but out of our combined (labour) incomes.

It is in the face of this imbalance, and the growing evidence of overall social and economic inequality, that there has been renewed interest in the taxation of wealth. The terminology used is rather unhelpful. We already have taxes on wealth (even if, as we have just seen, these are rather modest and not very progressive). A wealth tax is generally understood in the relevant literature to mean a tax imposed upon the value of accumulated assets. And analysts tend to draw a very firm distinction between a one-off wealth tax (which in the older literature is often referred to as a capital levy) and a recurring (usually) annual wealth tax. Although the general justifications may be very similar, much recent work (including the very detailed interrogation undertaken by the Wealth Tax Commission) argues that a one-off charge is much more likely to work. The sums are very large – the Wealth Tax Commission suggests that a one-off wealth tax payable on all individual wealth above £500,000 and charged at 1 per cent a year for five years would raise around £260 billion. But it is a one-off and/or an emergency measure; recommended, for example, to meet the exceptional costs of dealing with COVID-19. It is not designed to moderate the accumulation of wealth over time.[8]

One economist who *does* favour an annual wealth tax – as the only option that will address wealth inequality rather than fix an emergency shortfall in state revenues – is Thomas Piketty. In the later volume *Capital and Ideology* (2020), this is presented rather baldly and without attending to the objections of his colleagues (of the sort of which I have already hinted). In short, his judgement is that those with the broadest shoulders – and the most resources – can afford to carry the weight. Since Piketty imagines that these revenues will be used to fund a capital grant to young adults, the intention to redistribute wealth is absolutely clear. In his earlier volume, *Capital in the Twenty-First Century*, he makes out in some detail the case for 'a progressive annual tax on global wealth' (Piketty, 2014: 515–39). He recommends a pan-European progressive tax at comparatively modest rates (between 0 and 2 per cent) – though he insists that there is no reason not to impose much higher levies on the super-rich (say 10 per cent or higher on billionaires). Even at quite modest levels, he argues that such a tax would raise around 2 per cent GDP each year and, of course, narrow wealth differentials.

The arguments around the two modes of wealth taxation are rather arcane. As Stuart Adam and Helen Miller are honest enough to acknowledge, if we simply followed the logic of the 'standard economic approach' – where 'the government's presumed goal [is] maximizing a weighted sum of individuals' well-being' – it would make sense for government to confiscate *all* existing wealth![9] Between this and the real world, there is a very wide range of options. In the end, one of the main reasons for favouring a one-off tax is a practical-political one – that the costs of trying to sustain and administer an annual wealth tax regime would not be worth the revenues it could generate. Even Piketty admits that, while there is no technical or administrative barrier to what he proposes, the political logic means that, for now, it remains 'a useful utopia'. But it is not clear that a one-off levy would fare that much better. The one-shot solution relies upon an element of 'genuine surprise' which looks pretty implausible in a modern democracy.

But the fact that it may be difficult – though not necessarily impossible – to introduce a wealth tax does not mean that we have to give up on the idea of taxing wealth. Several of those who argue for a wealth tax insist that, if that is not presently possible, we still have the option of reforming a raft of existing taxes which almost no one is willing to defend as sensible and effective.[10] Inheritance Tax – which currently raises significantly less than the duties on beer and wine – is almost universally regarded as failing.[11] It is a famously unpopular tax, resented for the most part by those who would never actually be called upon to pay it (if anyone is, given that, in the long term, we are all dead). It is fairly easily (and frequently) avoided. It may be best simply to abandon it – as several reformers have suggested – and replace it with something which is more effective in getting at the familial transmission of wealth; for example, a lifetime gift limit or the transition towards a progressive charge on recipients rather than donors. It is not very hard to imagine something better than what we have – and there are models out there. Similarly, Council Tax looks overdue for reform. Its antiquated valuation base (from 1991) is only retained because the politics of revaluation look so unattractive to political incumbents. This and other reforms in housing finance – imputed rental taxes, CGT on house sales, the abolition of Stamp Duty (transparent, accepted but, in the eyes of most economists, irrational) – might make sense. But, as we have seen, tampering with the established perks of middle-income homeowners is politically very difficult. And (particular) losses of privilege are always much more keenly felt than (rather generalised) increases in social well-being.

There are other tax options out there. I will briefly consider just two. Land Value Taxation (LVT) has a distinguished pedigree, going all the way back to Adam Smith (2003 [1776]: Book V, Ch. 2). It is often described as, in principle, a model tax – as it is very hard to evade (hiding land isn't easy) and does not distort economic behaviour (since its supply cannot be altered). The Mirrlees tax review in 2011 recommended its introduction in these terms: 'the economic case for a land value tax is simple, and almost undeniable' (2011: 374). It is an enormous and rapidly rising repository of wealth. In 2018, the ONS reported that land made up 51 per cent of the UK's net worth (just over £5 trillion) and that, as a proportion of UK net worth, household land *doubled* (from 21 per cent to 41 per cent) between 1995 and 2017.[12] LVT does sometimes appear in the contemporary tax debate – though rather as an afterthought. Ever since it was popularised by the (non-economist) Henry George in the late 19th century, it has been tinged with an aura of crankiness (George, 1898 [1879]). But it is absolutely unclear why – apart from the weight of vested interests opposed to it – it does not get a fairer and more frequent hearing.

Finally, we come to the case for the taxation of carbon emissions. We saw this issue raised (in Chapter 4) by both Piketty and Gough. Anyone who takes seriously the challenge of climate change has also to take seriously the question of carbon pricing or carbon emissions taxation – as a way of changing existing patterns of usage and consumption. Like the taxation of other 'bads', the principal purpose of carbon taxation is not to raise revenue but to reduce consumption. For the foreseeable future, however, we do not need to worry that there will be too little carbon emission to generate revenues. The challenge is to create a tax regime that is effective (in reducing emissions), equitable (in its impact on different sections of the population) and feasible (in terms of public support). This is difficult, not least because, as both Piketty and Gough point out, poorer people spend more (proportionally) on carbon-emitting goods (primarily fuel and food) than richer people. Carbon taxes would need to be offset by payments to less affluent households simply to hold the line on inequality – or possibly used partially to fund a Basic Income.[13] It is possible to imagine a carbon tax that is broadly progressive – either by giving allowances to individuals or focusing upon luxury usage such as air travel – but less easy to see this commanding the necessary public support. More effective carbon taxation is a revenue-raising power that we need and that *could* be made progressive – but which we may struggle to put in place.

The last word

Anyone who wants to change our welfare regime is faced with a really wide range of possibilities. Given the challenges attending on ageing, the transformation of work and climate change, 'more of the same' doesn't look like a workable option. And, in any case, we don't want more of the same if that means a degraded social order in which the poor get (comparatively) poorer and social mobility has stalled. However we set about doing this, we have to find a way to change who owns what. We may reorganise the ownership structure of firms, institute a citizen's dividend, create a UBI, do something to unfreeze social mobility. None of this will be possible without an overhaul of our tax regime. Whatever the technical difficulties, we have to find a way to tax wealth, as well as income. And we have to do it like we mean it.

In politics, I have suggested, the first question is always this: 'What is to be done (now)?'. For that question, I think we have some pretty good answers. But a second question is almost as pressing: 'Who is going to do that (now)?' The answer to that one is, sadly and for now, quite uncertain.

Notes

Introduction

1. https://www.ons.gov.uk/peoplepopulationandcommunity/healthandsocialcare/conditionsanddiseases/articles/coronavirusayearlikenoother/2021-03-15; Edge Health estimated the incidence of COVID-19 in the English population at 12,400,000 in February 2021: https://www.edgehealth.co.uk/.
2. https://www.health.org.uk/news-and-comment/charts-and-infographics/covid-19-policy-tracker.
3. All data from: https://obr.uk/efo/economic-and-fiscal-outlook-march-2021/.
4. https://www.gov.uk/government/statistics/universal-credit-statistics-29-april-2013-to-14-january-2021/universal-credit-statistics-29-april-2013-to-14-january-2021.
5. See: https://obr.uk/efo/economic-and-fiscal-outlook-march-2021/.
6. See: https://obr.uk/efo/economic-and-fiscal-outlook-march-2021/.
7. See: https://www.insidehighered.com/news/2016/07/07/british-academics-consider-why-they-were-ignored-brexit-debate.
8. See: http://cdn.obr.uk/CCS1020397650-001_OBR-November2020-EFO-v2-Web-accessible.pdf.
9. https://assets.publishing.service.gov.uk/government/uploads/system/uploads/attachment_data/file/891155/Monitoring_report_2013-2020_-Web_version.pdf#page=17; https://researchbriefings.files.parliament.uk/documents/SN05585/SN05585.pdf.

Chapter 1

1. https://conservative-speeches.sayit.mysociety.org/speech/601526.
2. https://obr.uk/docs/dlm_uploads/Coronavirus_reference_scenario_commentary.pdf
3. See, for example, https://webarchive.nationalarchives.gov.uk/20130221121534/http://www.dilnotcommission.dh.gov.uk/our-report/.
4. https://conservative-speeches.sayit.mysociety.org/speech/601526.
5. https://www.gov.uk/government/publications/rates-and-allowances-corporation-tax/rates-and-allowances-corporation-tax.
6. https://assets.publishing.service.gov.uk/government/uploads/system/uploads/attachment_data/file/248096/0061.pdf.
7. https://commonslibrary.parliament.uk/research-briefings/sn06852/.
8. https://www.ifs.org.uk/uploads/BN263-public-sector-pay-and-employment1.pdf.
9. https://www.ifs.org.uk/publications/13791.
10. https://commonslibrary.parliament.uk/research-briefings/cbp-7405/.
11. https://www.ifs.org.uk/uploads/publications/comms/R132.pdf.
12. http://www.legislation.gov.uk/uksi/2012/780/pdfs/uksiem_20120780_en.pdf.
13. http://sticerd.lse.ac.uk/dps/case/spcc/WP11.pdf.
14. http://shura.shu.ac.uk/15883/1/welfare-reform-2016.pdf.
15. The original time frame envisaged a complete transition to the new system by 2017. The latest projected date for completion is September 2024 (as at 23 March 2021). https://commonslibrary.parliament.uk/social-policy/welfare-pensions/benefits/constituency-data-universal-credit-roll-out/.
16. https://assets.publishing.service.gov.uk/government/uploads/system/uploads/attachment_data/file/48897/universal-credit-full-document.pdf.

17 https://obr.uk/forecasts-in-depth/brief-guides-and-explainers/an-obr-guide-to-welfare-spending/.

18 https://www.resolutionfoundation.org/app/uploads/2019/02/Living-Standards-Outlook-2019.pdf.

19 https://www.ifs.org.uk/uploads/publications/bns/Universal_credit_and_its_impact_on_household_incomes_the_long_and_the_short_of_it_BN248.pdf.

20 https://obr.uk/docs/dlm_uploads/Welfare_trends_report_December_2019.pdf.

21 https://obr.uk/forecasts-in-depth/tax-by-tax-spend-by-spend/; https://www.ifs.org.uk/election/2019/article/how-high-are-our-taxes-and-where-does-the-money-come-from.

22 https://www.ons.gov.uk/employmentandlabourmarket/peopleinwork/employmentandemployeetypes/bulletins/employmentintheuk/march2020#employment.

23 https://www.jrf.org.uk/report/uk-poverty-2019-20-work.

24 https://www.gov.uk/government/speeches/chancellor-george-osbornes-summer-budget-2015-speech.

25 https://obr.uk/docs/dlm_uploads/Welfare_trends_report_December_2019.pdf.

26 https://commonslibrary.parliament.uk/research-briefings/cbp-7667/; https://obr.uk/forecasts-in-depth/brief-guides-and-explainers/an-obr-guide-to-welfare-spending/.

27 http://sticerd.lse.ac.uk/dps/case/spcc/RR04.pdf.

28 https://www.kingsfund.org.uk/projects/nhs-in-a-nutshell/nhs-budget.

29 https://obr.uk/docs/dlm_uploads/Welfare_trends_report_December_2019.pdf.

30 See: https://obr.uk/data/.

31 On the persistent official overestimation of economic growth, see: https://obr.uk/data/.

32 Needless to say, Piketty's claim is widely challenged. At the same time, very few argue that there has not been a real and substantial rise in income inequality since the 1970s. There is also widespread agreement that the inequality is especially pronounced at the very top of the income profile – for the top 1 per cent, or 0.1 per cent or 0.01 per cent.

33 https://www.ons.gov.uk/peoplepopulationandcommunity/personalandhouseholdfinances/incomeandwealth/bulletins/householdincomeinequalityfinancial/financialyearending2020.

34 https://www.ifs.org.uk/uploads/publications/comms/R136.pdf.

35 https://www.resolutionfoundation.org/app/uploads/2017/06/Wealth.pdf.

36 https://wid.world/country/united-kingdom/.

37 https://www.ons.gov.uk/peoplepopulationandcommunity/personalandhouseholdfinances/incomeandwealth/bulletins/totalwealthingreatbritain/april2016tomarch2018#trends-in-total-wealth-inequality-in-great-britain. ONS data are not fully consistent with Piketty's estimates, but they show very similar trends.

38 In 2018, the 'Bank of Mum and Dad' was reported to be the country's sixth biggest mortgage lender: https://familybuildingsociety.co.uk/Knowledge-hub/bank-mum-and-dad.aspx.

39 See, for example, https://www.centreforsocialjustice.org.uk/library/reforming-child-poverty-act.

40 For the most part, I deal with allocations after (differential) housing costs have been taken into account.

41 Tony Blair, 'Beveridge Lecture', London, 18 March 1999: https://www.bristol.ac.uk/poverty/downloads/background/Tony%20Blair%20Child%20Poverty%20Speech.doc. New Labour's record on child poverty is discussed in Chapter 2.

42 https://www.ifs.org.uk/uploads/publications/comms/R114.pdf.

43 https://www.gov.uk/government/statistics/households-below-average-income-199495-to-201718.

44 https://www.ifs.org.uk/uploads/publications/comms/R114.pdf.

45 https://www.ifs.org.uk/uploads/publications/comms/R136.pdf.

46 https://assets.publishing.service.gov.uk/government/uploads/system/uploads/attachment_data/file/622214/Time_for_Change_report_-_An_assessment_of_government_policies_on_social_mobility_1997-2017.pdf; https://assets.publishing.service.gov.uk/government/uploads/system/uploads/attachment_data/file/798404/SMC_State_of_the_Nation_Report_2018-19.pdf.

47 For a useful survey of some these issues, see Bukodi and Goldthorpe, 2019: 4–9.

48 See: http://csi.nuff.ox.ac.uk/?page_id=443.

49 https://assets.publishing.service.gov.uk/government/uploads/system/uploads/attachment_data/file/622214/Time_for_Change_report_-_An_assessment_of_government_policies_on_social_mobility_1997-2017.pdf.

50 All data from: https://assets.publishing.service.gov.uk/government/uploads/system/uploads/attachment_data/file/622214/Time_for_Change_report_-_An_assessment_of_government_policies_on_social_mobility_1997-2017.pdf.

51 https://assets.publishing.service.gov.uk/government/uploads/system/uploads/attachment_data/file/798404/SMC_State_of_the_Nation_Report_2018-19.pdf.

52 https://assets.publishing.service.gov.uk/government/uploads/system/uploads/attachment_data/file/447575/Downward_mobility_opportunity_hoarding_and_the_glass_floor.pdf.

53 https://assets.publishing.service.gov.uk/government/uploads/system/uploads/attachment_data/file/622214/Time_for_Change_report_-_An_assessment_of_government_policies_on_social_mobility_1997-2017.pdf.

54 *Inter vivos* transfers are also important but operate to a rather different logic. They are generally smaller and made to younger people. I do not discuss them here. See: https://www.ons.gov.uk/peoplepopulationandcommunity/personalandhouseholdfinances/incomeandwealth/articles/intergenerationaltransfersthedistributionofinheritancesgiftsandloans/2018-10-30.

55 https://www.resolutionfoundation.org/app/uploads/2017/12/Inheritance.pdf.

56 https://www.ons.gov.uk/peoplepopulationandcommunity/personalandhouseholdfinances/incomeandwealth/articles/intergenerationaltransfersthedistributionofinheritancesgiftsandloans/2018-10-30.

57 https://www.resolutionfoundation.org/app/uploads/2017/12/Inheritance.pdf, 34.

58 https://www.ons.gov.uk/peoplepopulationandcommunity/personalandhouseholdfinances/incomeandwealth/articles/intergenerationaltransfersthedistributionofinheritancesgiftsandloans/2018-10-30.

59 https://www.resolutionfoundation.org/app/uploads/2017/06/Wealth.pdf.

Chapter 2

1 These early commitments appeared in two DSS documents from 1998: *New Ambitions for Our Country: A New Contract for Welfare* (DSS, Cm 3805) and *A New Contract for Welfare: Principles into Practice* (DSS, Cm 4101), a Green and White Paper, respectively.

2 See: http://eprints.lse.ac.uk/51070/1/__Libfile_repository_Content_CASE_Labour%E2%80%99s%20social%20policy%20record.pdf.

3 http://eprints.lse.ac.uk/51199/1/__libfile_REPOSITORY_Content_CASE_CASE%20Social%20policy%20in%20a%20cold%20climate%20series_Working%20papers_swp05_full%20text.pdf.

4   DfEE, Annual Report 2001: https://assets.publishing.service.gov.uk/government/uploads/system/uploads/attachment_data/file/250879/5102.pdf, 6.

5   https://www.ons.gov.uk/releases/wealthingreatbritainwave62016to2018.

6   https://www.credit-suisse.com/about-us/en/reports-research/studies-publications.html; https://wid.world/country/united-kingdom/.

7   https://www.resolutionfoundation.org/app/uploads/2017/06/Wealth.pdf, 25.

8   https://webarchive.nationalarchives.gov.uk/20160107120404/http://www.ons.gov.uk/ons/rel/census/2011-census-analysis/a-century-of-home-ownership-and-renting-in-england-and-wales/sty-home-ownership.html.

9   Clearly, the future title to an income is not an asset in the normal sense; and how much wealth one draws down will depend on a number of contingencies, including how long one lives! For a brief guide to some of the problems – and the solutions – see: https://www.ons.gov.uk/peoplepopulationandcommunity/personalandhouseholdfinances/incomeandwealth/compendium/wealthingreatbritainwave4/2012to2014/chapter6privatepensionwealthwealthingreatbritain2012to2014#sensitivity-analysis-and-the-effect-of-annuity-rates-on-defined-benefit-and-pension-in-payment-wealth.

10   See: https://info.mercer.com/rs/521-DEV-513/images/MMGPI%202019%20Full%20Report.pdf.

11   https://www.ons.gov.uk/peoplepopulationandcommunity/personalandhouseholdfinances/incomeandwealth/bulletins/wealthingreatbritainwave5/2014to2016.

12   https://www.resolutionfoundation.org/app/uploads/2017/06/Wealth.pdf, 80.

13   Typically the data excludes small inheritances; in the widely used HMRC data, for example, those with a value below £5,000 (Karagiannaki, 2015: 187).

14   Reported at 2005 prices. Intergenerational transfers represent just under two thirds of these sums; the rest are inter-spousal transfers (Karagiannaki, 2015: 193–4).

15   Among them, Heffernan, 2000; Gamble and Wright, 2000; Fielding, 2003; Finlayson, 2003; Ludlam and Smith, 2004; Driver and Martell, 2005; Mooney and Law, 2007; Shaw, 2007; Faucher-King and Le Galès, 2010. A late and retrospective addition is Glen O'Hara, 2018. The most useful volume with a specific focus on Labour's welfare reforms is Powell, 2008.

16   Colin Hay's prescient *The Political Economy of New Labour*, published in 1999, was substantially based on articles written prior to 1997.

17   In the Swedish context, this is the story of the *löntagarfonder* [employee funds]; on which, see Pierson (2020, Volume 3: 151–5).

Chapter 3

1   For a brief survey of this history, see Jones, 1996 and Kenny and Smith, 1997.

2   Critics have always suspected that social democrats were only ever signed up to a sort of 'Sunday socialism', reserved for party conference platforms and set-piece speeches; see, for example, Fritz Brupbacker from 1935, cited in Frei, 1987: 56.

3   Attlee's Government is something of a 'special case'. It is certainly treated this way by Blair (1995: 2–10).

4   Famously, Laski's views changed significantly across time. I do not discuss him here.

5   https://hansard.parliament.uk/commons/1947-07-09/debates/5b400934-2716-4bfd-8971-654871aafba4/NewClause%E2%80%94(ReliefForPensionersInRespectOfIncreaseInTobaccoDuty).

6   Although there was some change of emphasis before and after the Second World War; see Durbin, 1949 and the commentary in Ellison, 1994: 77–9.

7   Although, at other times Cole argued just as confidently that it would be possible to impose high redistributive taxation without undermining economic incentives and activity (see Cole, 1929: 84–6).

8   This might be true of Tawney's early work. Tawney's recent biographer, Lawrence Goldman (2013), argues that there are two distinctive periods in Tawney's work. I am exclusively concerned here with the second – and more statist – period (after 1919).

9   And anticipating much latter arguments about the potential of Sovereign Wealth Funds to provide resources (collectively) for their citizens; see Pierson, 2020: 303–5.

10 The alternative argument that it fails because of the political logic of capitalist parliamentary democracy is one I return to in Chapter 4.

Chapter 4

1   https://www.ons.gov.uk/peoplepopulationandcommunity/birthsdeathsandmarriages/ageing/articles/livinglongerisage70thenewage65/2019-11-19.

2   https://www.ons.gov.uk/peoplepopulationandcommunity/populationandmigration/populationestimates/datasets/vitalstatisticspopulationandhealthreferencetables.

3   https://www.ons.gov.uk/peoplepopulationandcommunity/birthsdeathsandmarriages/ageing/articles/livinglongerhowourpopulationischangingandwhyitmatters/2018-08-13.

4   https://www.ons.gov.uk/peoplepopulationandcommunity/birthsdeathsandmarriages/ageing/articles/livinglongerisage70thenewage65/2019-11-19.

5   https://www.gov.uk/government/statistics/public-spending-statistics-release-february-2021/public-spending-statistics-february-2021.

6   https://www.ons.gov.uk/peoplepopulationandcommunity/birthsdeathsandmarriages/ageing/articles/livinglongerisage70thenewage65/2019-11-19.

7   https://www.resolutionfoundation.org/app/uploads/2020/06/Rainy-Days.pdf.

8   https://www.ons.gov.uk/peoplepopulationandcommunity/personalandhouseholdfinances/incomeandwealth/bulletins/householdincomeinequalityfinancial/financialyearending2020provisional.

9   http://www.ditext.com/morris/1563.html.

10 In 2016, the government spend on various tax credits was about ten times the expenditure on Jobseekers' Allowance. See: https://commonslibrary.parliament.uk/research-briefings/cbp-7667

11 https://www.ons.gov.uk/employmentandlabourmarket/peopleinwork/employmentandemployeetypes/datasets/emp17peopleinemploymentonzerohourscontracts.

12 For recent survey, see Brynjolfsson and McAfee (2016: 147–51). Martinelli (2017: 27–32) represents a more sceptical view.

13 https://www.ons.gov.uk/employmentandlabourmarket/peopleinwork/employmentandemployeetypes/datasets/employmentbyoccupationemp04.

14 https://www.measuringworth.com/datasets/ukgdpir/result.php.

15 A number of authors have argued that we *can* move towards a post-work society, built around the liberating qualities of new technologies, but only if we abandon capitalism. See, for example, Mason (2015) and Bastani (2019).

16 In the British context, this dates back at least to Fitzpatrick and Cahill (2002). The idea of the 'eco-social' is central to both Fitzpatrick (2017) and Gough (2017).

17 There is some evidence that existing welfare states already do something to enhance 'carbon equity' (Ottelin et al, 2018).

18 For a sceptical survey of the general idea of asset-based welfare, see Gregory, 2014.

19 'The *asset* in asset-based welfare has frequently become *property or housing asset*' (Doling and Ronald, 2010: 165; emphasis in original).

20 https://assets.publishing.service.gov.uk/government/uploads/system/uploads/attachment_data/file/461440/Chapter_1_Trends_in_tenure.pdf.

21 https://www.theyworkforyou.com/wrans/?id=2019-02-15.221988.h&s=Landlords#g221988.r0.

22 One UBI advocate who does see Paine's *really* radical intent is Standing (2017).

23 For a recent example, from Finland, see: https://julkaisut.valtioneuvosto.fi/bitstream/handle/10024/161361/Report_The%20Basic%20Income%20Experiment%2020172018%20in%20Finland.pdf.

24 See: https://www.greenparty.org.uk/assets/files/Elections/Green%20Party%20Manifesto%202019.pdf.

25 In the comparatively small literature on UBI and the environment, see MacNeill and Vibert, 2019; Malmaeus et al, 2020.

26 For a sober assessment of current prospects in the UK, see Martinelli and Pearce, 2019.

27 Henry George (1898 [1879]) was an enthusiast for private property – and its wholesale redistribution.

28 'Liberal meritocratic capitalism' is an unfortunate name, since the regime Milanovic describes under this label is neither very liberal nor very meritocratic.

29 Piketty also argues for a reform of the ownership of firms to give employees a greater stake in an enterprise's capital.

30 https://www.theguardian.com/politics/2016/jun/10/potential-benefits-and-pitfalls-of-a-universal-basic-income.

31 In 2016, Savills estimated the total value of the world's real estate assets at $217 trillion, nearly three times world GDP: https://pdf.euro.savills.co.uk/global-research/around-the-world-in-dollars-and-cents-2016.pdf.

Chapter 5

1 https://www.medicalnewstoday.com/articles/comparing-covid-19-with-previous-pandemics.

2 See Mary Ramsay of Public Health England (21 March 2021): https://www.bbc.co.uk/programmes/p09bd7kc.

3 Supporting data can be found at: https://sites.google.com/view/covidinequality/.

4 https://www.who.int/emergencies/diseases/novel-coronavirus-2019/technical-guidance/naming-the-coronavirus-disease-(covid-2019)-and-the-virus-that-causes-it.

5 Public health measures, including lockdowns, varied confusingly across the devolved administrations of the UK. These variations were significant. For the purposes of this brief summary, I focus on the English case.

6 https://coronavirus.data.gov.uk/details/deaths.

7 https://www.gov.uk/government/publications/nhs-test-and-trace-england-and-coronavirus-testing-uk-statistics-5-november-to-11-november.

8 https://committees.parliament.uk/committee/127/public-accounts-committee/news/150988/unimaginable-cost-of-test-trace-failed-to-deliver-central-promise-of-averting-another-lockdown/.

9 https://www.bhf.org.uk/informationsupport/heart-matters-magazine/news/coronavirus-and-your-health/covid-variant#UKvariant.

10 https://coronavirus.data.gov.uk/.

11 https://www.pfizer.com/news/press-release/press-release-detail/pfizer-and-biontech-announce-vaccine-candidate-against; https://www.ox.ac.uk/news/2020-11-23-oxford-university-breakthrough-global-covid-19-vaccine.

12 https://coronavirus.data.gov.uk/.

13 A useful source is the report prepared by the House of Lords Public Services Committee, *A Critical Juncture for Public Services: Lessons from COVID-19*: https://committees.parliament.uk/publications/3438/documents/32865/default/.

14 https://obr.uk/efo/economic-and-fiscal-outlook-march-2021/, 15.

15 https://obr.uk/efo/economic-and-fiscal-outlook-march-2021/, 14.

16 Coronavirus Job Retention Scheme statistics, November 2020: https://www.gov.uk/government/statistics/coronavirus-job-retention-scheme-statistics-november-2020.

17 https://obr.uk/efo/economic-and-fiscal-outlook-march-2021/, 188.

18 http://cdn.obr.uk/CCS1020397650-001_OBR-November2020-EFO-v2-Web-accessible.pdf, 177–8.

19 https://obr.uk/efo/economic-and-fiscal-outlook-march-2021/, 133.

20 https://obr.uk/wtr/welfare-trends-report-march-2021/, 4.

21 https://www.gov.uk/government/statistics/universal-credit-statistics-29-april-2013-to-14-january-2021/universal-credit-statistics-29-april-2013-to-14-january-2021.

22 http://cdn.obr.uk/CCS1020397650-001_OBR-November2020-EFO-v2-Web-accessible.pdf, 113–17; https://obr.uk/efo/economic-and-fiscal-outlook-march-2021/, 134.

23 https://www.health.org.uk/publications/long-reads/managing-uncertainty.

24 https://www.ons.gov.uk/peoplepopulationandcommunity/birthsdeathsandmarriages/deaths/bulletins/deathsduetocoronaviruscovid19comparedwithdeathsfrominfluenzaandpneumoniaenglandandwales/deathsoccurringbetween1januaryand31august2020#age-standardised-and-age-specific-rates-for-deaths-due-to-influenza-and-pneumonia-and-covid-19; https://www.ons.gov.uk/peoplepopulationandcommunity/healthandsocialcare/causesofdeath/bulletins/coronaviruscovid19relateddeathsbyoccupationbeforeandduringlockdownenglandandwales/latest.

25 https://www.ons.gov.uk/peoplepopulationandcommunity/healthandsocialcare/conditionsanddiseases/articles/coronaviruscovid19in10charts/2020-09-24.

26 https://www.ons.gov.uk/employmentandlabourmarket/peoplenotinwork/unemployment/datasets/unemploymentbyageanddurationseasonallyadjustedunem01sa.

27 https://www.ifs.org.uk/uploads/publications/wps/WP202026-Inequalities-childrens-experiences-home-learning-during-COVID-19-lockdown-England.pdf.

28 https://www.ifs.org.uk/uploads/WP201727.pdf.

29 https://www.resolutionfoundation.org/publications/caught-in-a-covid-trap.

30 https://www.ons.gov.uk/economy/governmentpublicsectorandtaxes/publicspending/bulletins/ukgovernmentdebtanddeficitforeurostatmaast/march2020.

31 https://obr.uk/efo/economic-and-fiscal-outlook-march-2021/, 22.

32 http://cdn.obr.uk/CCS1020397650-001_OBR-November2020-EFO-v2-Web-accessible.pdf; https://obr.uk/efo/economic-and-fiscal-outlook-march-2021/, 53.

33 https://obr.uk/efo/economic-and-fiscal-outlook-march-2021/, 49, 53, 68, 70.

34 https://www.gov.uk/government/publications/spending-review-2020-documents/spending-review-2020#responding-to-covid-19-1.

35 https://obr.uk/efo/economic-and-fiscal-outlook-march-2021/, 128–9.

36 https://obr.uk/efo/economic-and-fiscal-outlook-march-2021/, 22, 122, 149.

37 https://obr.uk/efo/economic-and-fiscal-outlook-march-2021/, 133–6; https://obr.uk/wtr/welfare-trends-report-march-2021/, 5.

38 The OBR had already anticipated a 4 per cent decline in GDP growth following on Brexit. They estimated that no-deal would add a further 2 per cent to these losses: https://obr.uk/wtr/welfare-trends-report-march-2021/.

39 https://www.ifs.org.uk/publications/15203; https://fabians.org.uk/wp-content/uploads/2020/12/Double-Trouble-Fabian-Society-report.pdf.

40 http://obr.uk/docs/pre_budget_forecast_140610.pdf; https://obr.uk/docs/dlm_uploads/EFO_November__2015.pdf; https://www.ons.gov.uk/economy/grossdomesticproductgdp/timeseries/ihyp/pn2; https://www.ons.gov.uk/employmentandlabourmarket/peopleinwork/employmentandemployeetypes/bulletins/averageweeklyearningsingreatbritain/february2020; https://www.ons.gov.uk/employmentandlabourmarket/peopleinwork/employmentandemployeetypes/timeseries/mgrz/lms.

41 https://www.resolutionfoundation.org/app/uploads/2021/07/Wealth-gap-year.pdf

42 http://cdn.obr.uk/CCS1020397650-001_OBR-November2020-EFO-v2-Web-accessible.pdf, 162–4.

43 http://cdn.obr.uk/CCS1020397650-001_OBR-November2020-EFO-v2-Web-accessible.pdf, 101, 18; https://www.resolutionfoundation.org/app/uploads/2020/11/Here-today-gone-tomorrow.pdf.

44 The number of households claiming UC that were subject to the benefit cap rose by 12 per cent between May and August 2020: https://www.gov.uk/government/publications/benefit-cap-number-of-households-capped-to-august-2020/benefit-cap-number-of-households-capped-to-august-2020#the-number-of-capped-households-in-gb; http://cdn.obr.uk/CCS1020397650-001_OBR-November2020-EFO-v2-Web-accessible.pdf, 114.

45 https://fabians.org.uk/wp-content/uploads/2020/12/Double-Trouble-Fabian-Society-report.pdf.

46 https://researchbriefings.files.parliament.uk/documents/CBP-7812/CBP-7812.pdf.

47 https://publications.parliament.uk/pa/cm201617/cmselect/cmworpen/59/5906.htm#_idTextAnchor037.

48 https://assets.publishing.service.gov.uk/government/uploads/system/uploads/attachment_data/file/935073/Capital_Gains_Tax_stage_1_report_-_Nov_2020_-_web_copy.pdf.

49 https://obr.uk/efo/economic-and-fiscal-outlook-march-2021/, 196, 188.

50 http://cdn.obr.uk/CCS1020397650-001_OBR-November2020-EFO-v2-Web-accessible.pdf, 16.

51 https://www.trusselltrust.org/2020/11/12/2600-food-parcels-provided-for-children-every-day-in-first-six-months-of-the-pandemic/; http://speri.dept.shef.ac.uk/wp-content/uploads/2020/12/Monitoring-responses-to-risk-of-rising-food-insecurity-during-the-COVID-19-crisis-across-the-UK-FINAL-1.pdf.

52 https://theconversation.com/food-bank-donations-surged-during-the-pandemic-but-look-closely-at-the-data-and-theres-trouble-ahead-142113.

53 https://www.heraldscotland.com/news/18471823.coronavirus---now-two-thirds-scots-support-universal-basic-income-poll-finds/. A useful survey of current party political positions is at: https://researchbriefings.files.parliament.uk/documents/CDP-2020-0096/CDP-2020-0096.pdf.

54 https://docs.cdn.yougov.com/5y7qpjzd6v/NEON_CoronavirusClimate_200417_W.pdf.

55 In Canada, for example: http://angusreid.org/universal-basic-income-covid19/.

56 https://www.gov.uk/government/publications/spending-review-2020-documents/spending-review-2020#shared-outcomes-fund.

57 https://questions-statements.parliament.uk/written-statements/detail/2020-11-25/hcws600.

58 https://researchbriefings.files.parliament.uk/documents/CBP-7667/CBP-7667.pdf.

Conclusion

[1] https://www.economist.com/graphic-detail/2019/04/13/american-inequality-reflects-gross-incomes-as-much-as-taxes.

[2] https://neweconomics.org/uploads/files/co-ops-unleashed.pdf.

[3] https://publications.parliament.uk/pa/cm200809/cmselect/cmpubacc/394/394.pdf; https://www.ons.gov.uk/news/news/theonsclassifiestrainoperatingcompaniesnowrunningunderemergencymeasuresagreements.

[4] https://docs.cdn.yougov.com/p54plx0gh9/NEON_PostCovidPolicy_200508_w4.pdf.

[5] https://researchbriefings.files.parliament.uk/documents/CBP-8513/CBP-8513.pdf.

[6] Ways of taxing wealth: Alternatives and interactions: https://www.wealthandpolicy.com/.

[7] https://obr.uk/forecasts-in-depth/tax-by-tax-spend-by-spend/property-transaction-taxes/.

[8] See the papers, including the Final Report, at: https://www.ukwealth.tax/evidencepapers.

[9] See Adam and Miller at: https://www.wealthandpolicy.com/wp/103.html, 24; an insight dating back to Jeremy Bentham (1843- []: 302).

[10] See: https://www.wealthandpolicy.com/wp/104.html.

[11] https://obr.uk/forecasts-in-depth/tax-by-tax-spend-by-spend/property-transaction-taxes/.

[12] https://www.ons.gov.uk/economy/nationalaccounts/uksectoraccounts/bulletins/nationalbalancesheet/2018.

[13] On which, see: https://www.carbontax.org/.

References

Ackerman, B. and Alstott, A. (1999) *The Stakeholder Society*. New Haven, CT: Yale University Press.

Advani, A., Chamberlain, E. and Summers, A. (2020) *A Wealth Tax for the UK*. https://www.ukwealth.tax/

Alvaredo, F., Atkinson, A.B. and Morelli, S. (2016) 'The Challenge of Measuring UK Wealth Inequality in the 2000s', *Fiscal Studies*, 37(1): 13–33.

Andersson, J.O. (2009) 'Basic Income from an Ecological Perspective', *Basic Income Studies*, 4(2): 1–8.

Arundel, R. (2017) 'Equity Inequity: Housing Wealth Inequality, Inter and Intra-generational Divergences, and the Rise of Private Landlordism', *Housing, Theory and Society*, 34(2): 176–200.

Atkinson, A.B. (2013) 'Wealth and Inheritance in Britain from 1896 to the Present'. CASE Working Paper 178. London: London School of Economics, Centre for Analysis of Social Exclusion.

Atkinson, A.B. (2015) *Inequality: What Can Be Done*. Cambridge, MA: Harvard University Press.

Bastagli, F. and Hills, J. (2012) *Wealth Accumulation in Great Britain 1995– 2005: The Role of House Prices and the Life Cycle*. London: LSE.

Bastani, A. (2019) *Fully Automated Luxury Communism*. London: Verso.

Beatty, C. and Fothergill, S. (2017) 'Welfare Reform in the UK 2010– 16: Expectations, Outcomes, and Local Impacts', *Social Policy and Administration*, 52(5): 950–68.

Benedetto, G., Hix, S. and Mastrorocco, N. (2020) 'The Rise and Fall of Social Democracy, 1918–2017', *American Political Science Review*, 114(3): 928–39.

Bentham, J. (1843). 'Principles of the Civil Code', in *Complete Works* (Volume 1). Edinburgh: Tait.

Blair, T. (1994) *Socialism*. London: Fabian Society.

Blair, T. (1995) *Let Us Face the Future: The 1945 Anniversary Lecture*. Fabian Pamphlet 571. London: Fabian Society.

Blair, T. (1998) *The Third Way: New Politics for the New Century*. London: Fabian Society.

Blair, T. (1999) 'Beveridge Lecture', in R. Walker (ed), *Beveridge Revisited: A Welfare State for the 21st Century*. Bristol: Policy Press, pp 7–19.

Blair, T. (2004) 'Reforming the Welfare State'. http://news.bbc.co.uk/2/hi/uk_news/politics/3733380.stm

Blair, T. and Schoeder, G. (1999) *Europe: The Third Way/die Neue Mitte*. London: Labour Party.

Blundell, R., Costa Dias, M. Joyce, R. and Xu, X. (2020) 'COVID-19 and Inequalities', *Fiscal Studies*, 41(2): 291–319.

Boyer, G.R. and Schmidle, T.P. (2009) 'Poverty among the Elderly in Late Victorian England', *The Economic History Review*, 62(2): 249–78.

Brooke, S. (1989) 'Revisionists and Fundamentalists: The Labour Party and Economic Policy during the Second World War', *The Historical Journal*, 32(1): 157–75.

Brooke, S. (1996) 'Evan Durbin: Reassessing a Labour "Revisionist" ', *Twentieth Century British History*, 7(1): 27–52.

Brynjolfsson, E and McAfee, A (2014) *The Second Machine Age*. New York: Norton.

Bukodi, E. and Goldthorpe, J. (2019) *Social Mobility and Education in Britain*. Cambridge: Cambridge University Press.

Christophers, B. (2018) 'Intergenerational Inequality? Labour, Capital, and Housing through the Ages', *Antipode*, 50(1): 101–21.

Christophers, B. (2019) 'A Tale of Two Inequalities: Housing–Wealth Inequality and Tenure Inequality', *Environment and Planning A: Economy and Space A*, 53(3): 573–94.

Chwalisz, C. and Diamond, P. (2015) *The Predistribution Agenda: Tackling Inequality and Supporting Sustainable Growth*. London: I.B. Tauris.

Clift, B. and Tomlinson, J. (2002) 'Tawney and the Third Way', *Journal of Political Ideologies*, 7(3): 315–31.

Coote, A. and Percy, A. (2020) *The Case for Universal Basic Services*. Cambridge: Polity Press.

Cole, G.D.H. (1917) *Self-Government in Industry*. London: G. Bell and Sons.

Cole, G.D.H. (1920) *Guild Socialism Re-stated*. London: George Allen and Unwin.

Cole, G.D.H. (1929) *The Next Ten Years in British Social and Economic Policy*. London: Macmillan.

Cole, G.D.H. (1932) *Some Essentials of Socialist Propaganda*. London: Fabian Society.

Cole, G.D.H. (1935) *Principles of Economic Planning*. London: Macmillan.

Cole, G.D.H. (1949) 'The Dream and the Business', *Political Quarterly*, 20(3): 201–10.

Cole, G.D.H. (1960) *William Morris as a Socialist*. London: William Morris Society.

Crosland, A. (1952) 'The Transition from Capitalism', in R.H.S. Crossman (ed), *New Fabian Essays*. London: Turnstile, pp 33–68.

Crosland, A. (1956) *The Future of Socialism*. London: Cape.

Crosland, A. (1962) *The Conservative Enemy: A Programme of Radical Reform for the 1960s*. London: Cape.

Crosland, A. (1974) *Socialism Now, and Other Essays*. London: Cape.

Crosland, S. (1982) *Tony Crosland*. London: Cape.

Dalton, H. (1920) *Some Aspects of the Inequality of Incomes in Modern Communities*. London: Routledge.

Dalton, H. (1936) *Practical Socialism for Britain*. London: Routledge.

De Man, H. (1935) *Planned Socialism: The Plan du Travail of the Belgian Labour Party* (trans and ed G.D.H. Cole). London: Gollancz.

Diamond, P. (2016). *The Crosland Legacy: The Future of British Social Democracy*. Bristol: Policy Press.

Doling, J. and Ronald, R. (2010) 'Home Ownership and Asset-Based Welfare', *Journal of Housing and the Built Environment*, 25(2): 165–73.

Dorling, D. (2018) *Peak Inequality: Britain's Ticking Time Bomb*. Bristol: Policy Press.

Driver, S. and Martell, L. (2005) *New Labour*, 2nd edition. Cambridge: Polity Press.

Durbin, E.F.M. (1940) *The Politics of Democratic Socialism*. London: Routledge.

Durbin, E.F.M. (1949) *Problems of Economic Planning*. London: Routledge and Kegan Paul.

Dwyer, P.J. (2018) 'Punitive and Ineffective: Benefit Sanctions Within Social Security', *Journal of Social Security Law*, 25(3): 142–57.

Ellison, N. (1994) *Egalitarian Thought and Labour Politics: Retreating Visions*. London: Routledge.

Esping-Andersen, G. (1990) *Three Worlds of Welfare Capitalism*. Cambridge: Polity Press.

Esping-Andersen, G. (ed) (2002) *Why We Need a New Welfare State*. Oxford: Oxford University Press.

Faucher-King, F. and Le Galès, P. (2010) *The New Labour Experiment: Change and Reform under Blair and Brown* (trans G. Elliott). Stanford, CA: Stanford University Press.

Fenger, M. (2018) 'The Social Policy Agendas of Populist Radical Right Parties in Comparative Perspective', *Journal of International and Comparative Social Policy*, 34(3): 188–209.

Fetzer, T. (2019) 'Did Austerity Cause Brexit?', *American Economic Review*, 109(11): 3849–86.

Fielding, S. (2003) *The Labour Party: Continuity and Change in the Making of 'New' Labour*. London: Palgrave.

Finlayson, A. (2003) *Making Sense of New Labour*. London: Lawrence and Wishart.

Fitzpatrick, T. (2017) *Climate Change and Poverty: A New Agenda for Developed Nations*. Bristol: Policy Press.

Fitzpatrick, T. and Cahill, M. (eds) (2002) *Environment and Welfare: Towards a Green Social Policy*. London: Palgrave Macmillan.

Frei, A. (1987) *Rote Patriarchen: Arbeiterbewegung und Frauenemanzipation in der Schweiz um 1900*. Zurich: Chronos.

Frey, C.B. and Osborne, M.A. (2013) 'The Future of Employment: How Susceptible Are Jobs to Computerisation?', Oxford: Martin School, University of Oxford. Available from: https://www.oxfordmartin.ox.ac.uk/downloads/academic/The_Future_of_Employment.pdf.

Friedman, S. and Laurison, D. (2019) *The Class Ceiling: Why It Pays to Be Privileged*. Bristol: Policy Press.

Gamble, A. and Wright, T. (eds) (2000) *The New Social Democracy*. Oxford: Blackwell.

George, H. (1898 [1879]) 'Progress and Poverty', in *The Complete Works of Henry George* (Volumes 1–2). New York: Doubleday, pp 3–568.

Giddens, A. (1994) *Beyond Left and Right: The Future of Radical Politics*. Cambridge: Polity Press.

Giddens, A. (1998) *The Third Way*. Cambridge: Polity.

Giddens, A. (2000) *The Third Way and Its Critics*. Cambridge: Polity.

Goes, E. (2016) *The Labour Party under Ed Miliband: Trying But Failing to Renew Social Democracy*. Manchester: Manchester University Press.

Goldman, L. (2013) *The Life of R.H. Tawney: Socialism and History*. London: Bloomsbury.

Gough, I. (2017) *Heat, Greed and Human Need: Climate Change, Capitalism and Sustainable Wellbeing*. Cheltenham: Edward Elgar.

Graeber, D. (2019) *Bullshit Jobs*. London: Penguin

Gregory, J. (2014) 'The Search for an "Asset Effect": What Do We Want from Asset-Based Welfare?', *Critical Social Policy*, 34(4): 475–94.

Greve, B. (2019) *Welfare, Populism and Welfare Chauvinism*. Bristol: Policy Press.

Griffiths, J. (1969) *Pages from Memory*. London: Dent.

Hacker, J.S. (2011) 'The Institutional Foundations of Middle-Class Democracy, *Policy Network*, 6: 33–7.

Hain, P. (2015) *Back to the Future of Socialism*. Bristol: Policy Press.

Hanlon, W.W. (2017) 'Temporary Shocks and Persistent Effects in Urban Economics: Evidence from British Cities after the U.S. Civil War', *Review of Economics and Statistics*, 99(1): 67–79.

Häusermann, S. and Gingrich, J. (2020) 'Welfare States Need Reinforcement, Not Reinvention'. Available from: https://www.socialeurope.eu/welfare-states-need-reinforcement-not-reinvention.

Hay, C. (1999) *The Political Economy of New Labour: Labouring under False Pretences?* Manchester: Manchester University Press.

Heffernan, R. (2000) *New Labour and Thatcherism: Political Change in Britain*. London: Palgrave.

Hemerijck, A. (ed) (2017) *The Uses of Social Investment*. Oxford: Oxford University Press.

Hemerijck, A. (2018) 'Social Investment as a Policy Paradigm', *Journal of European Social Policy*, 25(6): 810–27.

Hills, J., Bastagli, F., Cowell, F., Glennerster, H., Karagiannaki, E. and McKnight, A. (2013) *Wealth in the UK: Distribution, Accumulation, and Policy.* Oxford: Oxford University Press.

Hirvilammi, T. and Koch, M. (2020) 'Sustainable Welfare beyond Growth', *Sustainability*, special issue, 12(1).

Hobhouse, L.T. (1913) 'The Historical Evolution of Property, in Fact and Idea', in C. Gore (ed), *Property: Its Rights and Duties.* London: Macmillan, pp 1–31.

Hobson, J.A. (1896) *The Problems of Poverty.* London: Methuen.

Holland, S. (1975) *The Socialist Challenge.* London: Quartet.

Iacobucci, G. (2018) 'NHS Trusts Struggle to Produce Brexit Plans amid Continuing Uncertainty', *BMJ*, 363: k5346.

IPCC (International Panel on Climate Change) (2014) *Climate Change 2014: Synthesis Report: Summary for Policymakers.* Geneva: United Nations.

Jackson, B. (2005) 'Revisionism Reconsidered: "Property-Owning Democracy" and Egalitarian Strategy in Post-War Britain', *Twentieth Century British History*, 16(4): 416–40.

Jackson, T. (2009) *Prosperity Without Growth? The Transition to a Sustainable Economy.* London: Sustainable Development Commission. Available from: http://www.sd-commission.org.uk/publications.php@id=914.html.

Jay, D. (1946 [1937]) *The Socialist Case.* London: Faber and Faber.

Jay, D. (1962) *Socialism in the New Society.* London: Longmans.

Jones, T. (1996) *Remaking the Labour Party: From Gaitskell to Blair.* London: Routledge.

Joyce, R. and Sibieta, L. (2013) 'An Assessment of Labour's Record on Income Inequality and Poverty', *Fiscal Studies*, 29(1): 178–202.

Karagiannaki, E. (2015) 'Recent Trends in the Size and the Distribution of Inherited Wealth in the UK', *Fiscal Studies*, 36(2): 181–213.

Kautsky, K. (1910 [1892]) *The Class Struggle.* New York: C.H. Kerr.

Kemp, P.A. (2015) 'Private Renting After the Global Financial Crisis', *Housing Studies*, 30(4): 601–20.

Kenny, M. and Smith, M.J. (1997) 'Discourses of Modernization: Gaitskell, Blair and the Reform of Clause IV', *British Elections and Parties Review*, 7(1): 110–26.

Keskinen, S., Norocel, O.C. and Jørgensen, M.B. (2016) 'The Politics and Policies of Welfare Chauvinism Under the Economic Crisis', *Critical Social Policy*, 36(3): 321–9.

Keynes, J.M. (1936) *The General Theory of Employment, Interest and Money.* London: Macmillan.

Keynes, J.M. (1963 [1930]) 'Economic Possibilities for Our Grandchildren', *Essays in Persuasion.* New York: Norton, pp 358–73.

Labour Party (1934) *For Socialism and Peace.* London: Labour Party.

Labour Party (1961) *Signposts for the Sixties.* London: Labour Party.

Labour Party (1982) *Labour's Programme*. London: Labour Party.

Le Grand, J. (1982) *The Strategy of Equality*. London: Routledge.

Levin, K., Cashore, B., Bernstein, S. and Auld, G. (2012) 'Overcoming the Tragedy of Super Wicked Problems: Constraining Our Future Selves to Ameliorate Global Climate Change', *Policy Sciences*, 45(2): 123–52.

Lister, R. (2003) 'Investing in the Citizen-Workers of the Future', *Social Policy and Administration*, 37(5): 427–43.

Locke, J. (1988 [1688]) *Two Treatises of Government* (ed P. Laslett). Cambridge: Cambridge University Press.

Ludlam, S. and Smith M.J. (eds) (2004) *Governing as New Labour*. Basingstoke: Palgrave Macmillan.

Lupton, R. and Obolenskaya, P. (2013) 'Labour's Record on Education: Policy Spending and Outcomes 1997–2010', CASE Working Paper 3. London: London School of Economics, Centres for Analysis of Social Exclusion. Available from: http://sticerd.lse.ac.uk/dps/case/spcc/wp03.pdf.

Lupton, R. with Hills, J., Stewart, K. and Vizard, P. (2013) *Labour's Social Policy Record: Policy, Spending and Outcomes 1997–2010*, CASE Research Report 1. London: London School of Economics, Centres for Analysis of Social Exclusion. Available from: http://sticerd.lse.ac.uk/dps/case/spcc/RR01.pdf

Luxemburg, R. (2006 [1899]) *Reform or Revolution and Other Writings*. New York: Dover.

MacNeill, T. and Vibert, A. (2019) 'Universal Basic Income and the Natural Environment: Theory and Policy', *Basic Income Studies*, 14(1): art 20180026. Available from: https://doi.org/10.1515/bis-2018-0026.

Malmaeus, M., Alfredsson, E. and Birnbaum, S. (2020) 'Basic Income and Social Sustainability in Post-Growth Economies', *Basic Income Studies*, 15(1): art 20190029. Available from: https://doi.org/10.1515/bis-2019-0029.

Martinelli, L. (2017) 'Assessing the Case for a Universal Basic Income in the UK', IPR Policy Brief, September. Bath: University of Bath, Institute for Policy Research.

Martinelli, L. and Pearce, N. (2019) 'Basic Income in the UK: Assessing Prospects for Reform in an Age of Austerity', *Social Policy and Society*, 18(2): 265–75.

Mason, P. (2015) *Postcapitalism: A Guide to Our Future*. Harmondsworth: Allen Lane.

McKnight, A. (2015) *Downward Mobility, Opportunity Hoarding and the 'Glass Floor'*. London: Social Mobility and Child Poverty Commission.

Meade, J. (1948) *Planning and the Price Mechanism: The Liberal-Socialist Solution*. London: George Allen and Unwin.

Meade, J. (1964) *Efficiency, Equality and the Ownership of Property*. London: George Allen and Unwin.

Meade, J. (1972) 'Poverty in the Welfare State', *Oxford Economic Papers*, 24(3): 289–326.

Meade, J. (1976) *The Just Economy*. London: George Allen and Unwin.

Meade, J. (1990) 'Can We Learn a "Third Way" from the Agathotopians?', *Royal Bank of Scotland Review*, September. Edinburgh: Royal Bank of Scotland.

Meade, J. (1993) *Liberty, Equality and Efficiency: Apologia Pro Agathotopia Mea*. London: Macmillan.

Milanovic, B. (2016) *Global Inequality: A New Approach for the Age of Globalization*. Cambridge, MA: Harvard University Press.

Milanovic, B. (2019) *Capitalism, Alone: The Future of the System That Rules the World*. Cambridge, MA: Harvard University Press.

Miliband, R. (1973) *Parliamentary Socialism: A Study in the Politics of Labour*. London: Merlin.

Mirrlees, J. (2011) *Tax by Design: The Mirrlees Review*. London: Institute for Fiscal Studies.

Montgomerie, J. and Büdenbender, M. (2015) 'Round the Houses: Homeownership and Failures of Asset-Based Welfare in the UK', *New Political Economy*, 20(3): 386–405.

Mooney, G. and Law, A. (eds) (2007) *New Labour/Hard Labour: Restructuring and Resistance Inside the Welfare Industry*. Bristol: Policy Press.

Morris, W. (2003 [1890]) *News from Nowhere*. Oxford: Oxford University Press.

Mullan, P. (2000) *The Imaginary Time Bomb: Why an Ageing Population Is Not a Social Problem*. London: I.B. Tauris.

Nanda, S and Parkes, H. (2019) *Just Tax*. London: IPPR. https://www.ippr.org/files/2019-09/just-tax-sept19.pdf

Nolan, B. (2013) 'What Use Is "Social Investment"?', *Journal of European Social Policy*, 23(5): 459–68.

Nolan, B. (2017) 'Social Investment', in A. Hemerijck (ed), *The Uses of Social Investment*. Oxford: Oxford University Press, pp 43–50.

Norris, P. and Ingelhart, R. (2019) *Cultural Backlash: Trump, Brexit, and Authoritarian Populism*. Cambridge: Cambridge University Press.

Nove, A. (1983) *The Economics of Feasible Socialism*. London: Routledge.

O'Connor M. and Portes, J. (2021) 'Estimating the UK Population During the Pandemic', 14 January. London: Economic Statistics Centre of Excellence. Available from: https://www.escoe.ac.uk/estimating-the-uk-population-during-the-pandemic/.

O'Hara, G. (2018) 'New Labour's Domestic Policies: Neoliberal, Social Democratic or a Unique Blend?'. London: Tony Blair Institute for Global Change. Available from: https://institute.global/policy/new-labours-domestic-policies-neoliberal-social-democratic-or-unique-blend.

Obolenskaya, P. and Hills, J. (2019) 'Flat-Lining or Seething Beneath the Surface? Two Decades of Changing Economic Inequality in the UK', Social Policies and Distributional Outcomes Research Paper 4. London: London School of Economics, Centre for Analysis of Social Exclusion.

Ottelin, J., Heinonen, J. and Junnila, S. (2018) 'Carbon and Material Footprints of a Welfare State: Why and How Governments Should Enhance Green Investments', *Environmental Science and Policy*, 86: 1–10.

Paine, T. (1899 [1797]) 'Agrarian Justice', in *The Writings of Thomas Paine*, Vol. 3. New York: Putnam, pp 322–44.

Panitch, L. and Leys, C. (2001) *The End of Parliamentary Socialism*. London: Verso.

Phillips, T. (1954) *Report of the Committee on the Economic and Financial Problems of Provision for Old Age*. London: HMSO.

Pierson, C. (1995) *Socialism After Communism: The New Market Socialism*. Cambridge: Polity Press.

Pierson, C. (2006) *Beyond the Welfare State?*, 3rd edition. Cambridge: Polity Press.

Pierson, C. (2013–20) *Just Property*, 3 vols. Oxford: Oxford University Press.

Pierson, P. (1998) 'Irresistible Forces, Immovable Objects: Post-Industrial Welfare States Confront Permanent Austerity', *Journal of European Public Policy*, 5(4): 539–60.

Piketty, T. (2014) *Capital in the Twenty-First Century* (trans A. Goldhammer). Cambridge, MA: Harvard University Press.

Piketty, T. (2020) *Capital and Ideology* (trans A. Goldhammer). Cambridge, MA: Harvard University Press.

Pogrund, G. and Maguire, P. (2020) *Left Out: The Inside Story of Labour Under Corbyn*. London: Bodley Head.

Polanyi, K. (1944) *The Great Transformation*. New York: Farrar and Rinehart.

Powell, M. (ed) (2008) *Modernising the Welfare State: The Blair Legacy*. Bristol: Policy Press.

Rittel, H.W.J. and Webber, M.M. (1973) 'Dilemmas in a General Theory of Planning', *Policy Sciences*, 4(2): 155–69.

Scharpf, F.W. (1991) *Crisis and choice in European social democracy*. London: Cornell University Press.

Scheidel, W. (2017) *The Great Leveler: Violence and the History of Inequality from the Stone Age to the Twenty-First Century*. Princeton, NJ: Princeton University Press.

SEU (Social Exclusion Unit) (2004) *Breaking the Cycle: Taking Stock of Progress and Priorities for the Future*. London: HMSO.

Shaw, E. (2007) *Losing Labour's Soul? New Labour and the Blair Government 1997–2007*. Abingdon: Routledge.

Sherraden, M. (1991) *Assets and the Poor: A New American Welfare Policy*. London: Routledge.

Sherraden, M. (2018) 'Asset Building as Social Investment', *Journal of Sociology and Social Welfare*, 45(4): 35–54.

Smith, A. (2003 [1776]) *The Wealth of Nations*. New York: Bantam.

Soaita, M., Searle, B.A., McKee, K. and Moore, T. (2017) 'Becoming a Landlord: Strategies of Property-Based Welfare in the Private Rental Sector in Great Britain', *Housing Studies*, 32(5): 613–37.

Sobolewska, M. and Ford, R. (2020) *Brexitland: Identity, Diversity and the Reshaping of British Politics*. Cambridge: Cambridge University Press.

Standing, G. (2011) *The Precariat: The New Dangerous Class*. London: Bloomsbury

Standing, G. (2016) *The Corruption of Capitalism: Why Rentiers Thrive and Work Does Not Pay*. London: Biteback.

Standing, G. (2017) *Basic Income: And How We Can Make It Happen*. Harmondsworth: Pelican.

Stewart, K. (2013) 'Labour's Record on the Under Fives: Policy, Spending and Outcomes 1997–2010', Social Policy in a Cold Climate Working Paper 4. London: London School of Economics, Centre for Analysis of Social Exclusion. Available from: http://sticerd.lse.ac.uk/dps/case/spcc/wp04.pdf.

Stiglitz, J.E. (2012) *The Price of Inequality*. Harmondsworth: Penguin.

Streeck, W. (2014) *Buying Time: The Delayed Crisis of Democratic Capitalism*. London: Verso.

Tawney, R.H. (1921) *The Acquisitive Society*. London: Bell.

Tawney, R.H. (1932) 'The Choice Before the Labour Party', *Political Quarterly*, 3(3): 323–45.

Tawney, R.H. (1964 [1931]) *Equality*. London: Allen and Unwin.

Therborn, G. (2013) *The Killing Fields of Inequality*. Cambridge: Polity Press.

Thomson, D. (1991) *Selfish Generations? The Ageing of New Zealand's Welfare State*. Wellington: Bridget Williams.

Timmins, N. (2017) *The Five Giants*. London: Collins.

Van Der Veen, R.J. and van Parijs, P. (1986) 'A Capitalist Road to Communism', *Theory and Society*, 15(5): 635–55.

Van Mechelen N. and Bradshaw J. (2013) 'Child Poverty as a Government Priority: Child Benefit Packages for Working Families, 1992–2009', in I. Marx and K. Nelson (eds) *Minimum Income Protection in Flux: Reconciling Work and Welfare in Europe*. London: Palgrave Macmillan, pp 81–107.

Van Parijs, P. (1990) 'The Second Marriage of Justice and Efficiency', *Journal of Social Policy*, 19(1): 1–25.

Van Parijs, P. (1991) 'Why Surfers Should Be Fed: The Liberal Case for an Unconditional Basic Income', *Philosophy and Public Affairs*, 20(2): 101–31.

Van Parijs, P. (1995) *Real Freedom for All: What (if Anything) Can Justify Capitalism?* Oxford: Oxford University Press.

Van Parijs, P. and Vanderborght, Y. (2017) *Basic Income: A Radical Proposal for a Free Society and a Sane Economy*. Cambridge, MA: Harvard University Press.

Varoufakis, Y. (2016) *And the Weak Suffer What They Must? Europe, Austerity and the Threat to Global Stability*. London: Penguin.

Vizard, P. and Obolenskaya, P. (2013) 'Labour's Record on Health (1997–2010)', Social Policy in a Cold Climate Working Paper 2. London: London School of Economics, Centre for Analysis of Social Exclusion. Available from: https://sticerd.lse.ac.uk/CASE/_NEW/PUBLICATIONS/abstract/?index=4275.

Webb, S. (1918) *Labour and the New Social Order*. London: Labour Party.

Widerquist, K., Noguera, A., Vanderborght, Y. and De Wispelaere, J. (eds) (2013) *Basic Income: An Anthology of Contemporary Research*. Oxford: Wiley Blackwell.

Wilkinson, R. and Pickett, K. (2009) *The Spirit Level: Why Equality Is Better for Everyone*. Harmondsworth: Allen Lane.

Willetts, D. (2020) *The Pinch: How the Baby Boomers Took Their Children's Future – and Why They Should Give It Back*, 2nd edition. London: Atlantic Books.

Wise, E.F. (1933) 'Control of Finance and the Financiers', in R.S. Cripps (ed), *Problems of a Socialist Government*. London: Gollancz, pp 67–94.

Wright, A.W. (1979) *G.D.H. Cole and Socialist Democracy*. Oxford: Oxford University Press.

Index

Note: References to figures appear in *italic* type;
those in **bold** type refer to tables.